The Close

BASIC
BOOKS

A Member of the Perseus Books Group

The Close

A Young Woman's First Year at Seminary

Chloe Breyer

Published by Basic Books,
A Member of the Perseus Books Group

Library of Congress Cataloging-in-Publication Data

Breyer, Chloe.
The close: a young woman's first year at seminary / Chloe Breyer.
p. cm.
ISBN 0-465-00714-7 (alk. paper); ISBN 0-465-00715-5 (pbk.)
1.Breyer, Chloe, 2.General Theological Seminary (New York. N.Y.)
3.Episcopal Church–Clergy–Training of–New York (State)–New York
4.Women seminarians–United States. 5.Seminarians–United States. I. Title.

BV4070.G48 B74 2000
230'.07'337471–dc21

00-034296

The paper used in this publication meets the requirements of the American National Standard for Permanence of Paper for Printed Library Materials Z39.48-1984.

01 02 03 / 10 9 8 7 6 5 4 3 2 1

To Greg—

He found my hand, the hand with the pen. He closed his hand over my hand.

"Go ahead, bub, draw," he said. "Draw. You'll see. I'll follow you. It'll be okay. Just begin now like I'm telling you. You'll see. Draw," the blind man said.

So I began.

—RAYMOND CARVER, *The Cathedral*

To the community:

I am deeply grateful to all the community members of the General Theological Seminary, including faculty, staff, students, and their families. My classmates in the GTS class of 2000 deserve special thanks. This book would not have been possible without your patient, good-humored cooperation with my persistent questions and impromptu interviews during our first year—a time when you, no doubt, thought you had finally escaped your Commission on Ministry's queries about calling. Few of you expected your own actions, words, and stories to turn up in print. So, whether you see yourselves painted in broad brush strokes over many pages or in a one-sentence snapshot of a composite character, I thank you profoundly for all you shared.

In the telling of their stories, I have in some cases changed identifying details and used pseudonyms for the people I describe both on the Close and at Bellevue Hospital.

close (kləʊs), *n.* [a. F. *clos*: —L. *clausum* closed place, enclosure.]

†**d**. The precinct of any sacred place; a cloister.

—*Oxford English Dictionary*

Contents

Introduction
Coming into the Kingdom

"What made you want to do this?"

The questioners include my perplexed relatives, former employers, childhood friends, and people seated next to me on trains or airplanes.

When a question like this is asked of individuals in most degree programs, the answer is straightforward: "I'm studying music because I've loved the cello since my first lesson in junior high"; or, "I'm in a computer programming course because software is where the opportunities are." Usually, questioners go away satisfied.

"I'm studying for ordination at an Episcopal seminary because my bishop recommended I go to a place that emphasizes priestly formation" does not produce the same sort of gratification. In fact, unless our conversation is interrupted naturally—when the waiter comes with lunch or the aircraft cabin lights dim and a movie screen appears—my answer falls short. If the questioner is an old school friend—someone who showed me how to flick butter patties at the cafeteria ceiling or helped me organize antinuclear petition drives—this answer is definitely inadequate.

Most people who ask "What made you want to do this?" are not merely wondering why I like the sound of Anglican chant or when I became interested in fifth-century pilgrims' journeys to the Holy

Land. A deeper level of curiosity is detectable. The questioner might actually want to know why I believe in God, or she might be asking what made me want to serve God by working in the church. She might be curious about why a young woman with secular schooling and an interest in social change would forgo law or business school. Occasionally I detect a hint of judgment: "Why are you wasting that first-class education that has prepared you for success in the *real* world?" or "Why do you want any part of a hierarchical, patriarchal institution that historically has resisted social change and is hostile to women?" As I complete the final year at General Theological Seminary, I have often pondered these questions myself.

When seminarians address the "Why" question, we are not merely describing how we wound up in this line of work. We have the privilege and responsibility of explaining our daily vocational tasks, our relationship to the church and our views of it as an institution, and our personal beliefs about what gives life meaning. Indeed, addressing the question "Why?" is a daunting task. Not having a rule of life so intimately related to their professional responsibilities, doctors or hairdressers don't face this peculiar challenge. The story that really "connects the dots" for each seminarian requires effort.

For me, finding the right words to articulate my calling is not just an attempt to avoid the platitudes that much of secular America associates with Christianity. I'm not simply trying to convince my listener that the God I love is different from the one preached by cult leaders, antiabortion fanatics, or those who confuse nationalism and ethnic hatred with religious teaching. Nor is my deliberation over language only for the purpose of distinguishing myself from the fundamentalist who contends stridently that "Jesus is her personal savior," or from the skeptical student who studies Christianity as a sociological phenomenon.

Communicating my own explanation in a fresh way that doesn't sound like a hackneyed campaign speech or an over-the-top sales pitch helps strengthen my faith. Offering a testimony about God's work in my own life gives me faith in the gospel's assurance that with God there is strength and meaning to be found in seeking to put the interest of others before my own.

The story that links together my own scattered assemblage of dots begins in Cambridge, Massachusetts. I grew up in an interfaith, academic household, the daughter of a American Jewish father and an English Anglican mother, and I was baptized into the Church of England as a young child. During the few years my family and I attended an Episcopal church in Cambridge, each of us had different reasons for going. My mother liked singing the traditional Anglican hymns she had grown up hearing in England. My father respected the old Irish American rector and thought my brother, sister, and I should have some exposure to organized religion—even if it wasn't his own Jewish faith. We came to know more about our Jewish heritage when my father began holding annual Passover Seders and attending Rosh Hashanah and Yom Kippur services. For me, Christianity was associated with singing in the choir, listening to the Christmas Eve reading of *When the Grinch Stole Christmas,* and playing the lead in our Sunday school production of the Book of Esther—a role that took on far greater importance for me more than twenty years later at seminary, when I became reacquainted with Queen Esther's story in a deeper way.

As I GOT OLDER, my marginal church involvement ceased altogether and, like so many other children of open-minded academics, I turned to more secular explorations. I spent teenage summers traveling and helping to lead other young people on Outward Bound-type backpacking trips in the Rockies. Besides fulfilling a desire for adventure and independence, these trips also met a growing spiritual need. I was stirred, listening to the wind move through an alpine forest or watching stars emerge in the reflection of a mountain lake at nightfall.

But finding God in nature wasn't the whole story. I was also inspired to be in a community of high school students facing tough physical challenges, young people who, back in school lunchrooms, might not acknowledge each other's existence—but who, after three days on the trail carrying each other's heavy packs, grew close.

To call these wilderness ventures religious experiences would stretch a conventional definition of religion. Yet they showed me how little I required things and how much I needed other people and the earth. Also, adventures far from home contributed to a growing sense of independence.

When I began attending college within walking distance of my home in Cambridge, however, I could not easily continue to equate personal growth with physical distance from home. Adventurous summer excursions were no longer enough to prove my independence. "Going away to college" had to involve more than moving to another zip code or amassing credits.

Summer vacation between my freshman and sophomore year was the context of my 1988 "mountaintop experience" in the Texas Panhandle. While visiting my roommate on her parents' ranch near Amarillo, I met an old cowboy missionary. He was the first person I'd encountered who combined a powerful intellect with palpable spirituality and a child's sense of awe—qualities I somehow associated with holiness. We had a parting-of-the-waters conversation that included a fleeting but tangible sense of a reality different from this one.

"Imagine starting out each day setting a foot out on the unknown," this elderly cowboy had mused, half to himself and half to me. His words reminded me of the leap of faith that Kierkegaard describes, but this setting-out clearly had particular meaning for a man who had spent seven years walking through eastern China listening to villagers and telling stories about his own transformation. "What an exciting way to live," the old man continued, radiating delight. "It has all been such an adventure." As we talked, I became enraptured and began to feel my future taking shape right there under the cottonwoods.

Though fleeting, this early encounter is related to why I am at seminary. If our lives were written in the constellations, that conversation would have been the moment when the orange haze of city lights peeled back to reveal a hidden set of stars, bright against the dark sky.

ACCOUNTS of mountaintop moments impress some questioners. Such accounts do not tell the whole story, however. What, these fellow seekers wonder, is the connection between an epiphany of the sort I have just described and the narrow, circumscribed duties of a parish priest in the Protestant Episcopal Church of the United States of America?

This was the same question I had on my mind over ten years later, one dismal day in the February of my first year at seminary. I was obsessing about my life—spiritual and otherwise—comparing my own experience at seminary with the graduate school lives of friends. Here I was in a small, heavily indebted institution without computer rooms, an affluent alumni network, or even *one* professor whose name could be the answer to a *Jeopardy* question. My Texas mountaintop receded like a distant mirage. My faith in my calling fell to an all-time low. Coming to seminary had probably been a mistake, or, at the very least, a waste of time. "Formation," that murky concept valued so highly by my bishops and having something to do with character development, prayer, and living in a community, was, I feared, nothing more than the inculcation of a particular flavor of "churchiness."

I struggled to explain my unenviable condition to my spiritual director, concluding with a tearful "It's just so *different* here."

Brother Clark Berge, an Episcopal Franciscan friar from the Society of St. Francis on Long Island, himself a fairly recent General graduate, laughed at me in the nicest way.

"So . . . you're having trouble adjusting from your last educational experience at one of the biggest, most famous universities in the world, with gobs of money and hundreds of connections, to being in a small seminary of a small denomination of the Christian church?"

I dabbed my eyes as Brother Clark continued.

"You could think of your situation as a kind of voluntary poverty. By being here you've accepted a certain type of limitation that, beyond anything you do in chapel, is a kind of spiritual discipline. Who knows where and how you will be called in the future, but have confidence that with God nothing is ever wasted."

I looked at him quizzically.

"Well, isn't that what God did?" Brother Clark asked me. "Didn't God adopt a radical form of poverty when He chose to embrace the limitations of time and space by becoming incarnate as a human being?"

Gradually I began to see that we seminarians are not simply learning a craft; we are also being shaped as persons. Sung grace at meals, prayers before each class, and monthly meetings with a spiritual advisor offer evidence that the spiritual lives and character of seminarians weigh equally with grade point averages and liturgical literacy. We will not graduate simply as experts in a field of liturgy, worship, or prayer, like the Levites of Ancient Israel. Seminary formation is a step toward the Anglican priesthood, a step that lies between the role of an elder in a community of faith and the part of a mediator between God and God's people.

MY REASONS for attending seminary are uniquely my own. But what distinguishes everyone in my class from graduate students in secular fields is that each of us has a story woven into the Story that begins with Genesis and ends with Revelation. Our stories have distinctly personal settings: Detroit or Roanoke, a hike on the Olympic Peninsula or a talk by a Texas lake. But they are also part of something archetypal. In our minds, they are Paul's story or Mary Magdalene's story, or Deborah's or King David's story. Our personal stories are linked to the Christian story about a God who would limit himself in time and space and whose life, death, and resurrection offer us grace—the fruit of which is service to one another.

THIS BOOK is a confession in the ancient sense of the term, meaning a testimony rather than an admission of sins. I trace loosely my own path in following a calling to the ordained ministry through my first year of seminary, from August 1997 until August 1998.

When the last interesting dinner conversation about the nature of my calling is over and I've exhausted all psychological, sociological, and economic explanations—it is the story of Esther that I look to for inspiration. I hope to be alive for a purpose, and I pray that like Esther, who by the grace of God uses her bravery and wisdom to save her people, I, too, will be able to fulfill my calling. A young Jewish woman chosen as queen of the Persian Kingdom, Esther is asked by her uncle Mordecai to thwart plans by one of the king's evil advisors to massacre every Jew in the land. When Esther explains to her uncle the personal danger she would face in trying to persuade the king to withdraw his royal edict, Mordecai warns her that if she does not act, she, too, will be destroyed. And, he adds, "Who knows whether you have come into the kingdom for such a time as this?"

Who knows whether you have come into the kingdom for such a time as this?

AT SEMINARY, time is marked not only by exams and vacations, but also by seasonal collects and Lenten meditations. With each change in the liturgical season, the altar cloth and the priests' and deacons' vestments change from the green of Pentecost to the purple or blue of Advent, or from the purple of Lent to Easter's white.

At our community-wide Eucharists we hear stories of John the Baptist, the nativity, and the coming of the Magi, followed by accounts of Christ's temptations in the desert and his reassuring words to Mary on Easter morning. Sometimes, in addition to our twice-daily communal worship, we share a seasonal ceremony—a silent refectory meal on Ash Wednesday or an all-night Easter vigil. Worries about that final exam in early church history interweave with meditations for Advent, creating a tapestry of mind and spirit that at first seems strange to people such as myself who are used to compartmentalizing our experience. The overlapping of the liturgical and academic years is continuous. The tower bell's ringing summons reminds us that in worship, ordinary time and eternity intersect.

This book is organized around the themes of each season in the church year for several reasons. Everyone charts life's forward movement in days, weeks, and seasons, but for Christians who believe their stories are related to Christ's story, time is also measured in periods of expectation, penitence, exaltation, and redemption. I have tried, then, to describe my expectations about seminary in light of the larger Advent theme of expectation for the first and final coming of Christ. Likewise, the season of Lent—the church's time of looking inward and preparing for the resurrection—becomes the background for my own and other seminarians' experiences of doubt, temptation, and reconciliation.

In the case of Easter and Christmas, however, I borrow from the pre-Reformation priests who used to say 9:00 A.M. prayers late in the morning. Just as they said all the daily offices but did not always do so on time, so I have taken creative license with the chronological order of my seminary years to explore the message of every church season. The structure of the Christian year underlines that mine is not a journalistic account of the first year of seminary so much as a confession relating my experience of "coming into the kingdom" within classroom and chapel walls.

Advent

Drowned by piped holiday Muzak, the sacred themes of the West's most secular holiday tend to hide among our shopping lists and eggnog parties. However, the "eschatological expectation" aspect of Advent—the anticipation of Judgment Day—occupies a unique category of neglect. In the swirl of holiday activities, even Christians find it easy to overlook that Christ's birth into history relates directly to his promise, in the words of the Apostles' Creed, to "come again to judge the living and the dead." Besides, in today's easygoing, prosperous America, the idea of a time of reckoning is more than a little discomfiting.

Liturgical scholar Laurence Hull Stookey believes that each element of the church calendar helps believers to "know and live out the conviction that the whole human family dwells continuously at the intersection of time and eternity."

Advent is no exception. The first season in the church year, Advent begins four Sundays before Christmas. Advent is a period in which to anticipate the Feast of the Nativity on December 25—and, in the longer view, to prepare for Christ's Second Coming at the end of days. Most people in Western culture have an unparalleled sense of time and its speedy passage during the weeks preceding Christmas. For Christians, however, our heightened awareness of the passing hours and days is not just from fear of failing to finish our shopping. It comes from the realization that the birth of Christ promised a day when God's will would be done "on earth as it is in heaven." In Advent, we relive the promise that one day our time will become God's time. For Christians, living each day anticipating God's revelation of eternal time does not degrade the passing moments. Rather, living "at the intersection of time and eternity" invites a hearty respect for the here and now, as each temporal second offers us a portal into the infinite.

Discernment

Like almost every other master of divinity student entering General Theological Seminary in the fall of 1997, I started down the road to seminary more than a year earlier in my home diocese of Washington, D.C. Before even applying to seminary, Episcopal candidates face a "discernment process" within their own communities of faith. In a denomination that makes decisions based on the complex interplay between tradition, reason, and scripture, an individual's conviction of his or her "calling" alone is not sufficient qualification for the priesthood. With the help of a committee from our parish, a lay mentor, our rectors, the bishops, and a larger Commission on Ministry, we aspirants would have our calls to ministry tested over a fixed period of one year.

On a Saturday morning in early September 1996, I and nine others arrive at the Church of Our Savior in Silver Spring, Maryland. We, the 1996 class of aspirants seeking diocesan sponsorship as candidates for ordained ministry, are gathered for orientation. Our numbers are reduced from the introductory meetings we had had the previous spring. Each candidate is directed to a separate foldout table, one of a line ranged across the linoleum-tiled floor of the parish hall. The room seems as awkward as the ten of us. What is a thriving day care center filled with shrieking children during normal working hours has been gravely rearranged for our arrival. Dozens of miniature chairs huddle in the far corner of the room, while office dividers covered with taped-up Magic Marker pictures of the burning bush hug the back wall. Bagels and cream cheese lie on a serving table; aware of the early hour, the bishops have kindly arranged for several pots of coffee, too.

Each applicant brings an entourage and carries copious documentation. We have psychological assessments, medical and financial records, a stack of required reading, commentary forms for the Parish Committees on Ministry to fill out, and a schedule for interviews with both bishops of Washington. Our rectors and parish committee representatives are in tow, a group with whom we will continue to discuss our callings regularly over the next four months. Finally, a lay mentor —a person who, though not a member of the clergy, is very active in his or her church as well as in some community ministry—is assigned to each aspirant.

Clustered around each applicant's table, the rectors, lay mentors, and parish committee members swivel to face one end of the room. Seated there at a long table is the Commission on Ministry—a group of four lay people, four priests, and the suffragan bishop of Washington. Together, this group and the diocesan bishop will eventually grant up to five people the title of "postulants": people on the ordination track whose callings the church considers valid for ordination. And for those not selected? They can either pursue lay ministry or move to another diocese that might consider their aspiration more favorably.

Leafing through a booklet of questions to be discussed with my parish committee over four months, I am intimidated by their intimacy. "How has God spoken to you? Through silence? Through art? Through nature?" "What part does your need for love or desire for approval play in your pursuit of this potential ministry?" "How do you function in interpersonal relationships?" Despite trepidation at the prospect of sharing such private matters with near strangers, I wonder if perhaps people called to other professions might also benefit from such a thorough investigation of their motives.

Sitting behind the center of the long table, Bishop Jane Holmes Dixon, the "suffragan," or assistant, bishop of Washington, is the second woman ever to hold this position in the Episcopal Church—the U.S. branch of the Anglican communion. She taught eighth grade, raised a family, and at age forty entered the priesthood. Bishop Dixon, a warm, personable figure with dark curly hair and bright eyes, is at once inviting and a force to be reckoned with. I watched in awe the previous year when, after the diocese refused to accept even one aspirant for ordination, she had politely but unapologetically fielded hostile questions from a group of irate rectors and parish committees without appearing the least bit ruffled. Should any of us harbor doubts about the nature of our vocation, Bishop Dixon reminds us of the words of her own bishop: she might have chosen a marriage ceremony in which she eschewed the vow to obey her husband, but if she wanted to be a priest, she must vow to obey her bishop.

The diocesan bishop, the Right Reverend Ronald Haines, is a tall, somewhat austere figure who better fits the traditional image of a purple-vested member of the episcopate. Before entering the clergy, he had been in business and engineering and had led Bible studies and prayer groups as a lay minister. Despite his intimidating height and reserved demeanor, Bishop Haines is exceptionally pastoral. My rector praised the bishop's conscientious responses to individual priests in his diocese. This rang true during my first year at seminary, when Bishop Haines personally answered each of my four Ember Day letters. (Ember Days are a cluster of three days during each quarter set aside for prayer and fasting in the Roman tradition; during each three-day period Episcopal seminarians are required to write one letter about their experiences to the diocesan bishop.) Indeed, a quick survey of my classmates indicated that getting a response of any sort was the exception and not the rule.

About the priesthood as a vocation, neither bishop minces words:

Point number one: Only 10 percent of the job is doing holy things up at the altar—a full 90 percent is resolving conflicts. Priests must remain eternally vigilant in a world ridden by anxiety.

Point number two: The job absorbs twenty-four hours a day, seven days a week, and frequently the most difficult part is setting limits. "People never die on time," Bishop Haines intones. Inevitably, the morning you're packing to leave for a long-planned family vacation, an important member of the congregation faces the last painful stage of a long battle with cancer. In a certain sense, priests are public property, Haines says, and must compensate by being extremely disciplined about making time for themselves and their families.

Point number three: Several personality types don't mix well with the ministry. For example, take the Lone Rangers. Bishop Haines describes this type as slightly depressed individuals who do not rely on colleagues or family for support. "They probably work in an isolated or difficult parish and think that they are not appreciated for the sacrifices they make," says Bishop Haines. "If they are not careful, the Lone Rangers become susceptible to any flatterer that comes their way. Then boundaries fall between the clergy and the congregation, and that's when things can get dangerous."

In view of these rough realities, what could possibly make the priesthood worthwhile?

"The transcendent moments carry you through," acknowledges Bishop Dixon. "The times when you see God in the funeral of one person or in the birth of another, or in a parish adopting a new program. These times make it worthwhile, when life moves quickly from the irrational to the transrational."

I reflect on the examples of the two bishops themselves. In one week, Bishop Haines's responsibilities carry him from negotiations over an Anglican-Lutheran ecumenical agreement, to a discussion about the future of the church with a roomful of aspirants, to a conference on polygamy among Christians in Africa. The diversity of the tasks and questions these bishops wrestle with attracts me.

The bishops' talk makes clear that vestments, symbolically, weigh very heavily. Bishop Haines is occasionally sued by errant parishes; further, a recent study reports that bishops face a relatively high risk of contracting serious illnesses during their tenure. Research also underscores that the odds of enjoying a storybook career in the priesthood are slim. Ex-seminarians whom I'd queried had not always found a whole lot of God in their three-year training course. Still, I can't restrain my expectation that the mysterious magic of seminary would imbue my classes, my colleagues—and myself.

A FULL YEAR later, after four months of biweekly discussions, a litany of tests and interviews, and a report outlining at least two alternative lay ministries, three aspirants out of ten of us are accepted as postulants in the diocese of Washington, and I am one. Those who took themselves out of the process or were discerned by the bishops and the Commission on Ministry as best suited for lay ministry became eligible for diocesan grants.

The two other aspirants granted "postulancy"—both women—plan to attend Virginia Seminary in Alexandria. My hopes are set on General Theological Seminary, where I feel I can receive a better "formation" than at any university-based divinity school. It has the added attraction of being the only Episcopal seminary in New York City, where my husband-to-be has worked since graduating from college.

Take It from the Bottom

My personal advent at General Seminary began in August, the first week of orientation. Coming on the heels of my honeymoon hiking trip in the Brooks Range of Alaska, my late arrival lacked the thoughtful preparation typical of the Advent season.

Still, my first months at seminary mirrored at least one Advent theme. I expected that seminary would be filled with the same sort of epiphanies—understood as sightings of God's eternal time—that had led me to the priesthood. But I was surprised to find how much "regular" time occupied the place, too. Just as in the world outside the Close that defined the seminary's green core, epiphanies rarely occurred inside those walls. I was never more aware of the gulf between God's time and our time, of that apparently unattainable "intersection between time and eternity," than in my first months at General.

IN THE last week of August, at two in the morning, halfway through orientation, my husband Greg and I arrive at our Chelsea apartment. We had spent the previous three days marooned in an Alaskan fog bank —a frustrating ending to an otherwise picture-perfect honeymoon. For three fog-bound days in our tent, while Greg finished two John McPhee books and a history of Alaska, I plowed through my assigned summer reading, a tome by a former archbishop of Canterbury entitled *The Gospel and the Catholic Church.* Between footnotes, I tried not to think about the invaluable pieces of information being divulged to my future classmates at the orientation I was missing. Classes had not even started, yet I was already behind.

Mary, a classmate from Los Angeles whom I met briefly during the summer, is the sacrificial lamb assigned to stay up late to give us our apartment key. This is not a role, I would soon discover, that my colleague-in-faith takes to kindly. Short, with black hair and dark eyes, Mary has enormous energy, doesn't waste time, and doesn't suffer fools. Mary is a Canadian of Lebanese extraction and was granted postulancy in the diocese of Los Angeles. Before coming to General, she worked in Canadian television, ran her own cafe, sold Toyotas in Detroit, and worked as the verger—in her own words, "a liturgical roadie"—at All Saints, a thriving parish in Beverly Hills. In her last job at All Saints she acquired the two things she thought essential for any woman entering parish ministry—an extensive theological library and a large toolbox complete with electric drill and plumbing wrenches. I assumed her choice of "must-haves" meant that whatever happened at her parish during her adult classes on the works of Julian of Norwich, Mary could always look forward to a long soak in a fully functioning bubble bath at the end of her day.

Apparently, Mary had spent much of that day trying to reassure her mother in Canada that the decision to leave a secure job and comfortable life in Beverly Hills for a cell-sized seminary apartment and an uncertain future had not been rash. Mary was not amused by an administrator's request that she stay up until 2:00 A.M. to let her tardy neighbors into their new home. Christian guilt was not a powerful motivating force for Mary. The General Seminary tote bag she won for playing the "name-your-classmate" bingo game until the wee hours was small compensation. Mary was completely immune to the martyr complex.

Compared to the shoe boxes that pass for most New York apartments, seminary housing is very reasonable—after the East Village studio Greg had called home, our new apartment is downright luxurious. However, as we drag our backpacks and luggage up to the fifth floor—exhausted and already missing the vast Alaskan sky—neither of us is particularly mindful of home décor. Pushing aside the stacks of boxes and unopened wedding gifts that the movers had delivered in our absence, we unroll sleeping bags and stretch out on a slightly warped wooden floor. Two days ago, we were listening to water rushing down a stony arctic riverbed; now we drift off to the call of car alarms.

I AWAKE to the sound of the chapel bells. This is to be a familiar wake-up call, along with the accompanying panic, as I realize I can't possibly shower and dress in ten minutes and make morning prayer, which takes place directly across the street, inside the Close. I have no time to get my bearings on this concrete island of over 7 million people that will be Greg's and my home for the next three years.

Throwing on a pair of hiking shorts and a clean T-shirt, I race downstairs. Crossing the street, I realize I do not yet have a key to the seminary's side entrance, an easy-to-miss iron gate opening onto soft green lawns that are accessible to the public only through the main entrance on Ninth Avenue. I hover anxiously, awaiting a fellow seminarian or staff member to happen along and let me in.

Minutes later, patience rewarded by the kindness of strangers, I step into the Close for the first time, apart from a brief visit last spring. Recognized as one of the ten most peaceful spots in New York City, the Close enfolds green lawns lined with low boxwood hedges, star magnolias, and holly. London plane trees and American elms shade the flagstone walkways. There is enough silence to hear bird calls.

The word "Close" means "an enclosure, courtyard or quadrangle abutting a building . . . the precinct of any sacred place." I came to understand that it held additional meaning for General seminarians, for "The Close" was nearly synonymous with the seminary community itself. "Will you be moving onto the Close?" classmates or professors would ask prospective students. In discussing controversial matters such as the Lambeth Resolution on human sexuality, seminarians would debate the potential "response on the Close." In my mind, the term simultaneously implied familiarity, claustrophobic exclusivity, comfort, and intimacy. Sequestered as I was within it, the Close became physically and semantically the emblem of my call, of my first year of seminary, and of my evolving understanding of the church's role in the world.

My first experience of morning prayer in the centrally located Chapel of the Good Shepherd goes by in a blur of chants, readings, and frantic page-flipping. When the service ends, I am about to return to my unpacking when I remember the Bible study group for new students after the service. I loop to the right as I leave the chapel, following a garden path lined with patches of grass and park benches, to join the madding crowd in Seabury Hall, one of the seminary's many red brick buildings.

In the basement, a student-run lounge called "Seabury's Bottom," groups of new students circle chairs. Led by several returning seminarians, we gather in small groups to discuss the morning's lesson: the account in Acts of Paul's shipwreck. "When had we survived shipwrecks in our lives and what had they taught us?" is the question for contemplation.

Today, I can't remember many of my group's shipwreck accounts or, for that matter, if I divulged one of my own. I was too busy sizing up my classmates by the way they dressed, wishing I'd worn something less backwoodsy Alaskan. One young woman impresses me—athletic, short, with neatly cut hair and palpable confidence. On the whole, however, the observation of a friend who sometimes ate bag lunch on the Close seems fair: seminarians are a friendly bunch, but not out to win any fashion contests.

Other students in my group are older than I expected, and I hear a surprising number of southern accents. The long-haired man who leads our discussion sports a goatee. Like me, he seems to have just rolled out of a sleeping bag, appearing similarly bored and a tad cynical about the whole exercise.

The discussion livens up when we talk about what has brought us to seminary. Liz, a sprightly young mother and former actress from Chicago, starts off. Liz began to tire of playing prostitutes in off-Broadway shows, she says, confessing with amusement that her religious zeal as a fourteen-year-old member of a born-again youth group might have been prompted by a crush on Jesus: "He was this great-looking guy in all the posters, and I was at kind of an awkward age."

About that time, Liz set out to save everyone, including, but not limited to, her family and her Jewish classmates. Liz's teacher transferred her out of the high school speech class after she admonished all the non-Christians in her class that they were going to hell unless they accepted Jesus Christ as their personal savior. "I was a nightmare," Liz admits. "My parents and teachers didn't know what to make of me." Her family moved to Chicago, and she separated from the youth group. Settled in a new environment, she retired from zealous attempts to save souls and started down the well-worn path of a struggling artist.

A decade later, in her first job after leaving the theater, Liz worked with Jewish refugees from Russia at a Jewish institute in New York. She taught English and helped reintroduce basic Jewish traditions to these refugees who had lost their religious culture, an experience that urged Liz to investigate her own Christian faith in greater depth. By the time she entered the ordination process in her early thirties, Liz's spiritual priorities had shifted from saving souls to building communities rooted in shared faith.

Phoebe, the natty and confident woman I had admired earlier, seems inspired by Liz's frank description of her journey to General. With little hesitation, she tells us that for a long time she thought that going to church was obligatory—"like paying your taxes"—and that reading religious books on a park bench was just "a great way to shake off skanky men." On a college retreat with other students from Notre Dame, however, Phoebe found herself alone in a church. "It sounds so schmaltzy when you talk about it," Phoebe laughs, "but for a single nanosecond, I felt that I knew everything in the world. God had revealed everything to me." She went outside and heard the words of the sacrament's institution running through her head—"Do this in remembrance of Me." For the first time she felt a profound call to ordained ministry.

Only one thing stood in the way of Phoebe's call and her eventual ordination: she was Roman Catholic. Her epiphanic glimpse of God's eternal time, and her place in it, was immediately followed by two years of depression very much in human time, time during which she worked at a well-known Chicago teaching hospital as a researcher on post-traumatic stress disorder. As she traveled to and from the hospital, she reflected on how God could call her to something that she could not do. Phoebe compromised by pursuing a career as a psychologist, since becoming a priest in her tradition seemed impossible. She had joined a Roman Catholic church in her neighborhood, but soon discovered they were not interested in letting her act even as a lay minister. So she quit.

In 1991, Phoebe moved to San Francisco with a friend and started work at UC Berkeley. For the first time, she began to meet women who attended seminary at the Graduate Theological Union, and she found her call re-emerging. She circulated through a lot of different churches but found none where she felt at home. Opening the phone book, she came upon a church called St. Andrew's. Dialing the number, Phoebe heard the female assistant rector pick up on the other end. Phoebe explained that she was a Roman Catholic feeling a call to the priesthood. "Let me guess," the rector said, "they don't want to talk to you about that, do they?" Within weeks, Phoebe joined this Episcopal congregation.

MARY, THE sacrificial key holder who, by appearances, has suppressed the uncharitable thoughts she harbored toward me, announces that she'd been very fulfilled as a lay person. Her "burning bush" moment at the altar rail in a church basement had been a call to turn her life over to God. The idea of priesthood evolved much later. Within months of her conversion, she quit being a star salesperson for Toyota in Detroit and moved to Los Angeles, where she worked as a verger in a large Episcopal church in Beverly Hills. Mary had been happy to organize worship services and lead catechumens in preparing for baptism. She remembers looking at all the vestments hanging in the sacristy closet and thinking that there was no way she would fit the mold for ordination. "I was too short, too old, too *something*." Apparently her parish and bishop did not agree.

After the women in the class break trail, the men in our group begin to disclose their stories. Nathan and his wife Claire come from Asheville, North Carolina. Nathan, tall with dark brown hair, sports Bermuda shorts and an all-American, one-of-the-guys demeanor.

During most of his youth he was indifferent to religion. At college in Asheville, Nathan fell in with an evangelical student group whose generosity and dedication he found appealing. Although he grew discontented with their lack of tradition and intolerance for ambiguity, this group gave his life a focus that Nathan felt was missing, and he stayed involved through college. When Nathan's mother, a devout Episcopalian who brought him up by herself, asked him to attend church with her, he refused, saying, "What has the church ever done for me?" The Episcopal Church held no interest for him, and he didn't feel like he "owed" it anything. In fact, he later discovered, the church had done quite a bit. After his father left them when Nathan was still an infant, the church secretaries looked after him while his mother sought counseling to combat severe depression. "I wasn't aware of it then, but the church sure *had* done a lot for me," Nathan concludes, visibly moved.

WITH AN unholy wad of chewing tobacco tucked in his lower lip, Brad, a wiry young man from Alabama, leans back, grins, and says he came to seminary the way someone comes upon a car wreck. Usually, according to Brad, the first people on the scene end up playing crucial roles in the rescue. This accident analogy fits his call. The priest in his church had left their congregation while Brad was still an undergraduate, and other lay people who recognized Brad's leadership abilities asked him to fill in by giving the sermons. Gradually, congregants began to say that he might make a good priest. A position as chaplain at a mental hospital became available, and friends urged Brad to accept it. Buoyed by their enthusiastic support, he agreed to give it a try. After three years, his work came to the attention of the area's bishop. His "call" came quite literally over the telephone: Would he meet the bishop for lunch to discuss the possibility of becoming a priest? "Good Lord! What a strange thing to say!" Brad recalls.

We don't get much more than this out of Brad that first morning. After begrudgingly sketching his story, he abruptly rises and announces he's off to get some real coffee. Later, as I got to know Brad, it struck me that this first morning must have realized one of his greatest fears, that seminary is filled with people who are into soul-searching before breakfast. As I discovered, Brad came to General for one reason: his diocese told him to. Strict attendance at chapel services attracted him about as much as Mardi Gras without beads and feathers, or Friday night without a bottle (or at least a healthy pour) of Jack Daniels. Brad preached powerfully, studied hard, and was always the first person to cut to the quick when a theological discussion drifted, but memorizing the dates of the first four ecumenical councils didn't make him jump out of bed in the morning. Somewhere in Alabama, Brad had picked up the idea that salvation was a gift—something precious that people couldn't earn through striving, prayers, or penitential acts. Salvation came through grace—you couldn't bargain for it.

As only the second openly gay priest from the diocese of Alabama, Brad was asked by his bishop to remain celibate as a priest—an expectation that apparently did not apply to heterosexual candidates for ordination. Still, God's summons to the priesthood was not so all-consuming that it robbed him of his free time and spirit of adventure. I don't have to hang around Brad long to understand what he thinks of Episcopal piety and where the church can put it.

One person in our group is silent—uncharacteristically so, as we would learn. Mauricio, a robust Costa Rican of African descent, is already ordained. As eager as most of us are to stretch our legs, we are curious about what has brought Mauricio to General Seminary—

especially when a master of divinity degree is not required for the priesthood in Costa Rica.

The son of the bishop of Costa Rica, Mauricio is the youngest of the seven ordained priests in Costa Rica by about fifteen years. Permission to study overseas did not come easily, since his departure left his father shorthanded. However, given the future responsibilities Mauricio faced, he believed a seminary education in the United States was a worthwhile investment. The weight of his future responsibilities and the role he would likely play in the Costa Rican church had struck Mauricio suddenly, as he lay sunning on a Florida beach. If there was an epiphany that led him to General, it occurred there on the sand.

Although he doesn't advertise it in Seabury's Bottom, I later discover that Mauricio is a poster child of a future church leader. Twenty-two years ago, he won a prize for not missing a service in two years as an acolyte. Seventeen years ago, he led his parish's youth group. Fifteen years ago, he gave his first sermon to a Panamanian congregation. At age eighteen, he became his church's youngest senior warden—the head of an elected vestry. He was the only child in a family of five to join holy orders, but it was a role that fit Mauricio like a second skin—not that he displayed any sense of entitlement.

Mauricio had come to New York with little money, even though he had sold his car and most of his furniture in Costa Rica. Mauricio arrived at General with his wife Ebeth, two suitcases each, and a thousand dollars. Early in the year, he couldn't finish his tutorial reading because he had to spend Saturday nights preparing sermons for small churches in Brooklyn that offered him small stipends. Mauricio did not discuss how hard he worked. He wasn't looking for sympathy. When he had to choose between preaching at a small church or assisting at the Cathedral of St. John the Divine on St. Francis Day, one of the biggest services of the year at arguably the most visible Episcopal house of worship in the city, Mauricio went to the small church.

The stories continue as the members of General Theological Seminary's class of 2000 take the first tentative steps toward becoming a community of faith. More than one person's account hinges on a moment of epiphany—a revelation that changed the course of his or her life. Kathi, a sorority leader turned senior warden and Philadelphia suburbanite, felt a burning sensation and butterflies in her stomach every time she acolyted or took communion between the ages of twelve and fifteen. Kate, an editor at a large New York publishing house, had begun to explore academic master's programs in religion, until the day she burst into tears on the subway when her husband suggested she apply to seminary instead. George says his parents found him at the foot of his bed, age six, blessing Necco wafers and juice.

Whether in the "schmaltzy moment" during which Phoebe comprehended the whole universe or in a family member's idle comment, small things had assumed larger meaning for each of us. For people who feel called, mini revelations are especially significant. They are sightings of the eternal—God's time spied from our lookout posts in the everyday.

Panhandle Epiphany

My classmates' stories recall my own first sighting of divine time. The sighting occurred in the course of a conversation that, in the words of comparative religion scholar Mircea Eliade, "opened a gate to heaven."

The conversation took place the summer between my first and second years of college, two thousand miles from home. I was visiting my freshman roommate at her family's farm in the northern Texas

Panhandle. We were very busy attending barbecues, riding motorcycles along dusty ranch roads, and volunteering on an archaeological dig near the farm.

On our third day of the dig, someone pointed out an old man sitting beside our excavation, a rancher and missionary who spoke several dialects of Chinese. My interest was aroused. I left the ancient arrowheads and ambled over to introduce myself. The old man was stooped forward, balancing his elbows on his knees to brush dust from his trousers. His cane rested against his shoulder, and a straw hat shaded a pair of watery blue eyes from the hot summer sun. I sat on the ground to talk.

His name was Bransford Eubank, and he was ninety-two years old. He'd grown up on the ranch where he still lived. A long time ago, his relatively new wife, eighty-two-year-old Eloise, had been the girl next door. With help from their neighbors and a few hired hands, Bransford and Eloise continued to raise cattle, graft fruit trees, and pump oil. Bransford was a naturalist, amateur geologist, agricultural consultant, pastor, and teacher. Though he spoke five languages and knew how to shoe horses and rope cattle, Bransford was at heart a Christian missionary who had once dared to deny himself and, as he put it, "take up my cross." "I saw following the Lord as a big adventure," he told me. "I figured that I'd give it a whirl, and that was that."

Urged on by my curiosity, he described his first trip to China, when he had taken a herd of cattle all the way from Texas to Peking and then taught agricultural husbandry at Yenching University. After returning to Princeton Theological Seminary, where he earned his master of divinity degree and was ordained a Presbyterian minister, Bransford had gone back to China. For seven years, he walked from village to village, teaching and preaching. He would stride across the marketplace and start talking to the oldest man he could find. Soon, people would gather around, curious to learn why this foreigner was addressing a respected elder. When they asked Bransford his business, he would reply evasively—goading their interest all the more. Only when they insisted would he give a word or two from the gospel. Although he complained about being too old "to cut the mustard anymore," he could still quickly recall a Chinese saying for every earthly phenomenon. Rain was "heaven's breath spoiled," and a successful person was "a superior man who works at basic things."

That afternoon, when we unfold a pair of deck chairs beside a lake near our campground, I catch Bransford's sense of wonder. We discuss his painstaking observations of female wheel bugs laying their eggs and debate Stephen J. Gould's theories of evolution. Despite a caution that "relatives are like underclothes: they should be worn but not exhibited," he describes his imaginative genealogy, which includes Pocahontas and an English knight slain by Richard III. Finally, Bransford shares his youthful, exuberant love for his new wife—a love he once thought "only came in early years." "Mr. One-in-a-Million," Eloise later tells me, often takes her out in the rowboat on the pond in front of their house and sings to her by moonlight. Besides God, Bransford is the most important thing in her life.

Bransford did not fit neatly into any of my categories. His devout spirituality sat comfortably with deep intellectual curiosity and keen wit. Born before the invention of the light bulb, he had managed to keep his mind flexible and open. Bransford's humility was palpable and his ability to touch hearts incontestable.

"Would you dare?" This was the question that goaded Bransford after he'd read the crucifixion story and Christ's message to deny the self and follow him. The question followed him out of his college dormitory one night and changed his life. "Lord, that's a step out onto nothing," he remembers protesting. But, as Bransford confides with a smile, he was, after all, a Marines recruit—first you obey the command, and only later question the commander's authority.

A step out onto nothing. I found all this talk of Jesus alien and the analogy to the Marines disconcerting, but Bransford's challenge to wake each morning and walk out onto the unknown sounded like an adventure. I wanted to find, after ninety-two years, that I could still feel each day full of surprises. I, too, wanted to grow old in a way that let me, despite curved spine and failing eyesight, take pleasure in finding a fossil, or new buds on a grafted pecan tree.

I could not guess that more than a decade of awkward experimentation with these ideas would pass before the faith I admired in Bransford could begin to become my own. Indeed, Eliade's "hierophanies"—manifestations of a wholly different order visible through mundane objects or activities and part of every religion—offer no maps for day-to-day living. They do not imply anything except that something sacred has shown itself. So, although I did not return to Cambridge that fall convinced that every word of scripture and the creeds were true, my need to integrate this strange lakeside moment was so keen that it inspired a period of analysis and the practical testing that continues to this day.

I have found other ways to illustrate my lakeside hierophany. Take the medieval garden tapestry that Lawrence Stookey describes in *Christ's Time for the Church.* On it, swaths of green are intermittently dotted with gold buds. From the display side of the tapestry, the buds appear inconsequential, drowning in a groundwork sea of green. Yet, on the tapestry's hidden reverse, unbroken threads of gold stretch from one bud to the next, linking all so thickly that every inch of the rug is laced with gold. Through my conversation with Bransford I saw a small opening into the glowing firmament on the eternal underside of our time-bound human existence.

Studying under the Cross

When I contemplate the tension between our time and God's time, between 9:00 A.M. and eternity, seminary life seems firmly on the temporal side of the dial. Nowhere is this more pronounced than in chapel.

Seminary life centers on the Chapel of the Good Shepherd, an ornate, gingerbread-colored house of worship with dark wooden monastic pew benches and excerpts from the 1928 Book of Common Prayer Ordination Rite etched in gold Latin lettering around the walls. I quickly discover that many General students love liturgy. Caroline, for example, the outgoing chief sacristan in charge of the chapel service, confesses her passion for liturgy during a senior sermon. It had started innocently enough, Caroline tells us. She was drawn to church by the music and stained glass windows. The next thing she knew, she was suffering lower back pains from too many deep-knee genuflections, and her AOL bill skyrocketed as she spent more and more time on line debating purple versus blue vestments for Advent and how to remove wine stains from the fair linen. For Caroline, liturgy was serious business. Everyone, even the acolytes intensively recruited from large congregations three minutes before the opening hymn, was an important player.

As a "junior," shorthand on the Close for first-year student, my initial chapel duty was as an acolyte. Acolytes are on the lower end of the liturgical food chain, a version of election monitor whose role is mainly to attend the service and lead the procession at its beginning and end. Acolytes also supply the elements so the priest can bless the bread and wine without having frantically to count wafers or refuel wine halfway through communion. Caroline has no patience for participants who feel their job is less crucial than that of the priests and deacons.

In my pre-seminary salad days, I half imagined that anyone marching past the altar rail would enter the ecclesiastical counterpart of C. S. Lewis's Narnia, a magical world discovered by children who enter through the back of an old-fashioned wardrobe. The raised section at one end of a church where the altar and cross are usually planted only *appeared* connected with the rest of the building. In reality, I fantasized, it would yield a glimpse of the divine such as I'd seen during that lakeside talk in Texas.

MY FIRST experience as an acolyte in the Chapel of the Good Shepherd differs slightly from this vision. The morning of my duty, I prepare by exchanging my Tevas for a pair of black flats and by turning my T-shirt inside out so its design doesn't show through the thin white robe. Inside the sanctuary, I try to remember that as a candle bearer I don't bow to the altar like everyone else. In the Episcopal tradition, the flow of worship is not advanced if an acolyte goes up in flames.

The service itself is hair-raising. Remembering when to sit, stand, and bow is a full-time job. Whenever the priest stands silently in position for more than a few seconds, my mind races to remember what I'm supposed to bring to him. I have never experienced so much stress in worship.

Once, I told a college friend that I wanted to attend seminary partly to help create spaces in which other people could encounter the sacred. I imagined that a well-planned service would inspire the same feeling of peace that one experiences when watching an alpine lake change color when the wind moves across it. I wanted people to leave church feeling as if they have just returned from a mountain retreat. It was a mild shock, then, to discover early in my time at General that making sacred spaces involved so many tedious, mundane activities. Creating a sense of God's unfailing presence was commingled with assuring an adequate supply of communion wafers. On that first morning, the awesome mystery of the God who valued sparrows and numbered the hairs of our heads remained elusive. I was too busy calculating the expected rate of the congregation's consumption of bread and wine.

Mauricio snaps me out of it that afternoon. Robing up, I notice, he pays the same close attention to the folds in his vestments that my husband devotes to cleaning the apartment: "I try to make no mistakes so as not to distract the congregation from the experience of worship," he explains matter-of-factly. If he drops the Gospel book or trips over the altar rail, people will pay more attention to him than to the service. By Mauricio's logic, helping people concentrate on their prayers through a seamless performance on his part allows the congregation to participate more deeply in worship. This is fundamentally a selfless act. I can buy that.

Once, during a two-hour service in his Costa Rican church, Mauricio says, he welcomed the unexpected as evidence of the Holy Spirit. Although some clergy might panic when confronted by stocking-clad feet to wash on Maundy Thursday, Mauricio embraced this unscripted moment as a gift of the spirit. If Mauricio could revel in the unexpected during our regimented chapel ceremonies, perhaps all was not lost. Although I did not see much gold thread serving next to the altar in the Chapel of the God Shepherd, my faith reminded me that it was still there.

ONCE CLASSES BEGIN, I fall quickly into a routine. With the exception of chapel services, held twice daily, and smaller classes, General could be almost any small liberal arts college. The academic regimen is recognizable and comforting. A typical Monday schedule includes:

7:50	Wake-up chapel alarm bells
8:00	Morning prayer
8:20	Breakfast in Seabury's Bottom
10:00	Old Testament (New Testament and junior tutorial on Tuesdays)
11:00	Chapel practicum: Orientation to the dos and don'ts of chapel worship
12:00	Lunch in the refectory
1:10	Music
3:10	Greek
4:30	Library visit #1: Greek sentence translation
5:30	Evensong
6:00	Dinner in the refectory
7:00	Library visit #2: More Greek sentence translations and required reading assignments

Most of my classes are in Sherrod Hall, one of many brick buildings lining the Close, flanking the chapel. The cream-colored walls in every room have one set of windows overlooking the Close and another opening onto Twenty-first Street. With blackboards, clanging radiators, foldup chairs, and roller maps of the ancient Near East, these classrooms are characteristic of many small colleges around the country. The crucifix hanging above the blackboard in each room is the sole reminder of where we are.

The crucifix is a small symbol that makes a big difference. One of my later church history professors points to it as the ultimate reminder of the line in the sand that separates our approach to scholarship from other contemporary methods. Like the nineteenth-century Anglican scholars we study, seminarians at GTS are expected to "study and pray with the same mind." We meditate on the martyrs, for example, while memorizing the dates of their demise. Pious Hunter S. Thompsons, we Gonzo historians of the postmodern world put our assumptions up-front and in full view.

At the same time, our first lecture in Old Testament offers a thorough introduction to the branches of historical and literary criticism—standard academic fare. The diocesan requirement that I learn Koine Greek, a language helpful only for deciphering the earliest versions of the New Testament, demonstrates an expectation of serious scholarship as well. Finally, within two weeks of reading, I have gained a new view of King David as a far more complex character than the innocent slingshot-wielding warrior of God I once assumed him to be. King David's apparently generous gesture in sparing his enemy's life, I discover, may have been a calculated decision by a shrewd political leader to avoid establishing an uncomfortable precedent of regicide.

In my New Testament course, too, I employ familiar academic tools. Coming from a liberal arts background, I find it easy to see Luke's eschatology in his constant refrain that "the end has not yet come." Luke, we learn, wrote later than Mark and addressed a largely gentile Christian community. Luke's community knew that the first generation of apostles had died before Christ's reappearance, which many early Christians thought would occur in their own lifetime.

Doing a biblical "exegesis," or close reading, of the text is an academic exercise both familiar and rewarding. The major difference, however, of studying under the crucifix becomes apparent in our discussions concerning the Bible's authority. Is the Bible just another classic

Western text like the *Iliad* or *Moby Dick*? How will we describe the relation between God and scripture to our future congregations? Also, many of our assignments are practically useful as well as academically engaging. My term-end exegesis, for example, will be pastorally reincarnated as a sermon.

My Greek and music classes offer unique perplexities. Few undergraduate associations are there to help me, and, to compound the problem, the crucifix doesn't shed much light, either.

Our music professor, a renowned composer whose anthems and choral arrangements are sung in Episcopal churches around the country, instructs our class with an eye to the plumbing in music theory. He expects that we, too, may one day get down in the pit to wrestle octaves, half-steps, intervals, and accidentals. He assures us that even the most tone-deaf seminarian can be surprised by the hidden abilities of his or her vocal apparatus. I have not read a line of music since piano lessons stopped at "Für Elise." My only recent vocalization has been yodeling Neil Young songs in our living room while Greg picks at his guitar. Despite the professor's sonic confidence, I have my doubts.

Over Thanksgiving, I must develop a point of view about *In Tune with Heaven: A Report by the Archbishops' Commission on Church Music*. The current church debate over pipe versus electronic organs captivates me about as much as learning the difference between the burse and the corporal during acolyte training. From the perspective of the two-thousand-year history of church music, the problem could be my attitude, not the subject. However, there is no doubt that memorizing Recommendation 1.4, which urges clergy to be "scrupulous in their observance of the laws of copyright," leaves me cold. Worse, finishing the paper threatens to intrude on an energetic annual family football game on the banks of the Charles River.

At the beginning of the course, I expected that it might inspire me with a sweeping historical overview of music's part in Western spiritual life: the slave runner composing "Amazing Grace" aboard his ship; the evolution of monastic chants; the effect of the English Reformation on church music. Learning the different parts of an organ doesn't elicit the musical passion I hoped for. Nor is it much consolation to know we should appreciate this knowledge because one day we'll all have to raise money for our own parish organs.

And then there is Greek. Fresh from five years of French, I discover that nothing about *Candide* has prepared me to struggle with hundreds of forms of the Greek verb *luo.* My undergraduate semester of classical Arabic is the closest analog, but glottal stops don't help me decline Greek nouns.

The first day begins auspiciously enough. My classmates and I learn most of the Greek alphabet in the first class. Staring at familiar Greek letters like alpha, omega, gamma, and delta gives false confidence. This is easy, I think; this page looks like a sorority awning.

It takes all of five minutes—as I scan my first homework assignment, which asks for a translation of five short sentences—for the horror to strike. To survive, I will need the mind-set of a plainclothes detective. Before I know it, half my weekend has disappeared and I am staggering from the library clutching a tattered piece of paper dotted with a few fragments in English and many question marks. Although I take our professor's hint to tape all the endings of the first and second declension to the bathroom mirror, Greek vocabulary still goes in one ear and out the other. Apart from *agape, cosmos, theos, ecclesia,* and selected others, I retain few words. Mnemonic devices offer a little assistance. *Ballo* means "catch" because that is what you do with footballs, and I can remember that *dexomai* means "to receive" because my made-up mnemonic—*fedexomai*—is close to what I receive from the express driver.

Although the misery of first-semester Greek cements close friendships, I am discouraged, as with music, by the lack of immediate theological payoff. Greek's relationship to the crucifix above the chalkboard is apparent only in the suffering it produces. I have not envisioned spending hours translating the Greek equivalent of "see Spot run," and the romance of reading the Gospel of John in the original seems inconceivable to me that September.

Under the crucifix, rigorous intellectual analysis is not an end in itself. The cross reminds us that our academic pursuits, no matter how skeptical or far-reaching, lie within God's wide embrace.

Clerical Barbie

Free time during Advent goes to unpacking boxes and shuttling wedding presents from the mailroom to our apartment. Place settings, picture frames, paperweights, lettuce spinners, hand-dyed napkins, towels, sheets, and ceramic casseroles piled up in our kitchen and dining room—along with cardboard boxes and oceans of Styrofoam peanuts. Questions of where to put these things and when to use them (and for what) preoccupy my spare time.

Such questions epitomize the task of adjusting from living alone to living in a community of two. As a single person, I was proud of my lack of durable housewares. At heart, I saw myself as an explorer—able to move easily through life, unencumbered by possessions and free of appetites for expensive furniture, porcelain, or framed pictures. The chairs in my college rooms and my Washington studio apartment creaked home from flea markets; the bed, sofa, and desk were battered hand-me-downs. Household conveniences should occupy the least possible mental energy and income, I thought. If the second-hand bookshelf in my bedroom broke, a milk crate and two phone books were fine. I imagined that my unconcern for worldly possessions was further evidence of my calling. It never once occurred to me that my indifference to material goods might connect to never having experienced material want.

Greg, my husband, was a history of science major when we met as undergraduates five years before. A management consultant during the first year of our marriage and every bit the intrepid explorer of life that I conceived myself to be, Greg has a different philosophy toward material things. Rather than paying twenty dollars for a third-hand kitchen table, then spending three times that amount on duct tape to keep it upright, Greg considers himself a card-carrying member of the invest-up-front school of household purchasing. He prefers to spend time looking and to pay a little more for a table if it promises not to collapse under his dinner.

Now Greg and I have our first opportunity to live with our different views of home furnishing. As time wears on, however, my perspective evolves. The hand-carved African salad bowl from my godmother proves indispensable for holding nuts, key proteins in our vegetarian household. The toaster oven, which appeared so appallingly *chrome* when it first emerged from the box, becomes a dear friend as soon as I discover during midterms that dinner can be piping hot in minutes.

Our growing stash of wedding presents is also a reminder of time's passage. Like uttering the words "until death do us part," the unwrapping of our All-Clad saucepan with its forty-year warranty offers a small but sure reminder of our time-bound existence. Without turning my dinnerware into a Proustian madeleine, I can still say that the humble durability of many wedding gifts did prompt reflection. Life, as my marriage vows and our wedding gifts suggested, might not be an infinitely branching path, but moments are more precious when they are sturdy and serviceable. Our heightened sense of time's finitude was part of my first Advent in New York, an awareness well-suited to the themes of this first season of the liturgical year. In Advent, we are forced to acknowledge "the end"—both the final days of "our" time and the fulfillment of God's purpose for the world. In the readings, we hear Jesus telling us to "keep awake," for the end is at hand. We hear John the Baptist quote Isaiah's instruction, "Prepare ye straight the way of the Lord." Advent suggests that we should be mindful of minutes, that we should accept, as our earthly seconds tick away, that they are under-stitched and supported by a different form of time and that therefore we can cherish them for what they are: "a full-bodied, incarnational life with God now."

"So, how do you know they are not all weird church people?" Ellen, a nonseminary friend, demands over her beer. Greg and I are outside the Close, enjoying familiar company in a cozy bar in the West Village. Evensong seems like it occurred in another life.

A double major in biology and computer science at college, Ellen is doing a postdoctoral fellowship in New York and running a small Web-design firm on the side. She stopped by our apartment earlier in the evening, highly suspicious of the large number of people who greeted her between the front door and the elevator. A Nietzsche enthusiast during college, Ellen still feels social niceties are for the weak. Most likely, excessive friendliness is disingenuous—especially in New York City.

Ellen's insatiable curiosity manifests itself in many ways. It leads her to spend hours working in the lab, sitting in seminars listening to the latest developments in gene therapy, or systematically reading through the entire canon of nineteenth-century Russian literature at night. Religion, too, provokes her interest, when it appears "relevant." Buddhist monks teaching ex-gang members to build sand mandalas in L.A. qualifies; so does Sister Helen Prejean's work with death row inmates. Raffles, bake sales, and hymns sung off-key, however, do not make the grade. In Ellen's opinion, the Episcopal Church is too closely associated with lime-green corduroys and phony English accents. One glance at our bulletin board, replete with lengthy unsigned treatises on the appropriate and inappropriate use of the laundry room dryers, and Ellen deduces that direct confrontation is not the Episcopal modus operandi. Without knowing much about Anglican theology, Ellen suspects that the Episcopal Church lacks *soul.*

Along with another college acquaintance who covers politics for the *Village Voice,* we discuss Ellen's definition of "weird." Getting beyond couture and haircuts, Ellen makes clear that in her mind a "weird church person" is someone who uses religious sanctions to justify mediocrity and a closed mind. He or she identifies God with certain types of music, people, or behaviors that feel safe. A "weird church person" is someone who makes no effort to keep up with culture or public affairs and who avoids people who challenge his or her beliefs.

Ellen explains that Greg could never be such a person. Greg might be a baptized Presbyterian married to a woman who feels called to serve in the Episcopal Church, yet he is not conventional. He plays in a rock band. He is addicted to yoga. It does not appear to faze Greg that historically the clergy spouse has been female, deeply involved in her husband's work—certainly not in a career of her own. Nor does it bother Greg that for hundreds of years the church has reaped the benefits of an enormous amount of unpaid, often unacknowledged work from clergy spouses. When Greg looks ahead at the years to come, he is quite sure that baking cookies for coffee hour is out of the question. Running a music program might be possible—if he is allowed to choose the hymns.

When we first arrived in New York, Greg declined to join a support group of seminary spouses that met regularly. Greg made clear that having a spouse in seminary was not a debilitating disease. Unlike many of our neighbors in seminary housing, Greg felt a little cheated of the free anonymity of life in New York. It was no solace to him that General felt like a "small town in a big city"—rather, Greg said, the price was right.

REFLECTING later on our conversation, I realize that most seminarians are atypical, but they are not weird by Ellen's definition.

Conversations in Seabury's Bottom surely prove us a motley crew. There, Old Testament underlining and Greek flash cards meet the *New York Times* and the *Post,* a volatile mixture made even more potent by the mugfuls of stale, strong coffee that flow from the back bar for fifty cents a cup. Regulars at the Bottom include Phoebe, Liz, and a smattering of "senior," or third-year, women.

Sitting down at a Bottom table, mug and toasted bagel in hand, I land in the middle of a conversation between two seniors who have abruptly broken off arguing about New Testament theology to discuss an article in the *Times*'s business section about the CEO of Mattel Toys.

"So, why isn't there a Clerical Barbie?" the woman to my right asks. Clearly, she means a Reverend Barbie, not the Barbie who sits at a big filing cabinet.

"You're right! Come to think of it, I had Doctor Barbie and Businesswoman Barbie, but I never did find Clerical Barbie!" the student on my left pipes up, putting down her coffee.

"That would be so great!" the original toy enthusiast exclaims, clearly envisioning a mini ordination in a Barbie Dream Chapel. "Can you imagine changing her chasuble for the seasons and high holy days?"

"Or outfitting her in that simple black and white cassock and surplice for morning prayer!" someone else adds from her station by the toaster oven.

Other people, myself included, chime in with more trappings for a new doll in clerical vestments. It would be a big hit with little girls, and we wonder what has delayed Clerical Barbie's introduction for Christmas.

"What do you think the problem is? Barbie is usually so *hip*."

"Probably has something to do with the cost of starching all those itty-bitty collars."

"Uh huh. Sure, sure."

"I'm sure it doesn't have a *thing* to do with pressure from the American Conference of Roman Catholic Bishops."

"Oh no. Nothing whatsoever. Probably the Vatican wouldn't have an opinion on Clerical Barbie, either."

Not quick-witted enough to hang tough in the volley, I wait for the round of guffaws that signal the next topic for rock-Bottom analysis.

"So what would you have done if you'd been the South African Catholic priest who watched President Clinton get up to stand in line for communion?" I hear Liz ask Phoebe.

"I'd have given it to him, no question. I mean, it doesn't matter who, you can't just refuse a baptized person communion," Phoebe replies quickly.

"Yeah, but that wasn't this priest's reason for giving Clinton the bread," Liz retorts. "Look here, they quote the guy saying that he didn't feel right refusing the most important man in the world. That has nothing to do with the principle of extending communion to every believer who wants it."

"So, what are you saying? That the priest buckled under pressure?" Phoebe presses.

"That's exactly what I'm saying," Liz replies.

At this point, Caroline, the self-confessed liturgy addict, turns to the horoscope section of the *Post,* hoping to change the subject. "OK, who wants to hear Libra?" she asks, launching full tilt into the daily reading.

STEPPING into the Close during Advent of my first year requires a huge adjustment. Still, the quirkiness of church culture is not unlike the idiosyncrasy of other earthbound institutions. The only difference is that entering the seminary, I half expected heaven, not another temporal place mingling light and shadow.

After three months at General, I am more aware of God's time as distinct from my own. In my life, however, these two kinds of time are no closer to the intersection that Advent embodies.

Christmas

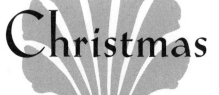

In *The Risk of Love,* Anglican theologian W. H. Vanstone describes a dream he had after encountering a drunk on the steps of his church one Christmas Eve. In the dream, a garbage collector comes to him for advice. "What shall I do?" the man asked, pointing in distress toward an enormous pile of refuse where—under a heap of rusted pipes, rotting food, and auto parts—he had found a buried human face. This face, Vanstone felt certain, was the face of God.

The next morning, Vanstone told his congregation that this vivid dream image of a suffering God buried beneath the pain and waste in creation portrayed God's self-emptying love as accurately as did his birth in a manger. We merely got lucky that God chose to reveal himself through the charms of a tiny infant rather than the horror of a battered human face. Ultimately, both images express the same inexhaustible love that bears the suffering of all creation.

FROM THE OUTSET, Christians have celebrated Christ's birth in light of the knowledge of his death and resurrection. The earliest parts of the New Testament—Paul's letters and the earliest version of Mark—do not even mention the nativity. The first evidence of any celebration of the savior's birth occurs in fourth-century Rome. The most likely explanation for the choice of December 25 as the day of celebration is not that it posed a Christian alternative to the pagan celebration of *Sol Invictus;* rather, it was a day calculated to fall exactly nine months after the early Christians' celebration of the Annunciation on March 25. As J. Neil Alexander, former liturgy professor at General, notes, the clichéd, greeting-card nativity scenes of Mary and Jesus surrounded by farm animals, shepherds, and wise men under the gleaming rays of a four-pointed star illustrate the important theological point that God's incarnation is ultimately known under the light of the four-branched cross.

For me, the "Christmas Spirit" becomes even clearer when I view it from the vantage point of the Easter event—Jesus Christ's death, resurrection, and forgiveness of even the enemies who killed him. God's love expressed in the nativity is not only a feeling of good cheer—although the amiable warmth of a holiday party should not be dismissed out of hand. Instead, though it may share a common attraction for what is good and beautiful, God's love at Christmas is unique in its extension to embrace the outcast, the downcast, and the enemy.

For all the genuine happiness associated with this season, a creative tension exists for me between the familial blessings I enjoy during the last week in December—the family football games, the delights of catching up with friends—and the sound of a real Christmas story. What is the connection, I wonder, between the warmth and comfort of the hearth during this holiday season and the challenging stories of forgiveness and reconciliation I have read or listened to over the years? One such story is the account I heard while traveling of an American couple who moved to South Africa to help develop the poor neighborhood where their daughter was murdered. Another illustration of a powerful Christmas witness is the report I read of the man who helped mentor the drunk driver who ended his wife's life. Are stories like these not the more genuine Christmas narratives?

"My True Love Gave to Me"

During my first year at General, my Christmas stories were more descriptive of easy devotions than of a more difficult, enemy-embracing love.

Although this most sacred holiday still lacked the heavy responsibilities I would have as a parish priest, I and many classmates encountered stresses of a different sort at this season. In the frantic rush of exams and list-making before Christmas break, I caught a glimpse of Christmas spirit at home.

"Where, in all your activity, in the fruitfulness of your days, do you find God?" Brother Clark had once asked me. This is an especially sharp question at Christmas because I'm easily bedazzled by its secular delights—the satisfaction of completing course work, the excited anticipation of returning home to Cambridge, the city's glamour of lights. Where, among all the pearls of this sparkling season, is the Bible's pearl of great price?

DURING final exam week, Greg and I have difficulty finding quiet moments. My exams coincide with the deadline for the final presentation on a consulting job he has been working on nonstop for six months. While I'm in the library, Greg adroitly draws together assorted personalities and views in order to prepare his team's recommendations. Our late-night dinners, a routine checkpoint all that autumn, cease altogether. We resort to leaving hand-written notes in our front hall. Thus Greg scrawls to me:

> Morning,
>
> Watched you for five minutes this morning to make sure you were still breathing. Walked, fed and watered the dogs. In that vein,
>
> - Would you mind picking up the dry cleaning today? Stock of fresh shirts running low.
> - Have you seen my Walkman? Didn't have time to excavate the dining room table. In fact, I'm afraid to go in there. Something was making ominous growling noises last night.

I scribble a reply on the other side of his note before heading off to my evening rendezvous with Bernhard Anderson's *Understanding the Old Testament.* My scrawled note and a plate of food I've filched from the dinner at the refectory will greet Greg when he comes home exhausted:

> Sorry, no time for dry cleaning—Old Testament tomorrow at ten. Come visit at the library. Also, can we schedule a time for Greek flash cards? Will move piles from dining room table after exams. Promise.

Greg's response appears the next morning:

> Thanks for dinner. Couldn't find you at the library.
>
> - Don't worry about the dry cleaning, but how about the laundry? I'll take what I can get. Will pay large sums for clean socks.

- Tried to straighten up a little. One thing: maybe try to keep the drawers and cupboards shut so we don't decapitate ourselves in a precoffee haze. Not that I bashed my head or anything.
- Got new pens to replace dead ones. You remain the Pol Pot of Pens. When you enter a room, most run screaming in fear. FYI, technically, caps should remain on when not in use.
- Still searching for my Walkman . . .

Soon, this abbreviated style of communication wears thin. Doesn't Greg know how much I have to do? This is no time to obsess about cupboard doors and bother me with ballpoints. I dash off a quick note reminding him that the laundry detergent is under the sink, adding that it is inappropriate of him to label me the Pol Pot of anything.

Over the next twenty-four hours our notes multiply and begin to conquer the earth. I confront at least two while getting dressed the next morning.

"*Please shut me!*" order two yellow stickies on the inside corners of a kitchen cabinet.

"*Mug- and plate-free zone*" says another note with an arrow pointing to the top of the toaster oven.

I appreciate my husband's sense of humor, but I wish he'd stow the quips until I finish my New Testament and music exams. Annoyed, I grab my books, push past the laundry basket (which has been moved to a strategic location blocking the front door), and head for the library.

The day does not prove very productive. Perhaps too little sleep is the main reason I have difficulty with Jesus' parables in St. Matthew's Gospel. All I can think about is the fact that it's Thursday, I have two exams tomorrow, and, in a fit of insanity, I've agreed to preach on Sunday—the same day Greg and I should leave for Boston. I have no Christmas presents for anyone. A panic I haven't felt since the last grim college all-nighter tightens my stomach. "Therefore I tell you, do not worry about your life, what you will eat or what you will drink.... Can any of you by worrying add a single hour to your span of life?" Matthew 6:24 could have been written in Sanskrit for all the sense it makes to me now.

By the time Greg finds me, I'm teetering on the verge.

"So, how's it going?" Greg asks, sauntering over to the table around which I've paced for an hour. "How was Greek? I'm sorry about the flash cards. I meant to test you this afternoon after my presentation. I called but you weren't in."

I shoot Greg a withering look, forgetting that congratulations are in order for him. "My Greek exam was yesterday," I snap.

"Hey, what's wrong?" he asks.

"Oh, nothing," I retort bitterly. "I just have two exams tomorrow that I'm completely unprepared for, a sermon to write for Sunday, and a flight right afterwards that we both have to catch. That's all."

"Well, it's nice to see you, too. You're a star and I'm sure you'll be fine, because you always finish and you always do a good job. So if you don't believe in yourself right now, at least believe in my opinion of you. Listen, I'll be doing the laundry if you want to come find me later or want help with anything or just want to take a break, decompress, and laugh a little. Sorry to interrupt you—just wanted to check in and make sure you still recognize me. By the way, my meeting went very well, since no doubt you've been dying to know." Greg leaves.

I stare at my books for another few minutes before giving up. At home, Greg is on his way downstairs with the laundry basket. Silently, I take one handle and help drag it to the elevator. We pull it out on the basement floor and start tossing clothes into the machines. Neither of us says a word.

I indulge my foul mood, tossing handfuls of dirty socks and T-shirts into the washer to the cadence of my complaints. There is no way I will pass the Bible content part of my OT exam (hurl Greg's yoga pants). I barely remember the difference between a major and a minor key (toss in running shorts), and I just learned that the music professor wants us each to sing as part of our final exam (throw in paint-speckled navy T-shirt). I never was so overwhelmed as an undergraduate—further proof that I am losing my edge (stuff in two sheets and an armful of pillowcases). From all I hear, seminary is a cakewalk compared to parish life.

Greg is deliberately loading the machines. Several minutes into my dramatic soliloquy, as we reach the bottom of the basket, I notice that Greg is staring into it with a quizzical expression. Taking in his curious look and running out of things to throw, I rein in my rant.

"What are you looking at?" I ask, anxiety slowly yielding to curiosity.

Greg says nothing, watching me again with the same bemusement before returning to the hamper.

"Look at what's at the bottom of the laundry basket," Greg says.

I glance down and see two socks, a shirt that needs to be dry-cleaned, and, hiding under the heap, a yellow Walkman. We look at each other, down again at the newly unburied treasure, and begin laughing.

Our surprise discovery pulls the week into perspective. Under a pile of dirty clothes, in the guise of a mass-produced material object, a humorous surprise reconnects us and puts me back in touch with the world. It might not have all the weighty significance of a human face under a rubbish heap, but it does the trick. Maybe seminary will work out after all.

A Family Christmas

After my last final, Greg and I pack and head for La Guardia with thousands of other family-bound New Yorkers. Along with warm clothes and a few stocking stuffers from the seminary bookstore, I carry a load of library books, my computer, and a set of Greek flash cards. These are security blankets, for Greg promised before we left that he would feed them to the Yuletide flames if he found me looking at them even once. Greg is prepared to do whatever it takes.

At Logan Airport, crowds of tired travelers crush around the baggage carousels. Porters with heavy Boston accents yell at the crowd to let them pass. Outside, where curbside traffic is equally chaotic and far noisier, I can see my breath. The damp bay air is slightly tinged with salt. Everything seems delightfully familiar.

I am first to spot my parents' dark blue station wagon. My mother pulls over in front of two Yellow Cabs and jumps out of the front seat to hug us. We pile our luggage in the back and are soon wheeling home to Cambridge.

As we pull onto Storrow Drive, which runs along the Boston side of the Charles River, my nostalgia grows. We pass the band shell and the esplanade, then Boston University; now Cambridge is near. The river sparkles in the setting sun, and I glimpse an MIT crew rowing upstream. As the river narrows and the low, grassy opposite bank comes into view, memories absorb me.

Before seminary or discernment or church of any shape or size, many of the major rituals in my life occurred around the Charles River. When I grew up in Cambridge, Memorial Drive was closed to traffic every summer Sunday. My parents took my brother, sister, and me roller-skating and bicycling along the river, and we sped under the canopy of towering sycamores. The commuter road, I remembered, was magically transformed into a peaceful passageway for pedestrians, and we were free to skate anywhere on the sun-dappled asphalt.

The river was also the site of the Head of the Charles Regatta, a point of pilgrimage for cooler-toting high school and college students from up and down the East Coast. The Harvard "River House" dormitories—Mather, Dunster, Leverett, Winthrop, and Eliot—lined the riverbank. My own college residence, Lowell House, lay a little inland, its white bell tower jutting above the massed red brick of the river houses.

Now, as we drive home for my first Christmas during seminary, the Weeks Footbridge passes on our right, evoking recollections of Lowell's annual May Day waltz—a dawn ceremony with ballroom dancing and mimosas to drink that went on during the Cambridge Pagan Society's maypole dance on the riverbank. Late one evening in the spring of my senior year, Greg and I had shared a bottle of champagne on that bridge.

Soon we cross the river to Cambridge, and my mother turns left onto Memorial Drive. I catch sight of the monastery of the Community of St. John the Evangelist, an austere gray stone building that houses an order of Anglican monks called the Cowley Brothers. The building sits inconspicuously between the park and the long row of Harvard-owned brick apartment buildings overlooking the river. For years I had bicycled and jogged past this building without noticing it. When I learned during college that the building was a monastery, I would pass it quickly with mingled fascination and dread. There was something awful about a group of people sequestered in darkness and mystery beside what appeared to be a center of freedom and power for the public good—the new Kennedy School of Government. Why would anyone choose a cloistered existence over such expansive possibilities? Such speculations unsettled me; the next day, I would choose a different route for my run.

Now, after three years working in a start-up nonprofit organization, one year of discernment in Washington, and four months of my first year at seminary, I see the monastery for the first time with simple curiosity. What is the ministry of this community? Who founded the order? What sort of liturgy do they practice? My interest is piqued when I hear that Tom Shaw, the new bishop of Massachusetts, is a member of this community and that he works directly with Suffragan Bishop Barbara Harris, the first woman bishop in the Anglican Communion. Although I have no canonical ties to the place, I've heard that this monastery plays a part in new, interesting work in the diocese of Massachusetts.

The Community of St. John the Evangelist is on my mind when, a few days later, we must decide where to attend church on Christmas morning. This is the holiday moment when the difference between traditional family rites and my newly forming church rituals is most pronounced. The special Christmas morning breakfast is followed by present-opening and phone calls to faraway relatives. Eventually, the time comes to attend a service. I'm elected to choose the church where some members of my family will go. I choose the Community of St. John the Evangelist.

We set off for the monastery at ten minutes to nine and arrive just as the service is beginning. On the way, I hear about the church service I missed last year while at my husband's home in Pittsburgh. "Our old church was so *depressing*!" my sister reflects. "We went last year and there were not more than five people in the pews on Christmas day!" Her words touch a nerve. Liturgy goes far in expressing the peculiar love of God at Christmas time, but luckily the gospel message does not rise or fall on the aesthetics of the service. Indeed, if the incarnate God whose love embraces enemies and outcasts is everything I banked on, then God speaks for Godself. However, in an interfaith family where regular worship is more the exception than the rule and individual religious beliefs are not easily decipherable, the temptation is to hope that my nearest and dearest will be touched by the Christmas story just as I am; and the responsibility for this experience rests on my choice of a church. Today I will have to make sure that my family gets its money's worth, so to speak, even though I know church is not a show.

The interior walls of the chapel are gray stone. Dark wooden beams rib the ceiling, and shiny marble covers the floor. Most striking is a tall, square canopy of polished stone covering the altar and transforming it into a small sanctuary within the larger one. The four gray marble pillars supporting this canopy are decorated with spiraling garlands of dark green pine. Long beams of light fall from the high windows onto the checkered marble floor. In the main sanctuary, monks and more lay people line the side walls, facing the center of the chapel in Quaker style.

The service itself is even more peaceful than the time we took to decorate our Christmas tree. The silence following each reading is charged; the monks' Anglican chants are haunting. The reading from John's Gospel—"In the beginning was the Word, and the Word was with God, and the Word was God"—has a dreamy, mystical quality. The gifts of the morning and the walk along the Charles River that we have planned for that afternoon fly out of my mind. The sermon offers an unsentimental view of the birth of Christ and what it means for us.

After the transport of the service, I am jarred into an abrupt return to the world when, after a few minutes of walking home in silence, I ask my sister what she thought of the service. I don't get much of a response beyond a comment about its length.

After more prodding questions about the sermon and readings, she tells me she enjoyed the reading that began, "In the beginning was the Word . . ." Both my mother and Greg had liked this passage, too. They agree that the cadence was lovely and that the passage was philosophically interesting. We discuss its meaning and sound until we reach the car. As I recall the Greek translation and open my mouth to enlighten everyone, I realize my audience has lost interest. We've moved on to a discussion of Christmas dinner plans. The service has been agreeable, but life goes on.

Tough Love at Harvard

THIS DISSONANCE between the Christmas celebrated at the Community of St. John the Evangelist and the one honored in the wider society—the difference between the love that is of God and the loves of secular society—was best articulated in a sermon by Professor Peter Gomes the following Sunday at Memorial Church in Harvard Yard.

As I remember him from my undergraduate years at Harvard, Professor Gomes, the Plummer Professor of Christian Morals, is a diminutive, fiery, brilliant African American Baptist preacher with an English accent who loves to tell the story about the time he answered the phone in his office, incognito, and heard the caller ask to speak with "that short, black man who preaches on Sundays." Professor Gomes's sermons helped sustain my faith through college.

More than any preacher I've heard, Professor Gomes seems to know how to interpret the gospel with so much humor and clarity that it resonates in his congregation's skeptical ears. He was fully aware that at least half the undergraduates in his pews, myself included, regularly sneaked out of their dorms on Sunday morning with the same fear of detection that a grounded teenager feels when slipping out for late-night carousing. He did not hesitate to bring our fears into the light of day in the most disarming, irreverent way. Gomes knew none of us had come to hear the news of a faith that was constantly apologizing for itself, trying to accommodate "all those people still sleeping back in the dorms." His take-no-prisoners approach to preaching the gospel worked as effectively on skeptical Harvard students and graduates as one of those university-led, full-on, multimillion-dollar fundraising campaigns.

When Greg and I take our seats in a Memorial Church pew on the Sunday after Christmas, we watch Professor Gomes climb a spiral staircase into the enormously ornate pulpit, knowing we're in for enlightenment. Gomes's message is, "Don't let the nostalgia of Christmas get in the way of your Christian faith."

Within minutes of his opening prayer, Professor Gomes has completely disarmed his listeners with witty stories of Christmas frivolities familiar to us all. People settle back in their pews like an audience digging in for a good film. There are chuckles and knowing looks and nods all around.

Before we get totally comfortable, however, Professor Gomes's tone changes and he launches into a story about a Christmas party he attended. A couple of eggnogs into the evening, the host of the party sat down at the piano and began playing Christmas carols with great gusto. Professor Gomes recalls watching the man's face when, after resounding renditions of "We Wish You a Merry Christmas" and "Jingle Bells," he attacked the second verse of "Hark the Herald Angels Sing." As the host began singing the words "Veiled in flesh the Godhead see" and "Hail the incarnate Deity," his voice faltered and he leaned forward, squinting and peering at the music as if uncertain of the correct words. For the preacher, this incident offers an excellent example of the "intrusion" of the Christmas message into a Christmas celebration.

I wonder if Professor Gomes and I attended the same party.

Gomes, warmed up by this time, is going full throttle in a slightly different direction. He lets us know what he thinks of Christmas pageants: "Those lovely little plays where we get to watch all of our delightful little children marching down the aisle playing harmless characters in an enchanting and endearing way." We put children in these biblical roles as a way of sugarcoating a very demanding, radical message about the nature of Christian love.

Christians, he continues, are the first to deny the power of the Christmas message. When Muslims and Jews complain about the crèches on courthouse lawns, we are the first to say, "They really don't mean anything—they're just holiday decorations." People of other faiths are fully aware of the radical claims the incarnation makes about God and human beings. In some respects, other people take these claims more seriously than we do, Gomes says wryly.

The atmosphere of lightness and comfort has all but disappeared. Professor Gomes's words hit close to home, inspiring reflection about our attempts to glaze over the Christian theology that may intrude uncomfortably upon our treasured holiday. We feel inadequate—hypocritical, even. At the very least, we are a people of weak faith, failing in our religious duties.

Sensing the wave of self-recrimination rippling through the pews, Professor Gomes is quick to stem the rising tide—the effect of a Puritan undertow still present in even the most liberal Cambridge Christian.

"This does not mean, however," he points out, "that as followers of Christ we are to nail ourselves to the cross. Despite what the history of certain types of piety might tell us, our savior sacrificed himself so that we might *not* have to do the same."

No, he continues, the answer is not to put away all the gifts and plum puddings. We do not serve the Lord if we react against Christmas pageantry by assuming a false austerity. The Christian call is not fulfilled by ignoring the message through either excessive celebration or meager self-denial. What matters is knowing that all those warm, peaceful feelings cannot be divorced from the difficult call to love and serve one another as God loved and served us.

I remember, much later, a homiletics professor telling me that the good preacher has a divided mind. One half of her brain must be steeped in the biblical tradition, while the other half must be able to walk through the "the valley of dry bones" in which she lives, naming the forms of death she sees there. "Cynicism," "elitism," "consumerism," and "self-absorption" were the skeletons that the Plummer Professor of Christian Morals identified in his own community surrounding Harvard Square. Speaking of vapid cocktail talk, precious pageantry, and apathetic public witness that Sunday, Gomes showed us a few of our own bones that needed resurrection. By linking our daily condition to the biblical promise of salvation, Gomes did what every good preacher does: he began a dialogue between God and God's people. ("And if you don't believe that *this* makes a difference," my homiletics instructor had concluded with relish, "then I'm afraid you're in the *wrong business.*")

Spirits of Christmas Past

Returning to New York as the twelve days of Christmas end, I discover that I am not the only student to feel tension between Christian faith and Christmas nostalgia. January finds Mary, Brad, me, and a few others gathered again in Seabury's Bottom. We are supposed to be cooking breakfast for the seniors who are taking their General Ordination Exams—four days of open-book exams on everything from scripture to pastoral care. (Most dioceses required us to pass these exams, in addition to our seminary course work, in order to be ordained.)

During our breakfast preparation, Mary has a distinctly uncommunicative air. Once described as having two gears—"on" and "off"—Mary normally shows the quintessential morning personality. On this day, possibly suffering jet lag, Mary is not her usual effusive self until the end of the meal. All of us who help cook sit down for coffee and the remnants of Mauricio's Spanish omelet.

We canvass the intelligence we gleaned from the seniors about the General Ordination Exams. Which was the more difficult question—analyzing the ethics of South Africa's Truth and Reconciliation Commission using two twentieth-century Christian theologians, or discussing a hypothetical situation in which a child in your congregation whose parent has just died asks you if her mother is in heaven and whether she will see her there?

Soon, however, conversation drifts to our Christmas vacations: culture shock for all. Phoebe spent much of her break defending the ordination of women and Darwinian evolutionary theory against her fundamentalist in-laws. At one point on Nathan's extended tour of family members throughout Maryland and Virginia, he heard himself introduced by a relative as "a first-year seminarian at General Theological Seminary in New York, where he's the only straight male member of his class." Others had weathered Southern Baptist jokes about "Whiskeypalians" and Christmas-party inquisitions by people who'd stored up all their existential questions for just such an opportunity.

Mary describes going back to her home in Windsor, Ontario, a border town for Detroit gamblers where Christmas Eve found more people in casinos than in pews. The joke around the table on Christmas

Eve, she tells us, was how many people would be up for a round of blackjack after the midnight service.

"To be honest, when I left New York, it was like I was all dressed up with no place to go," Mary mused.

She had not been home for Christmas for five years, since moving to All Saints in Beverly Hills. There, Mary reported, Christmas had been a "bang-out" celebration—a "standing-room-only event where people were hanging from the rafters." There were three services: a children's service at 4:00, another at 7:30, and the "real show-stopper" at 10:30 P.M.

On Christmas Eve of her first year at seminary, Mary decided to cross the river to Detroit. There she discovered a depressing church less than three-quarters full. The church used a 1979 Book of Common Prayer, but that was about all she found familiar.

Mary leans back in her chair, thinking how best to summarize the evening.

"Basically, it was a cold, rainy night in Detroit; I wasn't sure whether my car was going to be ticketed or stolen, and ... Well, let's just say I knew I was a *long* way from Beverly Hills."

L.A. was no longer home for Mary—and neither was Manhattan or General Seminary or even her hometown, except in a marginal childhood way. The Christmas holidays were emblematic of the whole seminary experience—a liminal period, similar to baptismal preparation or to initiation and other rites of passage.

BRAD CLEARS his throat because he has a Christmas story to top Mary's. He reminds us that he'd taken his music and Old Testament exams early so that he could fly home in time for a friend's ordination in Birmingham. When he got off the plane, he ironed his robes because he was to march in the procession. The ordination was beautiful, he said, but the whole thing was over very quickly.

"Suddenly it was December 20 and there was no more church," Brad says, "no priests, no bishops, no chapel, no clerical collars—the whole nine yards. It was all gone. All of a sudden I was free. It was weird."

Enjoying his freedom, Brad stayed in Birmingham for a few days before joining his family on the Alabama coast. There he again saw friends from his time as a chaplain at Bradford Psychiatric Hospital. Mostly, they were in their late twenties or early thirties and completing master's degrees in social work or counseling. Brad's friends worked in the hospital's adolescent program that taught teenagers outdoor skills using the team-building exercises of rope courses, white-water rafting, and climbing. These activities enabled kids to "face their demons" with the support of a group. After work, Brad used to go out a lot with these friends—to rock climb on weekends or watch videos at their houses. "One of our favorite things," Brad confessed, "was to rent *From Dusk Till Dawn*. We were serious Quentin Tarantino groupies."

I ask Brad to give us a clearer picture of his friends' looks and mannerisms. Other classmates also want to hear the real story.

"Oh that's easy," he replies. "Kinda granola-outdoorsy, weed-smoking types. Long-haired dudes who hate deodorant ... iguanas for pets and tattoos on their ankles, the whole thing. They were totally cool people, and I fell madly in love with them because they were so relaxed and easygoing compared to the other staff at the hospital. Either you could be indoors with the caseworkers and psychiatrists comparing notes on the medication levels of a patient's urine sample, or you could be outside swinging with the kids telling them when to jump from the top of the pamper pole. It was pretty clear where I'd rather be."

Brad met his friends again over Christmas, at a karaoke bar they frequented. "It was a dreadful little dive," Brad shrugs, "really horrid. Sandwiched between a motel and a waffle house, as I recall."

He and his friends constructed a tradition where he'd sing his theme, Barry Manilow's "I Write the Songs That the Whole World Sings."

"So I walk into this bar and sit down with my friends and the next thing I know, I hear my name over the loudspeaker, and what could I do?" Brad reflects ruefully. "I have to get up in the middle of this redneck bar and start singing Manilow hits, hamming it up. My friends take out their lighters like it's a concert. I mean, forty-eight hours earlier I was taking my music exam and going to chapel in THE General Theological Seminary of THE Episcopal Church with THE Book of Common Prayer, and now I'm singing bad '70s songs at a karaoke bar in the Birmingham suburbs! It's like, *hello,* will the real Brad please stand up?"

"Then I start wondering," Brad continues, "what am I going to do when I get ordained? Will I still be hanging out in karaoke bars? What will my bishop say? Finally the song is over and I head back to our table. All my friends are joking—'Have you changed? Can you still drink with us?' They are really glad to see me and want to hear what's going on, but I try not to get too deep because everyone's been drinking and no one really wants to hear about it. The atmosphere had begun to change, so I went home and crashed as soon as I could."

Though the evening "was a really good time," it had "a kind of melancholy to it as well." As a priest, Brad knew he'd have to socialize a great deal with his congregation and that karaoke would probably not rate high. Brad realized how much he would miss his former life and his old friends, who, at that moment, he wanted to keep just as they were.

"You know how you wake up one day and wonder whatever happened to those friends?" Brad asks. "That night I was conscious of those days with my friends passing, going away right before my eyes. So, even though it was Christmas, there was a sadness to it." Brad's words unsettle me. He has identified the cross of priesthood: the challenge of leading a solitary existence in the midst of community—a weight even heavier than low salaries and long hours.

Brad's family lives in Robertsdale, a small town near the Gulf of Mexico. His father is retired from a paper mill in Mobile, and his mother has been at home for as long as Brad can remember. Three sisters and one brother live nearby. None of his family, except his elder sister, is at all religious.

"Things were going along fine," Brad says, "when the next thing I knew it was Christmas Eve, and suddenly I realize that no one wants to go to midnight mass except me. My parents were at home, but everyone else was out partying or doing whatever. Part of me felt as if I were dorking-out a little, but another part really wanted to go—like it wouldn't be Christmas if I couldn't share something with other Christians."

I ask Brad how his parents reacted. Luckily, he had borrowed a parishioner's car in Birmingham. Borrowing his dad's truck would have been like trying to pass an act of Congress, he laughs. Brad picked a parish church almost at random, a place about twenty miles away where his grandfather was buried in 1992. He looked forward to attending the service anonymously. It would be a relief not to have to chat about seminary or his future plans. He was feeling a little bit down about his vocation, though. "While I was driving alone to this little parish on Christmas Eve, I was wondering why I'd chosen this life for myself, when all it did was take me away from the things I love," he says.

Knowing nods pass around our table. Who hadn't felt this way?

"But then, I got to the church," Brad continues, "and it was like a huge reunion. I knew so many people there! I saw college and high school friends, cousins who I knew lived in the area—but I'd been sure they wouldn't bring their kids to a midnight mass. I even knew the organist, who had moved from another parish across town. I couldn't believe it. All those people I knew in this one little church!"

For Brad, this was a revelation that validated his calling. As long as he was in the church, he realized, wherever he went, he would never be alone. He would always be near people who understood what it meant to be a disciple. Such moments assured him he was on the right track. Why couldn't they occur more often?

Possibly because Christmas had been our first re-entry into secular life since September, Brad, Mary, and I noticed that we felt some distance from a holiday that had operated by its own laws for so long. Common to us all was the jarring contrast between a reunion with old friends and familiar family rituals, on the one hand, and the call to worship a God who asks us to love enemies and outsiders, on the other. Our experience of competing Christmas stories differed only in degree from the challenge every person of faith meets in a largely secular society.

Once again, I saw clearly that preparing for ordination did not guarantee that I'd transcend the conflicting pulls of the easy and difficult loves symbolized by Christmas. I had not overcome my hunger for Christmas cake or been filled with the desire to hand over to the poor all my thoughtfully chosen gifts. My desire to preach to my family about materialism was matched by my delight at receiving a beautiful coffee-table book on St. Francis of Assisi. Indeed, my discovery of the Community of St. John the Evangelist and my new understanding of the liturgical side of worship and scripture had only strengthened the tension I felt between the easy and difficult loves that Christmas asks of us all.

Epiphany

Before Christmas became an important feast of the church, Justin Martyr argued that Jesus' real birthday "began for men when they first realized who he was"—that is, as theologian J.C.J. Metford writes, in the celebration of Epiphany. Two events helped identify Jesus as the Christ—first, the adoration of the Magi, symbolizing Christ's revelation to the Gentiles; and second, his baptism in the Jordan River, when the Holy Spirit descended and a voice from heaven named Jesus the Son of God. Centuries later, Christians celebrate the season of Christ's "epiphany"—from the Greek *epiphaneia,* meaning "a revelatory manifestation"—beginning on January 6 and continuing for nine weeks.

Although I was at home in Cambridge for the beginning of Epiphany, writing thank-you notes, going to the dentist, and savoring unhurried breakfasts with the *Boston Globe,* a light went on over winter break that changed second semester at seminary. Throughout the fall term, despite the stimulating interfaith roundtables and our animated chatter in Seabury's Bottom about Clerical Barbie, I couldn't forget Ellen's concern about my catching the church bug. Her voice was in my ear, offering a running commentary about our institution being out of touch with society. Although my secular critique of the church persisted, when I returned to General for a second semester, our priestly vocation—flawed and anachronistic as it may have seemed—became real.

I received no divine insight about being in the right place at the right time. My changed perspective may have come partly from going to visit English relatives over the break. We toured Westminster Abbey and Ely Cathedral, which finally made sense of our seminary chapel's rood screen and other obscure architectural elements. Whatever the reason, I had a restored sense of vocation and a newfound confidence that my calling was more than simply the sum of seminary activities.

My revelatory manifestation preceded an ankle injury on the basketball court and our class retreat in Connecticut. The accident was a blessing in disguise, making it impossible to keep up the frenetic pace I'd maintained first semester. I could concentrate on prayer, studies, and the grander purposes behind music theory and chapel duties. (Also, I became a walking pastoral opportunity for other seminarians, who competed to open doors and carry my lunch tray.) Our class retreat at the beginning of February allowed time to reflect on my calling.

The weekend retreat begins unpromisingly. Riding to Connecticut in a bus with eighteen other seminarians is like traveling to an away game with the high school field hockey team. Instead of gossiping or complaining about homework, however, we argue about chapel and discuss how best to distribute communion wafers. The rowdier group sits in back, while readers fill the front seats. Grumpily, I wonder why, after four months of worshipping, working, and eating together, we need more "ice-breakers" to get acquainted. I do not have high hopes for this weekend.

While reading my Old Testament I eavesdrop on the conversation behind me. Mauricio thinks that a priest should gaze directly into a parishioner's eyes while offering communion, to acknowledge the human element in the exchange. It is also important in his view to capture a visual cue as to whether someone prefers receiving the host in their mouth or in their palm.

Brad, however, is concerned about boundaries. "You don't want to make it like some spiritual power thing—like you personally absolve them of their sins—and you definitely don't want to give the wrong impression."

Another student two or three seats away chimes in that she knows a priest who was sued for sexual harassment for pressing the communion wafer too fervently into someone's hand.

"Puh-lease."

"Unbelievable."

Always-realistic Brad points out that most people take communion because they want to go to heaven, but a few needy members of every congregation want the physical contact. "It's pretty weird stuff." Almost as weird, he adds, as the psychiatric disorders behind those demon sightings by the desert fathers. (We were reading Athanasius's *The Life of St. Anthony* for church history.)

Shortly after arriving at the Trinity Conference Center in Cornwall, Connecticut, the class begins a series of meditations led by Father Stephen. Father Stephen is a doctoral candidate in Anglican studies who in his late forties left a parish of 2,000 members in Houston, Texas, to come to New York with his wife. In an unassuming way, Father Stephen is as enthusiastic about his calling as anyone I've met. Occasionally, I would run into him in the elevator of our building at seven on Sunday morning. Bleary-eyed, I was usually starting a brief sleepwalk around the block with our dogs. He was always crisp-collared, freshly shaven, and braced for a day that included leading mass at a convent uptown, celebrating two regular services at St.

Ignatius on West End Avenue, and working on his dissertation in the seminary library all afternoon.

Sitting comfortably around a fire in a large conference room overlooking a river, we hear Father Stephen reflect on twenty-five years in parish ministry. "The beginning of the twenty-first century is an odd season for ordained ministry," he begins. Popular models for the priesthood, he tells us, include the character Father Timothy in Jan Karon's book *At Home in Mitford.* A rural southern priest, Father Timothy worked eighteen hours a day and was loved by his congregation. Unfortunately, he had difficulty sleeping at night, was twenty pounds overweight, and had a lust for sheets of marmalade cake that aggravated his diabetes.

Father Stephen also mentions a scene in the recent British film *Priest* in which the main character knows of incest in a family but, because of the seal of confession, feels powerless to report it. In one scene, the priest collapses in his room before the crucifix, shouting, "Stop hanging there so smugly, you bastard, get down and *do* something!" This moment is the character's true ordination, Father Stephen insists, not the coronation that we probably anticipate, being "carried down the aisle in a sedan chair by six acolytes fanning you with palm leaves."

Whether we believe in them or not, encounters with powers and principalities will be unavoidable in our ministries, Father Stephen assures us. Indeed, at his Texas parish, he felt the full force of the "diabolical"—a word whose origin means "to separate." Father Stephen's understated manner and penchant for recreational hymn-singing leads me to expect that his description of an encounter with the "diabolical" will be a rather mild brush with unpleasantness, perhaps a vestryman throwing soup across the room in an argument about same-sex marriage. But it was soon clear that evil had indeed visited him.

"Halfway through a dinner party with friends and a few liberal professors from my alma mater, the Episcopal Divinity School," Father Stephen continues, "the telephone rang in the parish hall. The voice on the other end told me to come quickly. There had been a fire at the home of one of my parishioners. Arson and murder were suspected." Mrs. Jones and her family were the backbone of his congregation. She was the kind of person who always asked Father Stephen thoughtful questions after the sermon. She and her husband led fund drives and most of the congregation's service programs.

Father Stephen arrived at the Jones home to find a smoking ruin surrounded by fire engines and squad cars. "I ducked under the yellow crime-scene tape and told the officer in charge that I was the family's priest and needed to say last rites. The policeman told me this was the worst thing he'd seen in twenty years of duty." Father Stephen followed the officer inside. Signs of the diabolical were everywhere—a smoldering house, the stench of burnt flesh and five charred bodies, bound and gagged. Mrs. Jones and most of her family had been murdered.

Father Stephen prayed over the bodies and commended their souls into paradise "where there is no suffering." He thought this tragedy might bring the congregation together. Far from it. Later that evening, a woman parishioner shook him by the lapels, shouting, "Why did you do this to us? It's your fault! How could you let this happen?" She, like other parishioners, projected her anger and fear onto him. Father Stephen thought he knew who had committed the murder and that he himself might be in danger. The police agreed, sending a guard to his house. On Sunday, Father Stephen returned to his congregation and preached about the murder, afraid he might be shot during the sermon. He was intensely aware of the eldest son in the Jones family weeping in the front pew. At the end of the service, Father Stephen put his arm across the young man's shoulders; as they walked, the congregation gathered around. When they stepped outside, FBI agents who had been inside the sanctuary snapped handcuffs on young Jones.

"I knew that the eldest brother was responsible when I went with my wife to our favorite Mexican restaurant the day after the fire," Father Stephen continues. "Young Jones sat in a booth with a friend, laughing and ordering the biggest sandwich on the menu. Lynn and I were afraid, so we left." The press had film footage of the young man scratching his eyes so they'd look red during the funeral. Later, Jones told reporters he had doused his family with gasoline, setting them and the house on fire for the insurance money to start a muffler business in California.

"The man is now sitting on death row," Father Stephen concludes quietly.

After the murders, Father Stephen suffered from post-traumatic stress disorder, a condition common to war veterans and survivors of domestic violence. He saw a therapist three times a week for eighteen months. Eventually, his congregation did recover, and Father Stephen himself mustered the energy to move on, coming to New York to begin his Th.D.—a decision made in joy, not fear.

In addition to the bad times, inexplicable moments of peace also come to an ordained person, Father Stephen assures us in a later meditation. "Consolations" he calls them, little serendipitous events that tell us we are in the right place at the right time.

Father Stephen led a conflicted parish in Texas in the early '80s, when the oil well that funded the congregation dried up. He expected a $600,000 deficit and, distressed, began medicating himself with alcohol. His older sister gave him a book about addiction. After reading it, he had a dream in which a monk told Father Stephen that if he completed his assignment in two months, he would be allowed to visit the blue room—a beautiful chamber in shades of cerulean, azure, and marine with a white throne in the middle. Otherwise he would die. Father Stephen awoke and called his friend the substance abuse counselor.

Twenty-four hours later he was on a plane to Pennsylvania and a detox center where "all the Houston drunks went to dry out." Father Stephen arrived half an hour before registration. The man who took his bags asked if he wanted a moment alone first, since registration could be trying. He agreed, and the man proposed to take him to the blue room. "The blue what?" Father Stephen asked. "The blue room," the man replied. "The blue room is the center of our life here."

Although the room lacked a throne, Father Stephen sat down and wept. For the first time in years, he felt he was sitting in the palm of God's hand. "In Hebrew, the word 'blessing' is similar to 'bloodied,'" he says. "To bloody is to bless and to bless is to bloody. God had grabbed me by the scruff of my neck and shaken me till my teeth chattered."

AFTER Father Stephen's meditations, we sit for a few minutes in silence. The usual backchat is gone. Father Stephen does a good job of impressing upon us the solemnity of a vocation that, for me, has been obscured by the collegial quality of seminary life.

He powerfully reminds us that the time we spend poring over vestment catalogues or daydreaming about who will speak at our ordination ceremony should not distract us from the hard mysteries that lie ahead. We, too, will need patience to await the epiphanies that make us see God afresh.

Lives of the Saints

The glow of Epiphany spreads from our retreat into the classroom. With stronger faith in a priestly vocation and a new course on early Christian history, I begin to see priests, deacons, and bishops of all varieties sitting at nearby desks. In addition to Brad, Mauricio, and Mary, other classmates manifest early Christian archetypes.

The new light in which I see many of my fellows is partially due to the influence of Father Wright's 9:00 A.M. class on the patristic period in early church history. Typically, I stumble out of morning prayer into a flood of dates and details about Roman persecutions, three centuries of saints' lives, and a blow-by-blow account of how most of them met their colorful ends. Father Wright dramatizes the early days of Epiphany in a way that music theory can't match. I quickly come to look forward to the sight of our instructor hovering above the podium, nodding and grinning good morning as we take our seats, rubbing his palms in brisk anticipation of his lecture's dramatic disclosures.

"St. Xeroxius," as students call him, does not let the early martyrs die. His voluminous single-spaced handouts on the first 700 years of Christian history, while decimating acres of timber, also help many seminarians pass their General Ordination Exams. They're used as resource material in parish offices across the country. A canon in the diocese of New York, a well-respected scholar of church history, and a leading figure in ecumenical relations, Father Wright is passionate about his subject. With a flair for drama, he brings us to the foot of St. Blandina's cross in the coliseum and allows us to hear the Romans' bloodthirsty cries as the young woman is crucified for her faith. We vividly imagine a Eucharist served in a third-century house church in Britain. We are with Constantine at the battle of the Milvian Bridge. When the soon-to-be emperor looks skyward and beholds a sign of

Christ across the sun, we, too, imagine that we see signs in the upper corner of the chalk board.

For Father Wright, little in Christian history is purely academic. Besides the list of required readings by apostolic fathers such as St. Irenaeus, St. Hippolytus, St. Ignatius, and Origen, our syllabus includes a list of saints and the strong recommendation that we spend at least ten minutes a day meditating on their lives. Instead of mumbling a prayer into our desk at the beginning of the lecture, we stand as the early Christians did, in the Orans posture—facing east, arms outstretched, palms facing forward. The prayer might include an early collect on the "Good Shepherd" or a rallying cry from Tertullian, an early church father who challenged the authorities to "rack, torture, grind us to powder; our numbers increase in proportion as you mow us down. The blood of Christians is seed!"

Our spiritual forebears, we discover, were a formidable group who put our Sunday morning sacrifices in perspective, while defining a true counterculture. We read of Polycarp, the elderly bishop of Smyrna, who in 156 A.D. was routed from his home and burned at the stake. As the flames licked high, Polycarp proclaimed to his persecutors, "Eighty-six years I have served him, and he never did me any wrong. How can I blaspheme my King who saved me?" We read about Perpetua and her slave girl Felicity, both of whom went to the lions despite the pleading of Perpetua's family. Perpetua delivered a child in the dungeons of the coliseum only days before her death. Finally, Father Wright introduces St. Lawrence, an early martyr who infuriated Roman authorities by distributing the churches' wealth to the poor of Rome and, for his trouble, was roasted on a gridiron. Lest we think these early saints too serious, Father Wright points out that Lawrence managed to maintain a sense of humor throughout his ordeal, instructing his captors to turn him over when he was "done" on one side.

What sacrifices would we first-year seminarians willingly make for our faith? Father Wright inquires. The original Old Testament use of the word "martyr" meant simply "to witness." The earliest Christians were martyrs if they professed Christ's name aloud. Would we agree to take that step? Well, what about its current definition: to die for Christ? We're all willing to take salary cuts and give up chocolate during Lent, but what if we're asked to face the lions? Father Wright growls, sticks out his front teeth, and briefly paws the air to make sure we get the point.

When we reach the early heresies of Arius and Apollinarius, Father Wright requires us to evaluate our own theology about the divinity of Christ. Do we share Arius's view that Christ was another creature created by God, or do we subscribe to the Apollinarian idea that Christ was not only co-eternal with God, but also had a divine mind; his only "creaturely" aspect was to live in a human body. If we like to pray *with* Jesus instead of *to* him—preferring to think of him as friend rather than Lord—we are probably closet Arians. If our favorite hymns describe Christ as Immortal King, then we might be more Apollinarian. Our votes enter Father Wright's data bank, which covers a decade and graphs the rise and fall of heretical tendencies among juniors at General from the late 1980s through 1998. Our class falls squarely into the Arian camp, breaking a dominant Apollinarian trend.

FATHER WRIGHT also engages us by awarding prizes for extra work or for spotting typos in his handouts. A large collection of beloved icons and relics fills his apartment, including a Vatican-certified fragment of the cross of St. Peter. He also collects relics of modern luminaries. The person who can figure out why the alpha and omega on a fourth-century lead baptismal font were backwards, for example, might win a small piece of Pope John XXIII's clothing. Without documentation, we are told, one cannot be certain if this is a piece of papal clothing or part of a sheet from a bed in which the pope had once slept. Father Wright assures us, however, that such uncertainty is standard in the world of relic collection.

Dreaming of the See

A few patristics class discussions are devoted to writings of the early church fathers about the roles of bishops, priests, and deacons. Is today's Episcopal priest the successor of the Jewish elder or *presbyteros* who oversaw the administration of the Temple? Or is she the icon of Christ, standing in for him at communion and imitating his words at the Last Supper? Father Wright reminds us that, unlike many other parts of the church after the Reformation, Anglicans did not see their priests as simply extensions of the priesthood of all baptized persons. Confirming a theme stressed in my discernment process, I discover that priests in history are not simply holier counterparts of lay people. Rather, they have specific functions and responsibilities within the whole communion of believers.

Like many classmates, I wonder about the historical job description of bishops as well as priests. Patristic opinions differ on the subject. Does the bishop occupy the top rung of the ecclesiastical ladder, to be obeyed without question, or is his spiritual authority similar to that of prophets and teachers? Depending on the writer, the bishop can be a teacher whose primary responsibility is the transmission of doctrine, a president of the Eucharist, an overseer or administrator, or the pastor's pastor. According to the current church leaders, who come to General for the annual College of Bishops, additional modern responsibilities mean that a bishop is also the primary deflector of civil lawsuits, the foremost public relations official, and chief fire extinguisher—particularly when embezzlement or clerical sexual misconduct poses problems.

As far as I can tell, divergent profiles of the episcopate echo the different monastic orders in Christian history. As a monk once explained to me, when Benedictine monks need to purchase a new car, they might invest in a new Taurus rather than a secondhand Chevy. Their fifth-century rule requires stability, obedience, and conversion of life, but not strict poverty. A group of Franciscan friars who take a vow of poverty as well as of chastity and obedience would probably buy the cheapest automobile, even with 500,000 miles on the odometer. He wasn't sure what kind of car a Dominican would buy—but definitely something with good suspension, so that the brothers of this historically scholarly order could study on the road. Within the general parameters of Christian monasticism, the monk said, different orders reflect different temperaments.

The same seems to be true of differing models of priesthood and the episcopate. Most respected bishops have been servant-leaders who share, at a minimum, administrative skills, liturgical capability, and an ability to preach and teach. Beyond this, however, looking around the classroom at the future of the church, I can identify bishops in at least three different patristic molds. The first, articulated by St. Irenaeus, is bishop as teacher of the gospel. The second, described by St. Cyprian, is bishop as administrator. The third, a mold defined by Pope Gregory the Great, is bishop as chief pastor.

Mary was the bishop as teacher. Her spontaneity, quick wit, and willingness to drop everything for cheap opera tickets or a good bottle of champagne made her fun to be with; I always appreciated her classic utterances of street wisdom, too. I caught up with Mary's manic energy only as second semester began. As I got to know her, I came to appreciate her constant attentiveness to detail, and the intensity with which she attacked her studies.

For example, we might be idly speculating about whether a recent PBS Jesus special had done an accurate digitized simulation of Herod's Temple, and suddenly, Mary would be on the other side of the room riffling through the H volume of the *Anchor Bible Dictionary.* I might arrive at elementary Greek having struggled through a third of our assigned sentences and find, to my dismay, that Mary had gone two chapters beyond the requirement. She'd figured out that the word "acolyte" was rooted in the Greek verb meaning "to follow." I would tell myself that some people just had a gift for languages, before my neighbor leaned over to whisper that she had heard that Mary was saying the Lord's Prayer in Greek each night before bed.

Unlike some seminarians, Mary did not let the pressure to be chief pastor interfere with her interest in becoming a teacher. Although she was fully engaged in community life, Mary did not agonize if she accidentally left someone off her prayer list. Nor was her conscience overly troubled if she once forgot to ask about a classmate's sick aunt or an ailing pet.

One of Mary's greatest passions at All Saints, her home parish, had been leading a six-month catechumenate in which she prepared adult members of the congregation for baptism. Contrary to current church trends in which clergy lay down few requirements for baptismal candidates, Mary followed the early Christian practice, using an extensive program of study, prayer, and reflection for her catechumens. The baptismal journey culminated in the Great Vigil at Easter—a pivotal celebration in the liturgical life of the whole congregation.

Mary drew on her varied secular experience as an aid to teaching and reflection. She had once been Toyota's Salesperson of the Year and often marveled at the theological truths gleaned from the car business. "I've never really been one for mission work to the uninterested," she explained after we heard a sermon on spreading the gospel abroad. "It's like when I was in sales, I hated making cold calls." Whenever her manager walked by, Mary would phone her answering machine or her mother. This was her idea of "working the line." Nothing was worse than trying to sell a car to someone who didn't really want one. When a potential customer came into the showroom, however, things changed. "The minute they stepped onto the property," she grinned, "they were mine."

Her car sales experience also helped her understand ecumenical questions. The universalism of Christianity was profound, Mary reflected. Her faith was not tied to a particular race or place or time, a fact that overcame many questions of identity, from nationality to culture. At a certain point, however, that universalism broke down. Such a breakdown became apparent during our interseminary dialogues with Russian Orthodox, Roman Catholic, and Jewish seminarians, or when the Vatican released a papal letter in the late '90s making the prohibition against women's ordination nearly infallible. "What can we possibly say to the Roman Catholics?" Mary demanded. "I mean, what can we seriously say to them about papal infallibility or the ordination of women? In the car business, those positions would be *major* deal-breakers."

As clearly as Mary embodied St. Irenaeus's concept of the bishop as teacher, Nathan lived out Pope Gregory the Great's idea of the bishop as chief pastor. (Pope Gregory's sixth-century *Treatise on Pastoral Care* contained seventy-two individual "case studies" and was required reading for all bishops in the Western church.) For Pope Gregory, it was important that bishops as well as priests pay close attention to the spiritual needs of their flock.

During the fall, it became clear that one of Nathan's preoccupations was the welfare of everyone around him. If, for example, I mentioned that my husband Greg was reluctant to quiz me with Greek flash cards every night, Nathan would stop me in the hall a week later and ask if juggling school and home life was getting easier. If I had to miss a class, Nathan would be first to volunteer his notes.

Nathan felt that his whole life since his conversion during freshman year in college had been leading to ordained ministry. He loved God and wanted to share that love with the people around him. God's grace was radical, Nathan said. It was radical that God truly died. He didn't go out like a switched-off night-light—he died with his whole being, body and soul. "For God so loved the world that he gave his only son as a living sacrifice for us and for our sins." These words at communion meant a lot to Nathan, coloring his interactions with all of us.

Prayer was an essential part of his life. After reading *The Way of the Pilgrim,* by an anonymous Russian mystic, Nathan had decided to experiment more with prayer. He prayed when he was walking to class or sitting at lunch. Most of his prayers were thanksgivings, not petitions.

Nathan took his pastoral responsibility very seriously. Like his own pastor, Nathan questioned the decision of Bishop Browning, the twenty-fourth presiding bishop of the Episcopal Church, to demonstrate outside the gates of the White House during the Gulf War. President Bush was, after all, an Episcopalian and a member of the presiding bishop's flock. "George Bush probably needed spiritual direction at that moment," Nathan said. "And besides, doesn't Jesus tell us to forgive one another?" I disagreed, believing that Presiding Bishop Browning's stand outside the White House was the most effective way he could have lodged his protest against the bombing. The Episcopal

Church has respected moral authority, and I applauded the decision to take to the streets in this instance. Nathan, who had himself spoken out against the war, reminded me that there had been no shortage of outspoken Episcopal priests opposed to the Vietnam War. "I just think that the P.B. should have been there by George Bush's side," he added. "They wouldn't have had to agree on the issue. And it wasn't like Bush had an easy time making the decision to bomb."

Politics aside, Nathan was most chief pastor, however, when he was coaching on the basketball court. The minute Nathan and his wife discovered a gym under the refectory, they decided to resurrect the General Seminary basketball team. During the second semester, Wednesday nights and Saturday mornings became opportunities to play: first two on two, then three on three, and, soon, full court.

Seminary basketball was physically rejuvenating. I was always thanked for showing up, as if by tearing myself away from Greek for an hour I was doing a personal favor for Nathan. Choosing the teams was an exercise in diplomacy that Nathan passed with flying colors. "You three are high scorers," he would tell the next best players after himself. "You can play against the four of us." Phoebe, myself, and one other would join Nathan, and the game would begin.

Instead of starting with a jump ball, we usually shot to decide which team would take the ball first. Although a few players, like Phoebe, specialized in fast breaks and inside drives, Nathan and most of the others usually passed the ball on offense when they were not trying for an outside shot. Swearing was acceptable but not common. Competition was fierce. Nathan's encouragement on the court brought out the best even in clumsy people who hadn't played much. If I got the ball anywhere near the net, I heard "Great shot!" If I beat Nathan to the other end of the court, he'd exclaim, "Way to hustle!" or "Good running!" If I made a mistake and fouled, he would congratulate me on my "tough D." Our fifteen-point games ended with handshakes all around.

Once, I saw Nathan hotly angry with someone who pushed him to the ground. "That's not why I came out here!" he said, eyes flashing. As Greg pointed out, it was an exhibit of purely righteous anger.

THE BETTER I knew Mauricio, the more impressed I was by his organizational skills and the seriousness of his own vision for the shape of the church in his country. For Mauricio, church was more than a building with a distinctive-smelling carpet. It was not a sentimental place for the faithful to retreat to from the chaotic outside world but an ongoing institution with jobs to do in that world. Mauricio was my model of the bishop as administrator.

At a time in Christian history when martyrdom was common for church leaders, St. Cyprian set himself apart by putting his administrative responsibilities as bishop above the call to sacrifice his life. Unlike Origen, another apostolic father, whose mother reportedly hid his clothes to prevent him from running into the street to proclaim his love for Jesus at the height of the Severan persecution, St. Cyprian chose to flee Carthage in 250 A.D. rather than face death. For Cyprian, the bishop was less the pastor, less the teacher, and more the church overseer charged with preserving the community. During the third-century persecutions, the bishop as administrator became crucial.

Mauricio came to seminary with the very clear sense that he *was* the future of the church in Costa Rica. Although in some senses this is true of all seminarians, most of us do not live daily with the magnitude of this responsibility. Surrounded by dozens of Episcopal churches, schools, and a large number of Episcopalians in government, we imagine that our individual ministries may not greatly affect the small but secure foothold of the Episcopal Church in North America. In Costa Rica, however, Mauricio knew he would share responsibilities with only a handful of colleagues. He felt far more urgency than many of us did about finishing every reading, squeezing in extra credits, and discharging chapel duties.

Although Mauricio was no clerical operator, he had grown up breathing church politics, so he knew how to get things done. At the beginning of our second semester at General, his father was elected primate of the Province of Central America; he took part in the initiative to make the church of Central America an independent province of the Anglican Communion, rather than a part of the Episcopal Church of the United States. After attending his church's national convention, Mauricio reported that he didn't mind being absent from the conference floor in order to drive visitors to and from the airport. This task offered a far better opportunity than the convention floor to get acquainted with visiting dignitaries. Mauricio ended up translating the presiding bishop's convention speech from English to Spanish.

Mauricio had met several church leaders in the United States through the sister diocese arrangement between Costa Rica and North Carolina and New Jersey. Thus, when guests arrived for General Seminary's periodic College of Bishops and started each day with coffee from Seabury's Bottom, Mauricio did not need to make a new contact with each cup he poured. Equally, however, he made certain on those mornings that the muffins were fresh.

Although Mauricio's theology appeared more conservative than many of my classmates' and sometimes seemed almost smug in its certainty, the church was his element. For Mauricio, sound church administration was as dignified and important a part of the calling as presiding at the Eucharist. Whereas I made distinctions between the parts of my vocation that seemed most sacred and those that appeared more superfluous—preaching versus learning different types of incense for high holy days—Mauricio did not categorize his duties in quite the same way.

Mauricio saw his vocation much as he saw prayer. Like many Christian lay people and clerics, Mauricio believed that everything he did was a kind of prayer. His relationship with God was not limited to the time he spent on his knees saying sacred words or offering up petitions. Rather, it existed continuously—on the bus, during meals, while he listened to lectures. In the same way, for Mauricio, administration of the church was as sacred a part of the bishop's work as pastoral responsibilities, teaching, or liturgy.

THE QUALITIES of church leadership I find most inspiring are described by St. Cyprian and St. Irenaeus: teaching and administration. A quick survey of the images of saints in my office attests to the qualities I admire most in others and strive hardest to develop in myself.

Pinned on the corkboard above my desk, for example, is a postcard painting of St. Jerome. This giant of biblical scholarship, translator of the Latin Vulgate and possibly the most curmudgeonly individual ever to be canonized, glowers down at me, quill in hand. St. Jerome has not always held such an esteemed position in my life. Before my first year in New York, I had never heard of him. In a homiletics class exercise, however, I was asked to describe a 1625 Simon Vauvet painting of white-bearded, wiry old Jerome in intense debate with an angel who appears at his desk.

I was completely taken with the picture—the saint's passion for learning came through so clearly. The artist showed Jerome mid-thought. One of the saint's hands rests on a pile of papers, pen poised; the other is raised in an open-palmed gesture of emphasis. The presence of a messenger of God seems less consequential to Jerome than the point he wants to make. This is no cowering, eyes-averted encounter with the holy. Indeed, Jerome is so transported by the beauty of divine truth that the visiting angel appears to be a participant in conversation, not an object of adoration.

The picture reminds me of the way people change and are lifted out of themselves when they come into contact with beautiful ideas of the sort contained in the Bible (but not limited to it). The picture affirms the notion that God can be found in the pursuit of truth and learning; God is, as Paul says in Philippians 4:8, "whatever is true, whatever is honorable, whatever is just, whatever is pure, whatever is pleasing, [and] whatever is commendable."

St. Jerome may not occupy the niche above my desk after seminary, when exams are over. But my fondness for St. Jerome and his love of ideas is certain. This affection, and the great satisfaction I've found in debate inside and outside the classroom, suggests my tendency toward the model of church leadership that sees the bishop and priest as teacher.

For me, no single historical role model embodying St. Cyprian's idea of bishop as administrator stands out. I loved St. Augustine's *Confessions,* but his methods of instilling discipline as overseer of the early Christian community at Hippo, North Africa, struck me as draconian. Polycarp, bishop of Smyrna, was unquestionably a self-sacrificing Christian leader—yet martyrdom is not a fate to which I aspire.

When I think of leadership in a community of faith, Queen Esther comes to mind again. Although technically she is not a saint and appears not to have been a scholar of Jewish faith like her Uncle Mordecai, Esther's willingness to risk her own security for the welfare of her people exemplifies what it means to keep the bigger picture in mind. The strategic planning and timing involved in the banquets that led the king to accept her plea shows Esther's administrative competence. Though I do not share her taste for vengeance, which becomes clear later in the Esther story, the queen's original valor is admirable.

Like Esther, I trust that institutions can work and that authority may be used bravely, and to good purpose. My theological grasp of the differences between responsibility and authority in the church, rather than in secular institutions, may still be underdeveloped, but I assume that a Christian leader's spiritual authority may also be exercised toward virtuous ends.

During Epiphany, although no future bishops in my class wear the oval halos of sanctity, ancient models of church leadership appear all around me. We do not all have our predecessors' passion for crusading, so we do not try to convert strangers on trains or preach the Word before breakfast. Still, as we dream our futures, Mary, Nathan, Mauricio, and I envision ourselves standing squarely within a two-thousand-year history of apostolic succession.

Found in Translation

The task of translating ten Koine Greek sentences twice a week still epitomizes for me the struggle of first semester. Throughout the fall, half our class performed this difficult drill from week to week without much respite. The work involved parts of my brain unexercised for years; until Epiphany, I suffered under the siege of parsing and parts of speech.

Typically, panic would begin each Sunday afternoon. Plans for hanging curtains or moving our still half-unpacked boxes into storage would evaporate. I would dread yet another crisp, sunny New York afternoon spent staring down at a page of incomprehensible, slightly menacing symbols.

Rushing to the library, I would unpack my dictionaries, entrench at a table with a direct line of sight to a wall clock, and open J. Greshham Machen's *New Testament Greek for Beginners*. The assignment, as always, appears deceptively short. Early in the semester, a typical sentence might look like this:

ὁ κακὸς βλέπει τὴν ἔρημον καὶ τοὺς ἐσχάτους οἴκους

Problems begin with the first word, in this case a single omicron. As many times as our professor told us to begin our translation by identifying the verb before searching out the subject, my instinct was always to start the translation with the first word. With a little more confidence, I'd move on to the second word. This approach to translation might have worked, if only the Evangelists had arranged their sentences so that adjectives preceded nouns and direct objects followed active verbs. Unfortunately for me, logical word sequence in English was not a high priority in the ancient Near East.

Looking up at the clock, I realize it's 2:40. Having figured out that some people "see" something, somewhere, in this sentence, I need specifics. Nouns and their declensions come next. Rather than gaining a sense of the word's form through its position in the sentence, the Greeks decided to give each noun one of five declensions: nominative nouns are the subjects of sentences; accusative nouns are the direct objects; genitive nouns indicate possession; vocative nouns show command; and datives are the indirect object. Here again the clues lie in word endings. And the endings are copied neatly on green index cards sitting under a pile of books back in my apartment. Without a quick-reference guide, I have two choices. I can guess the ending from a similar-looking word on the last homework, or I can look it up in the chapter in Machen—an act that requires extreme manual dexterity, since I'm eager to keep my thumb-hold on the vocabulary at the back of the book.

Looking up nouns suddenly reminds me about the vocabulary quiz on the last two chapters we covered. Running back to the apartment for my flash cards, I take a break to memorize the words "baptism," "sin," "teacher," "gospel," and "that." My color coding system broke down after the first two weeks of class, so I resort to repeating the words over and over, hoping they'll stick. Now it's time to return to the unfinished sentence translation. Even after only a few minutes away, I find words that were on the verge of decipherability completely opaque again. The clock says 4:45 P.M.

After a question for Mary, staked out in a large chair behind the reference section, I conclude that my sentence translation might not be perfect, but it's time to move on to the next one. After much agonizing, page flipping, and erasing, ὁ κακὸς βλέπει τὴν ἔρημον καὶ τοὺς ἐσχάτους οἴκους has become "The wicked man/one/person sees the _______ and the last houses." I'm disappointed not to have something more poetic to show for my work, but there are four more sentences and three more assignments for other courses to go before I sleep. Just as my powers of concentration rally, a tolling bell sounds, signaling evening prayer.

For first-year students of Koine Greek, there was one more way to end the day. If you tried to return to other course work, invariably you would be searching for the last reserve copy of a book to anchor your exegesis on St. Mark's Gospel (due the next morning) when your concerned spouse showed up to announce that your parents are on the phone wondering if (a) they have the correct number and (b) it's still okay to visit this weekend. Every biblical language student knows the remorse brought on when your significant other announces wearily that you're welcome to continue studying, but he or she is heading home to heat up the leftovers.

DURING Epiphany a truce is called in my semiweekly armed struggle with Greek. Like the weight lifter who takes a day off to allow his muscles to rest, I find that, having relaxed my frontal lobe over winter break, I arrive back at General with more supple cognitive powers—at least in Koine Greek translation. Second semester, I find myself miraculously conjugating verbs and declining nouns with little effort. I begin to recognize word endings and grammatical constructions. I feel the same satisfaction upon completing a Greek sentence that I used to feel in solving an advanced algebra problem. The effort is still intense, but the siege of unknowing has lifted.

It also helps that our class in elementary Greek has shrunk by half. Many dioceses require at least one semester of Greek or Hebrew, and some bishops want more. Classmates who have fulfilled their requirements, along with others who treasure free weekends, are gone. The survivors include Mary, Kate, several students from Union Theological Seminary, and me. The atmosphere is more intense in a smaller class, since the odds are good that you'll have to read a truly disastrous sentence aloud. Repercussions for mangling a scriptural passage also seem greater than confusing the grammar in a Greek sentence equivalent to "See Spot run."

Our first passage is John, chapter 20, the resurrection of Jesus and his appearance to Mary Magdalene. Translating the passage is unexpectedly moving. Mary, Kate, and I take turns with our sentences. It is a constant surprise to discover that these words really mean what we know they do—almost all of them, anyway.

In the passage, Mary, overcome with grief, approaches the cave where Jesus' body was laid. Despite the early morning darkness, she can see that the stone sealing the grave has been rolled away. Jesus' body is gone. She runs to tell the other disciples. Simon Peter and the disciple John's Gospel calls "beloved" hurry to the tomb. They find the piece of linen cloth in which Christ was buried and believe that his body has been stolen. Then they leave Mary alone, weeping.

"Why are you weeping, woman?" Mary looks up and sees two angels sitting at the head and foot of the place where the body had been. Then she sees Jesus. Mistaking him for the gardener, she demands that he show her where he has taken her Lord's body. Jesus responds by saying her name out loud. "Rabboni!" Mary cries, rushing toward him. "Do not touch me," Jesus tells her, "for I have not yet ascended to the Father. Go to the other disciples and tell them that I am risen."

Christ's words to Mary when she reaches out to him, Μή μου ἅπτου οὔπω γὰρ ἀναβέβηκα πρὸς πατέρα, are usually translated, "Do not touch me, for I have not yet ascended to the Father." Sermons on this passage often explain that Mary's impurity prevents her from touching the Lord. The implication is that Jesus shies away from Mary because she is still in the flesh and might somehow contaminate him. As our professor points out, however, one form of the word ἅπτομαι means "to take hold of" or "cling to," not "touch." "Do not hold on to me" has different theological implications than "Do not touch me." So the transformation of a single word leads to a radical shift in theology.

Jesus had said the same thing to other disciples earlier in John's Gospel. And the Gospel of St. Mark records a scene that makes a similar point. During the transfiguration, when Moses and Elijah appear before the Lord, Peter proposes, in a moment of confusion, "Master, it is well that we are here; let us make three booths, one for you and one for Moses and one for Elijah." The most convincing explanation of

Peter's proposal I have heard is that it expresses the disciple's desire to make the moment of revelation permanent—to stay in the moment of spiritual exaltation rather than to return to the daily grind of healing and evangelizing down in the valley. Like Mary, Peter and the other disciples on the mountain wanted "to take hold of" the Lord.

The time I've devoted to trying to resuscitate a "dead" language bears fruit second semester. After several hard months as a frustrated tourist in Koine Greek, I have become an explorer able to enter territory uncharted by many globe-trotting contemporaries. After a brief but interesting journey through the intricate, subtle, and mysterious landscape of New Testament Greek, I am delighted to discover that εὕρηκα—*eureka*—is the first-person singular perfect form of the verb meaning "to find."

Job's Inscrutable God

During Epiphany, I remember conversations with Ellen during college vacations about different ways in which we had experienced the divine. For me it was watching sunlight on the floorboards of a Quaker meeting house or listening to prayer flags flapping in the wind on an Indian hillside. Ellen felt stirred when she was in the wilderness. At the time, we saw little connection between the source of this peace and the author of the Ten Commandments. Nine years later, I enter the second semester of Old Testament still not sure how to bridge the gap between the God of the Book and that visceral sense of a transcendent presence that Ellen and I had discussed over coffee.

When I first arrived at General, I was not one of the people whom Committees on Ministry warn about—someone whose faith crumbles upon learning that Moses, if he existed, probably did not write the first five books of the Bible. On the contrary, I was intrigued by the thought of the early biblical editors trying to reconcile the J (Yahwist) and E (Elohist) writers' differing accounts of the Joseph story. I enjoyed debates about which one of his older brothers decided to sell Joseph into slavery instead of leaving him to die in the desert. And I was delighted that the Chronicler, for reasons of his own, sought to present King David in the best possible light. Like a presidential campaign manager, the Chronicler conveniently omitted details about King David that other historians included: the seduction of Bathsheba, the rape of Tamar, and the slaughter of Saul's partisans. The writer's eagerness to demonstrate the blameless importance of King David in founding the Temple did not dilute the Word for me.

Source criticism and historical criticism were not faith-shattering either. My day brightened when I learned that the difference in tone between Paul's earlier and later epistles might be attributed to the possibility that Paul did not write the "pastoral" letters. It inspired awe that a collection of documents so riddled with the effects of historical circumstances and hidden agendas had been wept and prayed over for almost twenty centuries.

Still, it was one thing to find myself animated by a text's historical and literary value. It was quite another to read these ancient passages and find them resonating at my core. During Epiphany, when we turned our attention to Job and Jeremiah, I found descriptions of God and godly people that stirred me and moved my spiritually curious unchurched acquaintances as well.

Dr. Corney, our Old Testament professor, is in his sixties. He has a slightly hooked nose, glasses, a distinguished set of sideburns, and shoulder-length gray hair that evenly skirts his scalp just above each ear. He is well-cast as Ebenezer Scrooge in the annual Advent performance of the *Christmas Carol*—not because Dr. Corney is temperamentally suited to the part, but because he looks it. I've heard older General graduates wistfully recalling the heyday of "real characters" at General Seminary and, more widely, in the Episcopal Church. Having been at the institution long enough to watch six deans come and go, Dr. Corney is living proof that colorful personalities survive.

Class begins on Mondays, Wednesdays, and Fridays at 10:00 A.M., when Dr. Corney swirls through the door in a tacky black raincoat, doffs his tweed cap, and rummages around in an overflowing loose-leaf binder for a nightmarishly long list of biblical identifications. His IDs usually include a series of Israelite kings with ten-syllable names, numerous Babylonian and Assyrian texts, and the numerical codes for the day's relevant portion of the Dead Sea Scrolls. For good measure, Dr. Corney's list also contains nineteenth- and twentieth-century German biblical scholars and a few ancient Near Eastern deities.

In his haste to offer a critical analysis of all thirty-nine books in the Old Testament, Dr. Corney wastes no words. After a prayer, he stands at the podium and begins his lecture surrounded by a swarm of handheld tape players. The scene resembles a press briefing.

In our first-semester examination of the histories of Joshua, Judges, Samuel, 1 and 2 Kings, and 1 and 2 Chronicles, God appears to govern the fate of his people in a predictable pattern. Rulers who "do what is evil in the sight of the Lord"—commissioning golden calves to honor other gods, or marrying pagans—end their reigns in misery, violence, military defeat, or famine. Rulers who heed the prophets and dedicate themselves to Yahweh enjoy long reigns and many children. As Professor Corney explains, the Deuteronomistic Historian and the Chronicler (the writers mainly responsible for the sacred histories) are eager to forge the identity of their new nation by stressing its unique relationship with God. Their underlying message is that God takes care of those who take care of God.

The Yahweh described in the histories is difficult to communicate to nonseminarians, particularly in light of the divinely sanctioned exterminations that Joshua and his armies carry out against the inhabitants of Ai, Hazor, and other cities in the Promised Land. What kind of God *punishes* his people for saving the lives of a few innocent Canaanites?

The God described by many major and minor prophets, the same God who appears in wisdom books such as Job, Ecclesiastes, Proverbs, and Psalms, sounds less judgmental and predictable than the God of Deuteronomy. The God of the prophets is likelier to get the attention of curious, skeptical people. Since learning the difference between primary and secondary sources in high school history, many of us have been encouraged to look for hidden biases in everything from social studies textbooks to the U.S. Constitution. As a result, the God of the Old Testament histories appears heavy handed.

A discussion about the God of Job and Jeremiah, however, can easily hold its own in a dinner conversation with Greg that might otherwise focus on the media business. It's not that the God of the wisdom literature or the major prophets differs in essence from the God who describes himself to Moses as "I AM WHO I AM"; it's just that God, to a modern sensibility, appears more attractively inscrutable in the Books of Job and Jeremiah.

Part of the appeal of God in Job and Jeremiah comes from the sympathetic natures of those characters. Even Dr. Corney seems moved by the plight of Jeremiah, slowing his usual breakneck delivery to read the prophet's more poignant lines as sorrowfully as Jeremiah might. "I did not sit in the company of merrymakers, nor did I rejoice; under the weight of your hand," Dr. Corney recites mournfully, "I sat alone" (Jer. 15:17).

According to Dr. Corney, Jeremiah is a reluctant prophet in the line of Moses. He preached at the end of the sixth century B.C. during the unfortunate period of Israelite history directly preceding the invasion of Nebuchadnezzar and his forces. Jeremiah's job was to awaken the Israelites to their sins and warn of the coming destruction. At first he hoped that his words alone might reform the Israelites. Later, he realized there was no hope for redemption before the fall of Jerusalem.

Part of Jeremiah's appeal is that he complains so much and is entirely justified in doing so. He has a miserable life and is unafraid to share his suffering with God. He appears to be a naturally sociable person who wants nothing more than to be loved and accepted by his people, but because of the overpowering nature of his call to prophesy—the "burning fire shut up in [his] bones" (Jer. 20:9)—his desire for affection is unfulfilled. Jeremiah laments that he has to shout out destruction and become a "laughingstock all day long" (20:7). As Dr. Corney points out, once God has commissioned Jeremiah to preach a message more unpopular than tax increases and forbidden him to marry, he offers his prophet no support. Having driven Jeremiah from every form of human comfort, God refuses to provide any companionship himself. "Truly," Jeremiah cries in exasperation, "you are to me like a deceitful brook, like waters that fail" (Jer. 15:18). Dr. Corney reports Theresa of Avila's observation that if this was the way God treated his friends, it wasn't surprising that he had so few.

Jeremiah's love-hate relationship with God is more compelling to my spouse and nonseminary friends than the laudatory accounts of God by the Deuteronomistic Historian and the Chronicler. Something about Jeremiah's honesty, his loneliness and shame, his unwillingness to suffer in silence catches their imagination. At a time when nobody argued with God, Jeremiah was unafraid to stand up for himself. Both Greg and Ellen are struck by a God who offers his servants little besides the knowledge that he is God and that in the long run this assurance is enough.

Job is another Old Testament character who clearly occupies a soft spot in Dr. Corney's heart. Listening to his introductory lecture, one might think that the great crime against Job was not so much the injustices he suffered at God's hand as the amount of misguided scholarship about him. The Book of Job, Dr. Corney tells us, is not primarily a story of theodicy—the question of why bad things happen to good people. Although the issue of innocent suffering is certainly present throughout, it is not what makes Job an outstanding example of biblical wisdom writing. At the core of the Book of Job is the question of what relationship can really exist between a human being who is limited by mortality and a God who is infinite.

Dr. Corney takes a provocative tack. Satan's challenge to God at the beginning of the book suggests that the only reason for Job's blamelessness and righteousness is the good fortune God has given him. Dr. Corney thinks this challenge questions the whole created order in which God is omniscient and omnipotent. Of course human beings are good, says Dr. Corney (taking Satan's side), if they know that goodness will be rewarded—in this life or the next. God's only real choice is thus to demonstrate his own godliness and to determine that he should be worshipped for no other reason than that he is who he is. Whether or not God's need to prove himself demonstrates the Jungian hypothesis of divine insecurity, still, God's willingness to engage in a wager and his appearance to Job from the whirlwind say something important about his nature.

Job is equally interested in demonstrating his integrity, Dr. Corney continues. Job has no patience with his so-called friends, the false comforters who attempt to preserve their own sense of an ordered universe by telling him that either he has sinned, or his children have. All Job needs to do to appease God's wrath, according to Eliphaz, Zophar, and Bildad, is to repent of his evil ways.

"No doubt you are the people, and wisdom will die with you," Job responds to his comforters with biting sarcasm (Job 12:2). He sees the futility of trying to plead the rightness of his cause before a God who is both prosecutor and judge. Still, Job is determined to defend his ways to the end, with no support but the knowledge that he is justified. Dr. Corney closes his lecture by arguing animatedly that the "Redeemer" Job hopes for is not the Christlike savior or divine intermediary that modern Christian scholars often suggest. Instead, the "Redeemer" is simply another human being who, sometime in the future, will read his words and know that Job was right.

I report Dr. Corney's view over dinner that evening and watch Job rise sharply in my husband's estimation. With only vague recollections of the silent sufferer from his high school English workbook, Greg finds the new Job's perspective refreshing. He has always thought that most people downplay the importance of being right.

Job surfaces again a week later at a deli on West Fifty-seventh Street before a concert at Carnegie Hall. Greg orders bagel sandwiches and soup from behind the counter, while I wipe down a table next to the window. We are both preparing to enjoy our meal in the remaining twenty minutes before the concert. Since we are the only customers, I ask the Indian counterman if he'll turn down the radio. My gesture is partly an attempt to pretend we are having a relaxed evening away from the seminary, and partly to prepare mentally for Beethoven's *Missa Solemnis.*

Although uncertain what he thinks of God, Greg grew up saying grace before meals and was often the driving force behind our asking

God's blessing on food even when rushing. Tonight, we both look down at our lox sandwiches and say a brief thanksgiving for the fish we are about to consume. Our prayer brings me back to Dr. Corney's final lecture on Job that morning.

"Did you know," I begin breathlessly, as Greg prepares to take his first bite, "that when God speaks to Job out of the whirlwind and tells him what a totally inadequate witness he is, hardly once during his entire description of creation does God mention human beings?"

Greg raises an eyebrow, swallows, and darts a quick glance at the clock. "Really," he says.

"Yes, it's true," I continue. "God doesn't even talk about domestic animals. No pigs or sheep or dogs. Nothing. The closest God gets to describing anything domesticated is a war horse."

Greg agrees that war horses hardly qualify as household pets, and he continues eating.

Noting Greg's interest and realizing that we have at least eleven minutes before the orchestra begins tuning, I launch into an account of the significance of God's description of creation as a non-answer to Job's complaint. I explain the humbling effect that God's description of the vastness of creation must have had on Job. I bring in Dr. Corney's analogy from a geology professor he once studied with: if the Empire State Building is the history of the created world, then the existence of humanity is a nickel on the top of the tower, and all of recorded human history is a very thin piece of paper on top of that. Thus, although Job demands an accounting from God on the basis of his human integrity, God answers him only out of respect for his creatureliness. Also, to try and establish that . . .

"Wait a second," Greg interrupts. "So what does that make the Spice Girls? Atomic particles?"

In my enthusiastic diatribe, I had tuned out the Top Forty. "Actually,

I think they're more like a subatomic particle," I reply, taking in the tinny, rhythmic sounds from the radio behind the counter.

Greg ponders this suggestion for a second, listens to the radio, and considers this model of time in light of his history of science background. "No," he says, "a subatomic particle would probably be too small."

In this case, Greg is inclined to show greater charity toward creatureliness than I.

Perils of the Pauline

Like many people of my age and gender, I put most of St. Paul's writings into the category of things *despite which* I call myself Christian. My list of disclaimers includes the Crusades, the excommunication of Galileo, the pope's stand on abortion and birth control, and most of the activities of the extreme religious right.

Before seminary, I could never defend Paul's instructions for women to remain silent in church and for wives to be subservient to their husbands. It is clear that these statements have justified centuries of discrimination against women inside and outside the church. Nor could I deny that his command to the early Christian community in Rome to "obey the governing authorities" has been used to sanction oppressive regimes. That Paul had never meant his letters to the early Christian communities to become part of scripture was, to me, no excuse for the suffering caused in his name. Paul had a lot to answer for, I felt.

I ENTER the second semester of New Testament, or "NT 2," with a sizable chip on my shoulder. Of my five professors first semester, only one of them was a woman. My undergraduate experience drilled into my head that it was well nigh impossible to explore new perspectives without a teacher who was as untraditional as the insights I craved. Given the age and gender of my New Testament professor, I did not expect NT 2 to revolutionize my understanding of Paul. My initial prejudices proved unfounded, but on the first day, my hackles again arch skyward.

I am not the only skeptic about St. Paul's Epistles. Brad, as a gay man and trained therapist, is highly suspicious of the Apostle's self-proclaimed attempts in 1 Corinthians to be everything to everyone. During second semester, we sit in the back of the classroom and from this vantage point lob pot shots at Paul.

"I'm having this problem," Brad announces toward the end of an early class on 1 and 2 Corinthians. "I respect much of what Paul has to say, but he seems to give a totally different message about the Parousia to the Thessalonians than he does to the Corinthians." (As seminarians learn early in their education, *parousia* is Greek for the Second Coming.)

Professor Koenig hesitates, stroking his chin. He is a tall, thin man with a high forehead, soft blond hair, and delicate features reminiscent of the northern European Jesus who has dominated Western art for more than a thousand years. Making the sign of the cross with two extended fingers over the bread on the chapel altar, his head tilted thoughtfully to one side, Professor Koenig could have emerged from an early Dutch painting.

"Paul," Professor Koenig replies slowly, "never claimed to be a systematic theologian." As a practical tent-maker and passionate organizer, Paul tailors his letters to different parts of the early Christian community, each facing vastly different challenges and problems. To the Thessalonians, who are consumed by the fear of death—members of their community have begun to die and Christ has still not returned to earth—Paul offers reassurance. Christ will not forget those who have died before his final arrival, and the living "will by no means precede those who have died" (1 Thessalonians 4:14–5:21). Paul also reminds the Thessalonians that Jesus' return was not so imminent that everyone should stop working.

For the Corinthians, however, death is not real enough. Influenced by the Docetists, who taught that Christ was never truly human but rather swooped in and out of human form, the Corinthians do not fear death or judgment quite enough, in Paul's opinion. They feel assured of their place in the kingdom of God and consequently have time to light incense and throw parties, rather than worry about earning a place in heaven. Indeed, Paul spends most of 1 Corinthians reprimanding the Christian community at Corinth for sexual immorality, for filing lawsuits against one another, for abusing the Eucharist by eating at home instead of in community, and for following false teachers. According to Professor Koenig, Paul implies that the Corinthian infatuation with the Spirit leads them to neglect their worldly responsibilities to one another and to their community. By suggesting that Christ reigns incompletely and that his full dominion will occur only at an indefinite time in the future, Paul seeks to persuade the complacent Corinthians that they are not yet fully part of the celestial body.

Brad and I both grow more interested in Paul the following week when Professor Koenig argues, based on parts of 2 Corinthians and Acts, that the infamous thorn in Paul's flesh may have been a disfiguring eye disease. A physical disability would have been a huge liability for Paul, whose competitors were the beautiful people of early Christianity, false teachers whom he calls the "super apostles." For a first-century Greek, Dr. Koenig says, the messenger *was* the message, since health and God's blessing were interconnected in many ancient religious traditions. Were I a first-century Corinthian living in that ethos, I, too, might have followed the tall, square-shouldered young man with a firm handshake and a fresh toga, rather than the intense, wiry Paul with his rheumy eye. Before Paul, the Jewish philosopher Philo had written about Moses' transformation on descending from the mount. After his encounter with God, the prophet was so strong and beautiful that none of his people recognized him. So, Paul not only suffered shipwreck, jail, whipping, and stoning; he may also have had to contend with far less qualified apostolic competitors who were, nonetheless, more photogenic.

As sympathetic and interesting a picture of Paul as Professor Koenig paints, we can't avoid Paul's controversial reputation for long. Our class discussion of Paul's writings on slavery is revealing.

In addition to sitting together during lecture, Brad and I are in the same biweekly discussion group with Nathan and five other classmates. Our group assembles in a dingy room where the heating is so effective that we have to open the windows to breathe. Most people have plenty of opinions about Paul's belief that women should not speak in church and that marriage is a second-best condition for those who cannot commit to celibacy. John, our leader, is a third-year student, a lawyer by training. Occasionally, he interjects Professor Koenig's outline questions over the clang of the radiators.

"So, why doesn't Paul attack the institution of slavery?" John asks the class. "What does he mean when he urges the Corinthians to 'remain in the condition in which you were called?'"

One person suggests that Paul didn't condemn slavery because maybe slavery wasn't as bad then as it is now. Nathan, referring to our assigned reading, reminds us that perhaps it was more difficult for Paul to envision slaves as a single oppressed group that could be rallied into joint action, since in Paul's time over half of the Greek population was made up of slaves, and slaves were not of a single race or social status. Another classmate wonders if the church did perhaps secretly work to subvert slavery, even if it didn't promote liberation as part of its public platform in Rome. Maybe the early Christians had enough to worry about without being accused of leading slave revolts.

Brad is silent. I have the feeling he wants to talk but is awaiting the right dramatic moment. It clearly bothers him that our classmates are letting Paul off the hook.

"Hold on a second," he begins. "I mean, it's not like half of the population was clamoring to be sold into slavery. I bet you didn't see all these people running up credit card bills and then shrugging their shoulders and saying, 'That's it, time to sell ourselves into slavery!'" Brad thinks the gospel talks about physical, not merely spiritual, freedom. Nathan agrees.

Professor Koenig decides that to really understand the challenges slavery posed to the early church, we should each take a role in the cast of characters described in Paul's letter to Philemon. In the Epistle to Philemon, Paul appeals to a fellow Christian whose slave, Onesimius, converted to Christianity and served Paul faithfully. Paul suggests that Philemon treat his slave Onesimius well and possibly give him freedom. Since we do not know whether Onesimius ran away from his master originally, or how angry Philemon is when Onesimius returns, this letter is, as the New Revised Standard Version of the Bible says, "a masterpiece of church diplomacy." Paul suggests that Philemon take Onesimius back, "no longer as a slave but more than a slave, a beloved brother" (Philemon 15).

In our NT 2 preceptorial, each student is assigned a role as a member of the house of Philemon; on receiving Paul's letter, we will decide the fate of Onesimius. This exercise is clearly not one of our leader's favorite parts of the syllabus, but John dutifully tears up names and passes them around in a hat. The results are as follows:

Philemon, Christian householder
and slave-owner ....Nathan

Philemon's wife ....Kathi

Archippus, a lawyer and friend
of Philemon's ....John

Marcella, another slave in the
household of Philemon ....Brad

Gaius, a friend of the Apostle Paul
who has accompanied Onesimius
on his return journey to Philemon's house ....Kate

Onesimius, a Christian slave who belonged
originally to Philemon but has been serving
the Apostle Paul and is now being sent home ....Bob

Householder # 1 ....Phoebe

Householder # 2 ....Mauricio

The scene is a second-floor classroom in Sherrod Hall. Members of the household of Philemon are gathered in a circle. Onesimius, Philemon's slave, has just returned, accompanied by Gaius, a close friend of the Apostle Paul. Marcella, another household slave, has been asked to read the letter that Onesimius and Gaius have brought with them from Paul. The assembled group does not yet understand the gravity of the moment.

MARCELLA *(with flourish)*: Ahem! I have been instructed to read a letter from the great Apostle Paul. So y'all listen up now, y'hear!

> "Paul, a prisoner of Christ Jesus, and Timothy our brother, to Philemon, our dear friend and coworker, to Apphias our sister, to Archippus our fellow soldier, and to the church in your house . . .
>
> . . . I am appealing to you for my child, Onesimius, whose father I have become during my imprisonment. . . .
>
> . . . Perhaps this is the reason he was separated from you for a while, so that you might have him back forever, no longer as a slave but more than a slave, a beloved brother. . . . So if you consider me your partner, welcome him as you would welcome me. . . .
>
> . . . The grace of the Lord Jesus Christ be with your Spirit."

After Marcella finishes reading the letter, all eyes are on Philemon. What are the chances he will follow Paul's suggestion to give Onesimius his freedom?

PHILEMON *(clearing his throat)*: Ah, yes. This is indeed a grave matter. It was foolishness for you, Onesimius, to return after you ran away and *(Philemon looks around)* . . . yet not foolishness as well. Onesimius's decision to return shows the power of his witness and is a testimony to the greatness of our God! I will definitely consider what Paul advises me to do.

ARCHIPPUS *(sensing his friend is softening toward the runaway slave, he fears the dangerous precedent lenience might set for other householders like himself)*: What about all your other slaves, Philemon? What about Harold and Nancy—I mean, Demeter, Diana, and

Cassius? Do you plan to release them, too? What would happen if our slaves started thinking all they had to do to gain freedom was to become Christian? Overnight, we'd have mass conversions and there'd be no one to clean our villas!

MARCELLA *(jealous of his master's favoritism)*: What about the silver wine goblet that vanished from the guest villa on the night Onesimius disappeared?

ARCHIPPUS: And all the gold pieces in the floor mosaic of the bath house you reported missing?

PHILEMON *(countenance clouded, addresses his runaway slave again)*: So why *did* you leave, Onesimius?

Heads turn toward Onesimius, who sits slouched against the back of his chair with tousled hair and unlaced Timberlands. Clearly it had been a difficult morning for Onesimius. No doubt he'd spent the night hiding from wild boars and Romans. He looks bewildered, reaches for his book bag, then stops.

ONESIMIUS *(firmly)*: I left because I wanted to learn more about Jesus Christ.

PHILEMON *(breaking the hushed silence that follows)*: Well, Onesimius, what do you want to do now?

ARCHIPPUS *(interrupting before the slave can answer)*: Are you nuts, Philemon? What are you doing, asking your slave to give an opinion about his own fate? Have you forgotten who's the master here? Next thing you know, you'll be forming focus groups and handing out evaluations on customer friendliness!

ONESIMIUS: *(ignoring Archippus's outburst)*: I want to be free to go and proclaim the gospel.

A short silence . . . then panic.

PHILEMON'S WIFE *(pleadingly)*: But, Onesimius, why do you want to leave? Can't you serve God just as well in your job binding papyrus here in the villa? You do it so well, you know!

HOUSEHOLDER #1 *(furtively)*: What about the budget? Can the house afford this?

PHILEMON'S WIFE: Oh, Philemon, how will we ever explain this to the neighbors?

HOUSEHOLDER #2: What are the tax implications of this decision?

MARCELLA: If Onesimius goes, does that mean I can leave, too?

HOUSEHOLDER #2: Can I have his leather thongs and striped chiton?

PHILEMON: Quiet, everyone! Paul has never given me reason to doubt his motives. He's shared Christ's love with us all. He's transformed our lives with his words. These are truly difficult instructions ... yet, as Paul says, Onesimius is my brother in Christ.

ARCHIPPUS *(in desperation)*: OK, Philemon, suppose you agree to let him go, you obey Paul. Where does it end? You could be enslaved yourself, you know! Paul says so himself in his other letter, the one to the Galatians. I have a copy of it here, I'll show you. Now, where IS that letter?... Darn it! Has anyone seen Paul's letter to the Galatians?

PHILEMON'S WIFE *(bitterly)*: Well, I don't know where it is! I thought we were all supposed to have a copy of Paul's letters. *(Then pointedly to Archippus)* Clearly not *everyone* has been cc'd!

Despite the uproar, the decision stands. Onesimius is a new man. He lifts his Starbucks mug in tribute; he has earned his freedom, thanks to Paul.

AFTER ENGAGING Paul's writing through study, debate, and our imaginations, it is less easy to shelve his work as the product of a misogynistic zealot. In Professor Koenig's class I develop grudging respect for the Apostle's passionate, practical campaign to bring Christianity out from under the umbrella of Judaism and establish it as a universal faith. But more than one introductory course in New Testament history and theology will be needed to help me understand that what I abhor are the classical interpretations of Paul, not his writings themselves.

A year later, I enroll in an extraordinary Union Theological Seminary course on Paul, taught by an East German woman, Brigitte Kahl—a Lutheran pastor and theologian. She shows us how we can understand Paul's words differently by paying close attention to the text and its historical context—reading it, for example, in its original form without punctuation or chapter divisions. Paul is not, our close reading shows, the dead hand of church authority. By noting the number of reversals in the text and the considerable time he spends with outsiders such as women and gentiles, we determine that Paul, had he lived today, would have advocated forms of civil disobedience and supported the rights of gay men and women. Paul, after all, carries out his mission by aligning himself and other Christians with the marginalized, the ritually unclean, and the dispossessed.

Uncommon Prayer

A report on our prayer life is an important part of the quarterly Ember Day letters we write to our bishops. In Ember Day letters, seminarians are asked to share both academic and spiritual struggles. Also, one purpose of the monthly meetings I have with my spiritual director, Brother Clark, is to discuss prayer. Even my professors, aware that regular prayer is an important part of the seminarian's formation, factor in the time we are expected to dedicate to our spiritual life when they assign course work.

My first semester at General, the amount of time I was expected to spend in prayer was bewildering. Like most first-year students, I attended morning and evening prayer each day at the Chapel of the Good Shepherd. Mary and I calculated that the hours we spent in chapel were equivalent to at least one extra course. On Mondays, Wednesdays, and Thursdays, morning prayer at 8:00 A.M. was followed by the Eucharist at 8:20, and then we attended evensong from 5:00 to 5:30 P.M. On Tuesdays, morning prayer was again at 8:00 A.M., but evening prayer was at 5:30 P.M., followed by a well-attended "community" Eucharist at 6:00. Friday was a three-service day with sung morning prayers followed by a noon Eucharist and evensong at 5:30.

For all the time I spent in church, however, my prayer life seemed remarkably unaffected. For one thing, I was so busy in chapel, sorting through books in the pew rack and searching for the hymns, that there never seemed enough time to pray.

Typically, the service begins while I am still trying to wrench the GTS hymnal from its place, squeezed between six other books in the pew rack. Everyone else is already standing when the officiant walks down the center aisle and opens the service with the words, "Lord, open our lips." After opening prayers, the congregation sits, and I start looking up the psalm of the day. Once I figure out the position of the psalm numbers in the strange code slotted into a wooden wallboard, the search becomes easier.

The Old and New Testament readings of the day offer a moment's repose. All I have to do is listen. After the reading, there's even a minute or two of silence for reflection, which I assume means reflection that could be called prayerful. I soon discover that other worshippers use these moments to locate the Nicene Creed and the collects in their prayer books so as to avoid fumbling later on. Those who close their eyes for a second in the Chapel of the Good Shepherd get left in the dust, liturgically speaking.

Where exactly in this rigorous daily exercise of book juggling, recitation, and song was prayer? How could this so-called common prayer have anything to do with my prayer life when what I *really* did inside the Chapel of the Good Shepherd was riffle for page numbers?

Of course, as I become habituated to the liturgy, services seem more fluid. Many of the hymns and sung prayers, it transpires, are an acquired taste and grow on me like strong cheese. Learning in patristics about the delicate fourth-century negotiations that produced the Nicene Creed, I recite the words with deeper meaning. As my historical understanding grows, I feel the power of a prayer spoken by centuries of Christian worshippers. Although I still doubt that God would find a lovely hymn more pleasing than an act of charity, more often now, I leave evening prayer feeling refreshed.

At least one important development in my prayer life, however, occurs outside the chapel. One midwinter morning, Mary and I are at the French pastry shop around the corner, kvetching over coffee. The one really practical course I'm taking makes me doubt whether I'm cut out for pastoral ministry at all, I moan. How can I believe I'll make a good priest if already I feel like screaming at the thought of answering one more question about vestry "boundary issues" at St. Peter's-on-the-Pond? I resent spending time discussing what we can learn from congregations that go to war over the height of their pew benches, so I do other homework during class in protest. Under my irritation, however, is real fear that settling such parish squabbles might actually be most of the substance of my calling.

When she stops laughing, Mary puts down her cup and regards me closely.

"How do you pray about these doubts?" she asks.

When I do pray about what bothers me, it's usually in an all-purpose petition to God. "Dear God, please help me to know what to do..." is one of the most overused solicitations in my collection. Of *course* I pray to God about this, I tell Mary. I want nothing more than to know the right thing to do—in my relationships, in my work with others, in my courses, you name it. I am always looking to God for answers.

This is not the response Mary hoped for.

"I mean, do you ever *offer up* your prayers?" she continues. "Do you ever offer up something that upsets you and just leave it there with God—let it be, without pressing for an immediate solution?"

I ponder.

"For example," Mary goes on, "what about giving all your fears about pastoral ministry up to God and letting God deal with them once in a while? Maybe just for a couple minutes a day. Whatever."

This simple idea seems revolutionary. How had I made it this far without this insight into the possibility of prayer? Surrender my worries? For a short time each day leave them in the Divine In-Box with the confidence that they are God's problem and not mine? Give part of the weight of the world to God, acknowledging that I am not sole mistress of my universe? This thought is as startling as Brother Clark's earlier suggestion that I say thanksgivings for myself as diligently as I give thanks for other people.

I discover that making a thought-offering of my fears and anxieties about the future is something I can do anytime, any place—on my morning jog, climbing the stairs in my apartment building, even on the way to class. I remember how in Tibetan communities in Nepal and India, Buddhist monks and lay people piled the monastery altars high with oranges, flowers, money, sweet biscuits, and bowls of burning incense, leaving them for special holidays. Early Christians left similar offerings during the mass. These images help me regard my prayers as offerings. Some mental gifts are prettier than others, I suppose, and by human standards they must be more or less desirable to the recipient. However, I am more assured now that God will accept them all—thanksgivings and obsessive thoughts alike.

Lent

In early Christianity, Lent was the final stage of a rigorous program of fasting, prayer, and study for catechumens—neophytes of the faith—preparing them for Easter baptism. The length of the season varied from six to eight weeks. Fourth-century pilgrimage journals indicate that Christians in Jerusalem had extended Lent to equal the time that Jesus wandered in the wilderness. Judging from letters written by Bishop Athanasius to his colleagues around the eastern Mediterranean, not all members of the church agreed with this extension. Yet the dual themes of Christ's temptations and preparation for Easter through study and prayer still coexist in Lenten observance.

ALTHOUGH Lenten disciplines are the period's most familiar aspect, "Lent is not simply a time for self-improvement," Brother Clark told us during an 8:00 A.M. meditation on Ash Wednesday. Nor is Lent a time to feel virtuous about a successfully completed forty-day abstention from television. Any Lenten discipline we might adopt was for the larger purpose of reflection and reconciliation. For me, Lent brought a confrontation with fears and questions about my vocation.

If you were to ask the average pedestrian running errands between

Rite-Aid and Edison's Hardware on Ninth Avenue to define the word "sacristan," you would probably get a blank stare. Before seminary, I, too, was largely ignorant of the sacristan's role. Nothing could have prepared me for the significance of this title inside the Close.

The Guild of Sacristans first came to my attention in the thick packet of orientation materials. It had been established for the unglamorous mission of "maintaining the chapel and the oratory in an orderly manner," but the considerable space the organization received in our Community Life Handbook suggested that it played an important role at General Seminary.

At the end of the first semester, everyone in the class receives a letter about the Guild of Sacristans and an invitation to apply. Joining the guild is competitive, and applicants must write a short essay telling why they want to serve the guild, what qualifies them, and what they will bring to the group. New sacristans will be installed at the Feast of the Presentation on February 2, the beginning of the Easter term, and will serve until they graduate. With the exception of the chief sacristan, who serves for one year, other guild members serve throughout their time at seminary.

I can't understand the apparent gap between the guild's prestige and its work—setting up for services, polishing chalices, ironing the altar linen, and cleaning the chapel once a year before Easter. Nothing in the handbook explains how the sacristans' mundane responsibilities open windows onto a rich liturgical tradition or how their custodial activities might glorify God. Nor do I understand the noble history of the office, beginning with the first sacristans, who worked in Syrian churches around 400 A.D., as Christian worship moved from the household into the basilica. The sacristans' rigorous attention to the shine of the holy vessels and the crispness of the priest's vestments emerges in part from Anglican theology of the nineteenth century

Oxford Movement in the U.K. and from Archbishop Laud's idea of "the beauty of holiness."

Mauricio, usually a reliable authority on such matters, is in no position to educate me. Sacristans do not play major roles in his church in Costa Rica, and as the only ordained member of our class, Mauricio spends much of his time during services as a deacon or celebrant. Missing the significance of the theological and practical importance of the sacristan, then, I don't see joining the guild at General as an unusual opportunity. The sacristans' duties seem *adiaphora,* not essential for salvation—mine or anyone else's—so I decide not to apply.

A week or so later, I'm scanning the paper in Seabury's Bottom and overhear someone congratulate Mary on being accepted to the guild. Despite all my carefully considered reservations about applying—not the least of which is the fact that the guild flunks Ellen's church-weirdness test—I still have the passing sensation of being back in sixth grade, counting valentines, and realizing that I need five more cards to re-establish my popularity rating. My usual attempt to regain perspective by recalling the number of malnourished children in the Sudan and Ethiopia fails miserably. I desire acceptance, even though the qualifying grounds escape me.

The lobby bulletin board soon posts the list announcing new members of the Guild of Sacristans. As I ruefully scan a few classmates' names, Nathan appears out of nowhere with words of encouragement. "Apply," he urges. "They don't have enough applicants to fill the spots, and they're looking for two more people. Being a sacristan would be a great opportunity, because you would learn a lot and you'd be serving the community. It would be fun," he insists.

Having grown up in a community where "serving" meant collecting signatures for a disarmament campaign, I am still unconvinced that my best service to God or the community is to polish brass candlesticks.

However, I've underestimated the influence on me of my peers' enthusiasm. Also, I reason, there are probably few better places than the guild from which to view the supporting apparatus behind the sacramental glories of priesthood. I type a short application and, with mixed feelings, submit it to the chief sacristan.

The chief sacristan who followed Caroline is a tall, authoritative man with kindly, melting brown eyes and a resonant voice that sounds prophetic from the lectern. On special days, he walks up the aisle in measured pace, resplendent in black and gold robe, carrying a long, finely carved ebon mace that, during the Middle Ages, served to shoo cows and chickens aside to let the procession move unhindered toward the altar. Resting on his shoulder, the mace serves an equally important function as a symbol of authority in the liturgy at General.

Naturally, when my application for the guild is rejected, I approach the chief sacristan to find out why.

"Yes, I am sorry. We ended up receiving so many qualified applicants this year," he begins, as soon as it becomes apparent why I've phoned. He, too, is disappointed and unsure why I haven't been selected. It is hard to say why others have been picked and I have not, especially when, at first, too few applicants competed for the available places. One does not really know how these things happen, he says. If I want to look into the Guild of Chimers, I should think about that for next semester.

I might have reacted differently if I'd known that the birth of the sacristan in the early fourth century A.D. was an important moment in the evolution of Christianity from a home-based countercultural movement to an established religion with large public worship spaces, thus making the guild a chance to bring history to life. I might have avoided inflating this rejection into a symbol of everything I disliked about seminary and much of what I doubted in the church.

As it is, however, the significance of the job is lost on me. Rejection by the Guild of Sacristans brings into bold relief a question that has already appeared in many guises. Just what sort of place *is* this where I've landed? Would I ever really become fluent in the language or comfortable with the culture and currency? I usually liked traveling; during a year abroad I had lived and studied in India and Nepal. At times like this, however, the culture shock and isolation I feel here at seminary make me more homesick than I ever was in Asia.

Now, the salt doused liberally on my wound of rejection is that I have to admit I'd not even *wanted* to be a sacristan until I found out that membership was competitive. To my unchurched eyes, the guild appears a cohort of smartly dressed, very efficient housekeepers who have managed to turn a few repetitive tasks into a prestigious set of holy responsibilities.

Hanging up the phone after talking with the chief sacristan, I'm furious. If this institution spent the same amount of energy and attention to detail on intellectual exploration as on liturgical correctness, I fume, it might not have to pay thousands of dollars in lost tuition subsidies incurred by students who no longer qualify for their federal loans because they have received so many "incompletes" in their course work. Maybe if these people paid less attention to thurible-swinging and more to academics, I would not feel that I sin against the Holy Ghost because I, unlike some classmates, prefer to read actual sections of Hooker's *Lawes of Ecclesiastical Polity,* not the Cliff's Notes version.

My internal tirade escalates as I remember my gripes about the lack of community service activity around the Close. If General directed even one-*tenth* of its concern about chapel lighting toward witnessing the gospel in Chelsea, not a soul would be left on welfare, not a prostitute on the corner, not a homeless person in our neighborhood. Indignantly, I reflect that here at seminary we're neither conducting cutting-edge scholarship nor doing our part in neighborhood service.

By dinnertime the guild not only represents everything wrong with seminary, it suggests sad limits to the church in the world. Perhaps the priesthood is the only profession that rewards shabby scholarship and second-rate social work, I growl. No wonder membership among the mainline Protestant denominations in North America has declined drastically. If I want to succeed in the church, I might—without tripping on my cassock or moving out of step—have to become artful at reverently rearranging the chairs on the deck of our spiritual *Titanic.*

During first semester, I'd written a paper about Luke's account of the temptation of Christ in the wilderness. I argued, based on one translation of the Koine Greek word πειράομαι, meaning "to exert oneself, strive, or undertake," that his temptations were more a testing of God than purely satanic temptations, because they fit the Old Testament pattern of preparation in the service of God. Although, according to our Ash Wednesday meditation, Lent is not supposed to be exclusively a time of striving for self-improvement, I believe that my own Lenten struggles are tests to be overcome and strengthened by.

Reading the temptation narrative in Luke in my post-sacristan-rejection funk, I find new meaning. Satan's mocking voice echoes through the text in an oddly familiar way. I imagine him as incredulous, impatient, perfectly reasonable—and stunned by Jesus' indifferent response to his enticements.

"LET ME get this straight," Satan says to Jesus, to whom he has appeared from a cloud of ancient dust on a windswept plateau east of the Dead Sea. "I know you are the Son of God. It will take a while for your disciples to fully comprehend this, and you yourself appear to have occasional doubts, but I and the other spirits know it's true. You were the cocreator of the universe. Talk about gifts and talents—you've cooked up miraculous phenomena, a bunch of random carbon atoms bonding to create self-reflecting life forms! You put together the second law of thermodynamics before anyone knew how to spell. You have the *power*!"

Silence. Jesus sits unmoved.

"Given your outstanding abilities, explain to me your problem with the stones and the bread. If you're hungry, why don't you eat? You have a responsibility to take care of yourself. I mean, let's not forget you're God!" Satan pauses, chewing the end of his cigar, awaiting a response. Getting none, he continues.

"And another thing, why turn down leadership of all the kingdoms of the earth? David's legacy would be small potatoes next to the glory you'd get in that position. Think about it . . . God takes over the IRS, the Defense Department, the social security system. Talk about reinventing government!" He laughs loudly. Quickly realizing he's making no headway with the Son of God, Satan tries one more tack.

"If you're really stuck on being the Messiah, really think you can save humanity as the Lamb of God, not as an earthly king, explain why you won't at least demonstrate that you hold all God's supernatural power? [With this question, Satan is referring to the temptation that Jesus throw himself off the Temple to test scripture's assurance that angels will bear up those who fall.] Hey, if you know that the angels have been given charge of you, why not let them take charge? If God is asking you to die on a cross as a way of redeeming humanity, why not make him pull his own weight and support a few more miracles to guarantee your status as his only son?"

Again, silence.

"Well, it's just very bizarre," Satan concludes, now agitated, "that when you could have been or had or done anything in the universe, you'd choose to accept all the limitations—every last nasty, brutish, and short one—of human life. It's a little strange. Personally, I think it's an example of seriously wasted potential. And, I might add, you have a pretty negative self-image."

With that, the devil departs from Jesus until an opportune time.

The Kingdoms of This World

When Satan took Jesus up, he "showed him all the kingdoms of the world in a moment of time" (Luke 4:5) and offered them to him in return for his discipleship. The temptation here, we assume, is authority and glory—sumptuous palaces, adoration by millions. Perhaps, however, for someone like Jesus, who felt compassion for the poor and outcast, the real temptation of kingship might be slightly different.

"So, Jesus..." In the desert, Satan has materialized again out of swirling Judean dust, still devilish but beginning to sound like Billy Crystal. Jesus sits cross-legged on the cracked ground, examining a tuft of shrunken grass.

"Maybe you're not thrilled by the prospect of a great marble palace or the world's most powerful army ready to annex more territory for you at a moment's notice," Satan begins. "I can understand how someone with your temperament might not find the perks of absolute power as gratifying as others do."

Narrowing his eyes, Satan continues. "But before you tell me again about your undying love and loyalty to God, just think about the *good* you could do as ruler of the earth for the whole suffering mass of humanity you're so fond of."

Jesus is silent.

"Where would the Israelites have been without your ancestor King

David to drive out their enemies and gain a peaceful kingdom without slavery? What if he had decided that he wouldn't dirty his hands in affairs of state? Where would *you* be today?" the devil asks in a reasonable tone. "Say it's world peace you want, not a fleet of private jets and an Olympic-size swimming pool. Well, this is your chance. Be my disciple, and I'll help you get things done."

Satan crouches near Jesus, exhaling cigar smoke. "Call me your all-in-all," he says, "and whatever your agenda is—less infant mortality, higher literacy, saving the rain forest, you name it—I can help make it happen." Satan cocks his head; he can't resist a jab. "Who do you think is going to help humanity more? A smart ruler with strong backing, or a wandering homeless man who thinks he'll lead a lot of people to God by looking gift horses in the mouth?"

Jesus shifts a little, about to speak.

"Wait!" Satan shouts, sensing he won't like the reply. "When you hear me say that I will give authority and glory of the kingdoms of the world to him who worships me, use your imagination ... think 'U.N. secretary general' or 'president of the Ford Foundation' or 'director of the International Red Cross' or 'president of the United States before Watergate.' Just because I offer you all the kingdoms of the world, you don't have to be Hitler, Stalin, or Nebuchadnezzar.

"Before you pass this up, take a minute and *think* about giving up the opportunity to improve the standard of living for millions of people in *this* lifetime, for the sake of some abstract idea of happiness in a future life." Satan pauses for breath, satisfied he's scored a point.

At that moment, Jesus could have countered in many ways. He might have said he well knew that God valued a just ruler. After all, the Son of God had come to fulfill the Law upheld by such powerful administrators as King Solomon, who built the Temple in seven years, ran a profitable trade in horses and chariots, and constructed a world-class fleet of ships at Tarshish—or Nehemiah, governor of Jerusalem, who rebuilt the city walls in only fifty-two days after the Israelites returned from exile.

Jesus could have suggested to Satan that powerful government positions were not so enviable in their own right. They definitely were not worth attaining at the cost of devil worship. If God had asked Jesus the Nazarene to overthrow the Romans by force, he would have been happy to oblige. As Christ, the "anointed one," however, his calling was very different.

Satan's taunts made Christ sound as if he thought joy in the next life could be purchased only at the price of suffering in this one. True, Jesus told his followers not to lay up treasures for themselves upon earth, but to lay up treasures in heaven where "moths and dust did not corrupt and thieves did not steal" (Matt. 6:35). He also said that everyone who is persecuted for his sake should rejoice, for great will be their reward in heaven (Matt. 5:11–12).

However, Jesus also conveyed that heavenly rewards are more than an individual's post-death prizewinnings and that deliverance is not the result of a specific formula. Most of his parables make it painfully clear that beyond being in loving relationship with God and neighbor, there is no strict code of conduct that guarantees eternal life. Jesus never said that the kingdom of God on earth and in heaven profiles its participants. In addition to the poor in spirit, the meek, the merciful, those who mourn, and those who hunger and thirst for righteousness, he names others blessed as well.

A servant risks investing his talents rather than saving them (Matt. 25:29), and wise bridesmaids refuse to lend their foolish sisters lamp oil for fear of missing the bridegroom's return (Matt. 25:1–13). There is the tax collector who did not tithe or follow any of the correct religious laws of the time (Luke 18:7). A laborer begins work late and receives the same wages as his fellow workers who've been in the vineyards since sunrise (Matt. 20: 1–16). All these men and women participate in the kingdom, Jesus implies, not through calculation but because they recognize the Truth and are willing to take risks for it.

Finally, Jesus could have explained to Satan that the kingdom of heaven is not like Hades, a place limited exclusively to the spirits of the dead. Isaiah and the writer(s) of John's Gospel made the point that for some people the kingdom is present here and now. The person who hears Jesus and believes in the Father while he or she is living "hath everlasting life, and shall not come into condemnation but is passed from death into life" (John 5:24). All this happens in the present tense. Eternal life is abundant life, right now.

Jesus could have offered Satan any of these answers, but instead he chooses to rebut Satan in a few words. "It is written," he replies, quoting Deuteronomy 6:13, "that you shall worship the Lord your God and him only shall you serve" (Luke 4:8).

I remember that Queen Esther, too, recognizes this first and greatest commandment, deciding to risk her status in the court for the sake of her conscience and the lives of her people. As much as she loves the royal dignity into which (Mordecai reminds her) she had come from another place, Esther uses her elevated position as a means toward something greater. For her, power was not an end in itself.

DURING second semester, I set up a Bible study course at St. Clement's near Hell's Kitchen, a parish run by a rector I have long admired. My job includes teaching Genesis stories to Jehovanna, Zachary, Souhay, Ralique, and several other eight- to twelve-year-old children from P.S. 51 who participate in the church's after-school program. After spending most of my life in the library first semester, I believe a kids' Bible study might challenge me to put my learning into practice.

The walk from the subway stop on Fiftieth Street and Eighth Avenue to the church on Forty-sixth Street, between Ninth and Tenth Avenues, is a pilgrim's progress. In the very short walk down four blocks and crosstown a block and a half, I encounter a surprisingly large number of dragons and wild beasts.

From my research for Father Wright on Athanasius's *Life of St. Anthony* I knew that for the fourth-century desert fathers, demons came in all shapes and sizes, depending on the time of day, the nature of the temptation, and other contingencies. To St. Anthony, demons appeared as women, "little black boys," lions, bears, scorpions, leopards, wolves, and other wild beasts. For Evagrius Ponticus, another skilled demon-spotter, one of the more troublesome was "the noonday demon" who "makes it seem that the sun barely moves, if at all, and that the day is fifty hours long."

In class I hesitate to argue categorically for or against the objective existence of demons in the lives of these early saints, but my walk from the Fiftieth Street subway to St. Clement's assures me that manifold forms of temptation are not unique to the desert.

THE FIRST spiritual distraction across my narrow path is the glass skyscraper on the corner of Fiftieth Street and Eighth Avenue. Its powers to divert my attention arise not so much from the fact that it contains the offices of Cravath, Swain, and Moore—a prestigious old law firm that employs several friends from undergraduate days; corporate law lost its glamour when I discovered how much time goes into copyediting 100-page contracts. Rather, buildings like this distract because they are emblems of power.

Inside the golden lobby of marble and glass, people are going places and making things happen—good things and bad things. I had never spent enough time working in a downtown high rise to develop the ashen complexion and the vulnerability to Sick Building Syndrome that my husband and some other management consultants were susceptible to. I hadn't faced "Fear of the Man," as Greg refers to it—the invisible force that can reel a hapless employee back to his or her desk at any hour, interrupting dinners, ski trips, and family vacations.

Buildings like the sleek tower at Fiftieth and Eighth remind me of exciting trips from Washington, D.C., to court corporate and non-profit support for *Who Cares,* a magazine start-up for social entrepreneurs that two friends and I had started. Barely out of college, I'd been thrilled to meet with corporate executives and foundation officers who often were impressed by our bright ideas, boundless energy, and fearlessness about making cold calls. Themes from our sales pitch come to mind—our mantra about the power of young people's idealism to change the world.

BY SHEER force of will, I struggle free of the alluring skyscraper and walk on, passing delis and tourist traps with Empire State Building mugs in the windows, racking my brain for good questions about Esau and Jacob. (Which son was older? How did Jacob disguise himself as Esau?) I join the sidewalk traffic of Hispanic moms and toddlers, guys hanging out in doorways of T-shirt shops to eyeball the crowd, and old women deliberately wheeling shopping carts along the curb.

All is well until I reach the billboards at a construction site between Forty-eighth and Forty-seventh Streets. After an eight-month assault on my visual sense, I can ignore bus-length clothing ads that appear to be selling the hollow-eyed, full-lipped young women wearing the clothes, or the vodka ads that promise abundant life. If anything, the ads' repugnance lends importance to my mission and keeps me firmly on track. More insidious is a huge maroon poster with an edgy, quasi-intelligible background design. Enormous white letters in bold relief read:

AMBITION
WILL
CURE
AIDS
BEFORE
LOVE

Just as I suspected. Nietzsche, Marx, and a couple of Athenian orators were right. Jesus, Socrates, and St. Paul got it wrong. I remember a quote from Callicles, a serious challenger to Socrates' proposition "that it is better to suffer wrong than to do wrong." In one of Plato's dialogues, much to the consternation of many classmates, Callicles argues that human conventions, moral codes, religious laws, and such were "made . . . by the weaklings who form the majority of mankind," who say that "ambition is base and wrong, and that wrong-doing consists in trying to gain an advantage over others; being inferior themselves, they are content, no doubt, if they can stand on an equal footing with their betters."

This AIDS poster confirms my deepest fears about where the power to do good really lies. Maybe it isn't in church service or the sacrifice of personal ambition to work directly with the poor. Perhaps human altruism and idealism *are* inspired by ambition—although they embody a different sort of power than Wall Street. Love is for the weak. What's more, in human society, familial love and even love of neighbor are biologically determined, selected for in the same way as hair color. Could it be that we have not adequately considered the evolutionary psychiatrists who argue that members of the human species who exhibit unselfish behavior or self-sacrifice may have as great a chance of perpetuating their genetic code as people who are physically attractive or highly intelligent?

From Eighth Avenue and Forty-sixth Street, it's another long block and a half to St. Clement's. All I have to do is stay on the pavement and keep moving.

For all the temptations along my route, St. Clement's doesn't welcome me in through pearly gates. Nor are the children I teach particularly angelic. The church occupies an old brownstone. Inside the sanctuary on the second floor, a colorful set for the off-Broadway productions performed there backs the freestanding altar. Clarence, the office manager and kitchen organizer, buzzes me in at the battered wooden front door. I stick my head through the office door to glance at the bulletin board. According to the news, St. Clement's is holding a special actors' Eucharist, participating in homeless shelter actions at city hall, and thanking contributors to roof repairs.

I breathe deeply and push open the doors of the basement parish hall, where a swarm of thirty-five elementary schoolkids buzz and shriek. Some are doing homework. It's my job to gather ten to fifteen children whose parents have given them permission to attend Bible study once a week and who haven't hidden out in the costume closet or suddenly developed severe stomach aches. I line the children up at the door and, hoping not to lose anyone along the way, start to lead them up three long flights to a small attic classroom.

I've long since given up hope of engaging my spirited pupils in discussions about the role of corporate versus individual salvation in Genesis or about the creation story in light of Darwin. (It took all of one afternoon to realize that more urgent than the question of Abraham's monotheism was the challenge of convincing my students that we could get to class more quickly by *walking,* not crawling, up three flights of stairs.)

I divide the kids into two groups, the "Stingers" and the "Flipmodes." After reading a story aloud, I ask questions about the text, and the kids compete, game-show style, for correct answers. These matches between the kids, after offering stunning insight into the number of Jacob's wives and the color of Joseph's coat, actually yield theological reflection. "How could Moses not speak if he was speaking to God when he said he couldn't speak?" Jehovanna asks. "What made Pharaoh so bad? Why couldn't he be good?" someone else puts in.

Although I spend a lot of time taking away superhero dolls and making sure no one escapes out the window, there are days when the Spirit enters our class. My students learn the names of many heroes and heroines in Genesis and begin to make connections between these stories and their own stories. Zachary is outraged that Jacob stole his brother's inheritance, and Souhay says the Joseph stories made her think differently about her own little brother. On good days, I can uproot biblical people and events from history and deliver them to my class in a way that hits home. Returning to giant Manhattan apartment blocks, the kids may wonder briefly before turning on the TV why Jacob got away with tricking his father.

By the end of the semester, I've grown quite attached to the kids. I will miss the Stingers and the Flipmodes. Besides the promised party and the tally of cumulative points earned over the past few months, I will try to give each child a button reading "Stingers and Flipmodes" to remind them of our time together.

On the way back to the subway after the second-to-last class, I hunt down a store that prints T-shirts and buttons. After an afternoon's worth of negotiations between the saleswoman, the manager, and me—along with several phone calls to the church to ask if they'll consider thanking the business in their Sunday bulletin—the shop agrees to lower the price from $7.00 to $5.00 per button.

I walk out of the store into early evening commuter traffic, happy and hopeful. I feel as good as if I've just brokered a corporate merger. Maybe this shows there's a place for entrepreneurial skills in the body of Christ, despite everything. If volunteer programs can have sponsors, perhaps parishes can. I have forgotten the final line in the temptation story in Luke—Satan departed from Jesus only "until an opportune time."

OF THE THREE temptations Christ faced in the desert, the second—the offer of worldly power—is perhaps most intriguing to a seminarian living in Manhattan. With the exception of subsidized housing in Chelsea, apartments are mostly too small and parking too expensive to make material needs a serious consideration. However, the multitiered city, its blatant economic stratification packed into a few hundred acres of bedrock, still cannot segregate the very poor from the very rich, the upwardly mobile from the totally disenfranchised. There are plenty of opportunities for envy.

Since, as with Rome, all roads lead to New York, odds are excellent for encountering a childhood friend from camp on the subway or finding an old drama teacher driving your taxi. In Manhattan, the likelihood of encountering someone living in a world quite different from your own is greater than in other places.

Full of self-congratulation about my button deal, I continue toward the subway. The crowd parts to reveal a manifestation that Evagrius Ponticus might classify as the Temptation of the Alternate Lifestyle or the Rush Hour Demon. The demon manifests itself in the image of a college acquaintance whom I haven't seen in years. She falls into Callicles' class of people "who have the ability to carry out their ideas, and will not shrink from doing so through faintness of heart."

We greet each other enthusiastically. The last time we met, she had just founded a nonprofit venture offering money and contacts to business people interested in helping local entrepreneurs start companies in developing countries. She remains as buoyant as I remembered.

"So, how is your project going?" I ask. It's the right question.

"Oh, it's *amazing,*" she replies exuberantly, unleashing a torrent of supporting evidence. "Things have barely even started and we've already collected 250 applications from B-school students for our five slots in South Asia!"

"Are you serious?" I marvel.

"Yeah. Can you believe it? Over fifty people in Josephine's graduating class at Stanford applied. Babson Business School is fighting to get us to come and present. Harvard had thirty-six people applying. We're swamped."

"That's fantastic!" I say.

"And you're not going to believe this. . . . We just had a meeting with the president of the World Bank. He was so supportive. The bank offered us $250,000, but we turned it down because we didn't want to send people only to places the bank cares about developing. We don't want to limit ourselves."

That makes sense; I nod.

"It's okay, though," she continues, "because tons of venture capital people are interested, too. I think it's really going to take off."

"That is so great!" I say. "What incredible news!" It *was* really great. Without doubt, it *was* incredible news.

When she asks me how I like seminary, I tell her I'm studying for an Old Testament exam; Greek was a nightmare in the fall, but now I enjoy it. We agree that sounds pious. Otherwise, things are good. I refrain from mentioning my own recent entrepreneurial efforts.

In parting, she gives me her card and asks me to call. I spend the rest of my trip home along the strait and narrow path calculating how upset my bishop will be if I call my friend the next day to ask for a part-time job.

JESUS' TEMPTATION did not end in the desert. The angels who ministered to him after his encounters with Satan in the wilderness healed his wounds, knowing that his battles were not over. Although sometimes I am filled with the grace-given assurance that button swaps and international business deals are less unlike than they appear, such moments of peace are fleeting. They often merely presage the next onslaught of misgivings. My commute to St. Clement's dispels any question in my mind that temporal desires can be conquered once and for all. I feel fairly certain they are here to stay.

Philosophers or Prophets?

In *Temptation,* Diogenes Allen describes Christ's temptation to turn stones into bread as a temptation to reject the limitations of humanity. We seek God, Allen says, "as beings who must eat, who are vulnerable to starvation ... and who therefore can become greedy, covetous, [and] envious." Jesus must have been tempted to use his awesome powers to satisfy his own bodily needs and those of others. Instead, saying "man does not live by bread alone," Christ chose to recognize the claim of our physical needs while asserting that deeper satisfactions lie elsewhere.

Few creature comforts were out of reach for a young couple living at a beautiful seminary in a thriving downtown neighborhood of Manhattan. Our apartment, with its dining room window overlooking one of the city's few manicured green spaces, cost much less than similar apartments in the same area. Classes, companionship, dining facilities, and a mailroom were twenty yards' walk from our front door. The Close's tennis and basketball courts and dog run were free to seminarians and their guests.

The cherished bit of Hudson horizon so many New Yorkers long for lay only a block west of us. A dozen newly planted art galleries off Tenth Avenue offered culture and aesthetic stimulation. The ethnic restaurants crowded along Eighth and Ninth Avenues extracted extra pocket money for sushi, vegetarian steamed dumplings, cream cheese and lox, or plain old fresh tomato pizza. In late summer and early fall, fireworks over the river rained shimmering drops of color on the rooftops of our brownstone block.

Another kind of hunger, however, had gnawed off and on since the beginning of the year. It grew particularly acute during Lent. At first, I did not identify it as the kind of physical need that, like other cravings, reminds me of my human frailty. After all, Luke's Gospel does not mention Jesus' boredom with his own stale thoughts during his forty-day retreat or how he must have missed the charge of rabbinical debate with the Pharisees.

There were times when, if I had been offered the chance to turn stones into bread, I would have traded my M.Div. at General

Theological Seminary for a more prestigious set of academic credentials at a more illustrious institution. For me, the tree of knowledge sprouted up on 120th Street at Columbia University. Its fruit appeared in Ph.D. diplomas for the study of religion. The desire for academic accolades was familiar to me, but this craving became palpable during Lent.

I head uptown one midwinter afternoon, after Nathan and I discover that the book we need for our NT 2 essay on the history of conflict and community in Corinth is missing from the shelves of St. Mark's Library. Thinking I'll have a chance of finding it in a library in the cluster of academic institutions uptown, I ride the subway twelve stops to the Upper West Side and get out at Morningside Heights—the Harlem neighborhood containing Union Theological Seminary, Jewish Theological Seminary, Barnard College, and Columbia University.

My intended destination was Union Theological Seminary, the interdenominational seminary where Dietrich Bonhoeffer studied and Reinhold Niebuhr taught, but when I discover that the book is checked out there, too, Columbia's Butler Library is next. While I'm above 116th Street, I might as well explore the university. Robert Thurman, a renowned Western scholar of Tibetan Buddhism, teaches in Columbia's religion department, and I want to see what courses he's offering.

Entering Columbia through massive wrought iron gates on Broadway at 116th Street is like starting a college admissions tour. The grandeur of the campus is overwhelming—its contrast with the street world of Morningside Heights is extreme. Only a few steps from heavy traffic on Broadway, a quiet stone plaza is surrounded by academic buildings. Taking College Walk, I reach the center of campus, turn left up the wide marble steps in front of Old Low Memorial Library, and sit down with my back to the wall, taking in the whole campus. Butler

Library towers against the sky. The quadrangle's layout directs the eyes upward to the names engraved on the frieze of the library:

HOMER · HERODOTUS · SOPHOCLES · PLATO · ARISTOTLE ·
DEMOSTHENES · CICERO · VIRGIL

Here were luminaries around whom isolated communities of learning were truly meant to be founded. The philosophers, whom Plato called "lovers not of part of wisdom, but of the whole," had led Western societies toward the Enlightenment and all that followed. To seclude myself from the life of the city and the world to achieve distinction in a university is a vocation requiring no justification. This kind of Close I understand.

Inside the admissions building, beside the marble bust of Athena, goddess of wisdom, is the visitors' office. Waiting for the young man at the information desk to finish his phone call, I watch an orientation video for prospective students. Undergraduates gather on the same steps I was musing on a few minutes ago. A blond student says he came to Columbia to major in economics but, a year later, is studying literature. An Indian woman had aimed to become a doctor, but at Columbia she grew fascinated by Islam and decided to double-major in biochemistry and religion; she loves leaving lab to run to her class on Sufism.

Sighing, I find all this comforting. It recalls a time in my life when biblical literature was just one of five courses, of equal weight with political theory or Romantic literature, not the focus of my whole day. The rules for success remained the same from course to course; the method of analysis was uniform whether I studied the diaries of nuns in medieval Europe or Marx's dialectical materialism. My job had been to interpret my subject, using tools refined by experts. The subject did not master me. The process of scholarly exploration owed more to

Aristotle's legacy than to Jesus, whether I was in the lab or reading the New Testament.

Glass-paneled shelves along one wall of the visitors' office hold books by Columbia faculty and graduates. *Orientalism* by Edward Said catches my eye because I read it for a college tutorial in comparative religions. Volumes by Margaret Mead, Franz Boas, and Allen Ginsberg give me a twinge of longing. These familiar books, like well-known faces, make the university a safe haven compared to seminary.

I decide I'll just look into the Department of Religion in Kent Hall. I walk up six floors to the department, where nostalgia really takes hold. Pinned to cork squares, posters announce opportunities for National Endowment for the Humanities awards and Ford Foundation predoctoral fellowships. Rustling through the notices, I see that the South Asian Institute will hold a brown-bag lunch on Mahatma Gandhi's dialogues with Americans.

As I scan this rich menu, I admit how much better I understand a community founded on a hunger for knowledge than a community based on a life of common prayer. I have begun learning at General about the kingdom of God, but it is still far too abstract a concept to avow that it's a vision I share with my classmates. Do we really have a common ideal to overcome our differences? For all the answers I gave my Commission on Ministry about my calling, I realize that I still feel more at home in a setting where academic fellowships, not pastoral opportunities, dominate the bulletin board.

I overhear two graduate students chatting in a way more familiar to me than the conversations at General on assistant rectorships.

"I've been trying to get into my dissertation, and I'm going on the market next fall."

"Really, that soon? You know, I've heard that it gets hellish if you're trying to teach and finish up your dissertation at the same time."

"It'll be rough, but I've decided to get a job, then start teaching when I've finished writing."

"Really. That's great!"

I want to congratulate him, too. His dissertation sounds like genuine achievement to me.

My watch says it's time to get back to the computer and that essay on 1 Corinthians 15. I'll do a quick computer search at Butler Library, grab my book, and go.

To get past the security desk, I need a Columbia ID. The guard directs me to the office that issues temporary cards. I wait impatiently behind a Lithuanian woman who lost her visiting scholar's card. When my turn comes, I say I'm a student at General Theological Seminary.

"General *what*?" asks the man behind the typewriter.

"General Seminary."

"Is your institution based here in New York?" he asks.

"It's General Seminary, down in Chelsea," I say irritably.

"I need to see your metro card, then," he says, holding up a form that reads Metro Title Referral Card. "Get your librarian to fill out this card saying the book is not available at your library or any New York public library, then bring it back so I can give you a day pass. You need a new pass every day. You get fourteen days per semester."

"Can I take out books?" I ask despondently.

"No," the man replies, "unless you want to pay a $200 monthly borrowing privilege fee. This is a private library, you know."

The fruit of this tree of knowledge is beyond my grasp. Like the seminary, the university is a closed community isolated from the world. Worse, no matter how enticing this manifestation of secular academia looks, I am no longer part of it.

Dogs and Doormats

"If anyone strikes you on your right cheek, turn to him the other also; and if anyone would sue you and take your coat, let him have your cloak as well; and if anyone forces you to go one mile, go with him two," Jesus says in Matthew 5:31–49.

Historically, Christians and non-Christians alike have leapt to misinterpret this passage. Rather than accepting it as a teaching about how active, nonviolent resistance and presence of mind can undermine what the New Testament scholar Walter Wink calls hierarchical domination systems, we interpret Jesus' words as an instruction in meekness—the source of Christian doormat theology. Although the passage can be read like the Beatitudes, as a saying that does not condemn ambition but instead seeks to channel it in a radical new direction, we still use these words from Jesus to support submission in the face of injustice—or so I decided during my first Lent at General Seminary.

Perhaps because I was living, working, and praying among about 150 people housed on a single block in Manhattan, I found little room for idealization. For all the prayerful aspiring priests who lived in my building at 422 West Twentieth Street, the seminary-owned residential housing across the street from the Close at times lacked any sign of the lively power of Christ's message. Wherever I looked, inside myself and outside in the community, all I saw was human limitation.

Jane Seminarian may not have the aggressive tendencies of Jeff Law Student or the material ambitions of Sue Business School Student. Nonetheless, it became painfully clear during Lent that our weaknesses—our willingness to give up authority, our fear of confrontation, and our tendency to "turn the other cheek" as a submissive rather than subversive act—just as clearly indicate the fallen nature of the human condition as do greed and aggression. Acknowledging these limitations was all the more unsavory because of the high spiritual ideals we professed.

My own response to an irregularity in a piece of decaying New York real estate became an episode where "turning the other cheek" meant the opposite of what Jesus probably intended.

Only one of two elevators in our five-story building worked consistently. On the noisy ride from the first to the fifth floor, I could count on a short conversation about the cuteness of our dogs or about the suitcase I was dragging. On occasion, however, noise and small talk were replaced by mechanical malfunctions that disabled the left elevator. Sometimes the safety eye would shut down, catching me on one side of the elevator door and my dogs on the other. The elevator would also stall between floors—more than once with passengers inside. Understandably, the person lodged between floors three and four, rather than taking the opportunity to meditate, would begin to press the alarm frantically. Signs were posted after the elevator began acting up, but until the repairman arrived, riding the left elevator was like playing Russian roulette.

To an outsider, the problem might seem straightforward. If complaints are ignored, then you do what it takes to fix the problem. At General Seminary, for some reason, solutions weren't that simple. Fear of confrontation and an inappropriate application of Jesus' instruction to "walk the second mile" would turn a small problem into a large one. Even when I was irritated for the third time at the familiar sight of a darkened, dysfunctional elevator, I hesitated to report the situation.

Was this a minor suffering to be embraced, not avoided? Who was I to complain that other people were not doing their jobs? A white, privileged young woman with great opportunity and a fine education, I was complaining that the elevator was not working. Most of the guys in maintenance were African Americans or Latinos and had never enjoyed my opportunities. I was friendly with the head of the maintenance department, had heard how proud he was of his daughter, and listened to his hopes for "his guys." How many times had I heard how much better it was to serve than to be served? Yet I was moaning about bad service. And I called myself a Christian? More to the point, perhaps I would have to pass the custodian of my building in the hall the following morning and would run into him in the laundry room for the next two years. We were already in dialogue about the correct way for students to tie up boxes for the recycling pile so the city wouldn't ticket the seminary. Protesting the elevators would be uncomfortable, even embarrassing.

Given the fearful consequences of direct action, it was preferable to let my anger erupt in unforeseen ways. I could waste forty-five minutes bemoaning incompetence with my neighbor or snap at my husband for interrupting me while reading. It was easier to avoid confrontation by manipulating a piece of scripture in order to give my fear divine sanction. Better to write off my silent irritation as yet another Christian sacrifice. Better to suppress prejudice and to erupt in irrational outbursts at small inconveniences than to risk being labeled racist, elitist, or—worst of all—a spoiled seminarian. What would the neighbors think? The eleventh commandment—not to confront others on the strength of one's own conviction—was supported by the Christian doormat interpretation of the fifth chapter in Matthew.

Direct communication on the Close was difficult. Passing observations in the hall about the "interesting collection of boxes outside your door" meant, "Please take out your trash." "Was that Bach or Beethoven you were playing last night?" meant, "Your music kept me awake." I understood this language well only because I was a native speaker. "Do you want me to clean the apartment?" Greg knew meant that I'd noticed he'd forgotten his promise to vacuum. He found this habit as irritating in me as I found it in others.

OUR WILLINGNESS to give up our claims on authority, to submit unbiblically, is manifest in other ways. Perhaps because of Manhattan's dislocation from the natural world, more people in our neighborhood own dogs than cars. At 6:30 A.M., the sidewalks of Twentieth Street are thick with bleary-eyed owners walking their corgis, labs, golden retrievers, poodles, bulldogs, German shepherds, and Yorkshire terriers. Perhaps 70 percent of us in seminary housing own dogs. We either brought pets from home or, as Greg and I did, felt left out of the dog culture and in a weak moment adopted puppies of our own.

Like other animal-loving New Yorkers, seminarians are subject to strict regulations requiring dog owners to clean up after their pets, inside and outside the Close. We never venture out without a handful of baggies. It is unequivocally communicated that General's lush green lawns are not designed to accommodate our pets' intimate needs.

In March, a lengthy memo from General's business office appears on our building's notice board among the baby-sitter ads. Scanning its length, I expect a proposed hike in tuition due to the $250,000 budget deficit. Instead, a painstakingly crafted memorandum alerts us that someone in the community has failed to clean up after his or her dog. It is highly regrettable, the memo intones, that members of the community cannot show greater consideration.

For the next three weeks, dog owners inevitably slip into elevator avowals that their dogs are guiltless. We spend an embarrassing amount of time discussing the memo and speculating about the guilty parties. We think of everything the business office could have accomplished in the time it took to draft this elegant note. But, above all, we want to clear ourselves and our pets.

More notes appear, threatening disciplinary action if the perpetrator strikes again. Puppy owners like Greg and me feel particularly vulnerable. Like a seven-year-old who is highly susceptible to suggestion, I wonder if I'm already guilty of this crime. Possibly on an early morning wander through the Close, my dogs have performed and escaped notice. The fuss is absurd, I tell Mary on the way to church history. "I'm tempted to take the blame and post a note just so we don't all have to talk about this anymore." Rising above the fray, however, is not as easy as I think.

At the height of the dog to-do, I decide to return my two pups from their afternoon walk via the main lobby to pick up our mail. We greet the person at the front desk, and then I make the mistake of walking down the hall to glance at a new exhibit on T. S. Eliot. A few steps in the direction of the display cases, and one of the leashes wound around my wrist tugs sharply. One puppy, sensing the opportunity to partake in a truly subversive, sensational act, is relieving himself beneath a nineteenth-century painting of the seminary grounds in Dean Hoffman's day.

Panic sweeps away my resolve to rise above anything. If I'm caught red-handed by the powers that be it will confirm their deepest suspicions. I stumble over my dogs, baggies flailing. No sooner have I bent down to erase evidence of the crime than, as if on cue, a member of the administration strides around the corner.

"Well, that's *lovely*," she sniffs. I rise from my knees to stammer some explanation. But the other puppy, as a good sibling should, has already followed suit. My dogs' brilliant sense of humor and dramatic timing are totally lost on me. Humiliated, I'm ready to hurl both pups across the hallway. How *could* they do this to me?

Later, I realized during a New Testament exam that the true embarrassment for me in this episode was that I had missed my dogs' cue. Were they inviting me to join an honest act of what biblical scholar Walter Wink calls active, nonviolent resistance?

Wink's historical research, reported in *Engaging the Powers* (1992), shows that "turning the other cheek" and "walking the second mile" were acts that symbolized resistance, not capitulation. Roman military law during Jesus' lifetime stipulated that soldiers could force citizens to carry their packs only one mile, or face punishment. A Christian who volunteers to walk a second mile thus confronts an oppressive system directly yet nonviolently by putting the Roman soldier himself at risk. Likewise, when a slave turns his right cheek toward his master in anticipation of a blow, he robs his assailant of the opportunity to deliver a backhanded slap—traditionally, a shaming gesture delivered by someone of higher social status to an inferior. Turning the right cheek forces the oppressor to strike with his right fist, a blow reserved for fighting between equals.

Wink directs his activist interpretation of these passages mostly toward totalitarian governments or patriarchal family systems. But his conclusions apply well to the oppressive overscrupulousness that can sometimes invade a close-knit community like the seminary. The uproar over dog messes on the Close suggests that grown men and women—who have raised children, fought in wars, and occupied positions of considerable authority—in this instance submitted to a trivial preoccupation. As much as any member of the administration, we were all guilty of participating in a debate that a free system would hardly tolerate. Active, nonviolent resistance would have been the only truly biblical response, yet only my dogs grasped that.

Might there have been other ways of responding to the situation to remind ourselves that dog doo is not graver than sin against the Holy

Ghost? Truly turning the other cheek in this case might have meant dealing with the situation more lightly through humor. I could have quoted Luther on the theological importance of dung, the symbol of our true creatureliness. I might have praised my dogs loudly, as my puppy-training book by the monks of New Skete advised. The list was endless, but the moment had passed. The incident was another Lenten reminder of the distance my community and I still had to travel to attain our ideals.

Easter

The fifty days beginning on Easter Sunday and ending on Pentecost celebrate the resurrection of Jesus Christ and his appearances to the disciples. Christians believe that after Christ was betrayed, beaten, hung on the cross, and left by his loved ones to die alone, God raised him from the dead. At the first Easter, the disciples received the good news that Christ's promise was true: through him, not even death could separate them from the love of God. The fruit of this promise is what we continue to celebrate each Easter season.

For a postmodern mind, Christ's resurrection—more than his incarnation or his miraculous healings—is the most difficult episode in the Christian narrative. Inconsistencies in Gospel accounts of the resurrection appearances don't make it easier for the skeptic. In John, Matthew, and Luke, Christ himself appears before the disciples after his death and directs them to Galilee, whereas the earliest version of Mark never refers to a postresurrection appearance. According to John, Christ also appears in Jerusalem. According to Luke, he materializes in Emmaus as well.

All four Gospels, however, agree on one central point: what happened on the first Easter was momentous and strange. They concur that the resurrection was no mere resuscitation. Jesus Christ did not simply resume his old life as Lazarus did, after he had been raised from the dead. Luke and John describe Jesus appearing inside a locked room, and Luke writes that Jesus was taken up into heaven after issuing the great commission to his disciples. At the same time, none of the Gospel writers portrays the resurrected Christ as merely a ghost. John's Gospel relates that Jesus ate fish on the beach with James and Peter and allowed Thomas to touch his wounded side.

The only consistency in the Gospel accounts of events after the crucifixion is the Evangelists' awe and mystification about Jesus' "spiritual body." Their astounded confusion explains why our Easter is not just a seasonal fertility rite named after the Anglo-Saxon goddess Eostre to celebrate flowers, eggs, and conception.

THE "OTHERNESS" of the resurrection makes most sense to me in the story of Christ's appearance to Mary Magdalene. Mary, shattered by the loss of her savior, comes to the grave to anoint his body days after the other disciples have left. Arriving at the tomb, she discovers that his body has been taken and begins to weep inconsolably. To her, the empty tomb means nothing but more loss. Grave robbers might have stolen the body, or the Roman authorities seeking to stop the place from becoming a pilgrimage site. Mary is so distraught that even when she turns and sees Jesus standing behind her, she mistakes him for the gardener. Like the other disciples, Mary has heard Jesus say many times that he will come again, but, also like them, Mary doesn't connect the disappearance of Jesus' body with any possibility of resurrection—until she hears her name called.

"Mary," Jesus says to her.

"*Rabouni,*" Mary cries, which means "teacher" in Hebrew.

By the end of Lent, I long to hear my name called in a way that will show me with as much certainty as Mary felt that Christ's resurrection is real.

I am tired and homesick in my struggle to understand the language and customs of a place that sometimes I think would be more sensibly located in the corner of a distant continent. The effort of excavating meaning from things that at first seem absurd is exhausting. Nor do I always wish to "Rejoice" as the signs on the bulletin board instruct me to do whenever a senior is called to St. Martha's in Minnesota or St. Edward's-by-the-Sea. During my spare time, I still prefer to read *The New Yorker,* not *Episcopal Life,* and I prefer receiving e-mail updates from the Environmental Defense Fund, not Anglicans Online. The struggle to make General Seminary home and myself a poster-child seminarian is tiring. As Easter Sunday comes and goes, I begin to wonder if I would even recognize my name if it were called.

DURING spring term, first-year seminarians start applying to churches for two-year, part-time internships. "So where are you doing your field placement?" echoes around the Close during Easter. Although a few classmates announce over lunch that they know exactly which parish they want to work at, many find the process more painstaking.

All fall, we were supposed to attend services at the more than sixty Episcopal parishes in Manhattan and the surrounding area. Independently or in groups, our class visited places like St. Luke in the Fields, St. Ignatius, St. Thomas, St. James, St. John's in the Village, St. Mark's-in-the-Bowery, Heavenly Rest, Holy Apostles, and Trinity Church. We went out to Brooklyn, up to Harlem, down to Chinatown, and into Greenwich Village. We came away from these services weighed down with church bulletins about adult education classes and parish programs. A few conscientious classmates might even have taken notes on the difference between this service and the sixteen or seventeen others we attended.

There are many questions to consider. Who will be our mentor? What are the preaching requirements and liturgical responsibilities? Typically, we can go for a big midtown church like St. Bart's or St. James, look out over a congregation of several hundred, perhaps offer the chalice after a month or two, and maybe see the rector twice a semester. Alternatively, plenty of tiny, struggling churches with congregations of twenty-five are eager for a young seminarian to organize a stewardship campaign or start a membership drive. Neither of these options greatly attracts me.

The search's intensity seeps into my home life. Greg, who has grown accustomed to 10:00 P.M. tortellini dinners and the frequent exercise of prying me from the library late at night, finds his patience and husbandly good will stretched to the limit on Sunday mornings. On his consulting schedule, Greg's weeks frequently end at 9:00 P.M. on Friday, unless he has a project to finish, in which case his office claims him on Saturdays and Sundays as well. On top of it all, Greg usually dedicates the little weekend free time he has to cleaning our apartment, consistent with his "I don't mind clutter, but I don't like dirt" philosophy of living. Greg's dream is that one morning a week he can wake up, fully rested, to indulge in some time alone: walking at a leisurely pace to the corner coffee shop to chat up his friends behind the counter; reading the paper; trekking to the roof of our building with his guitar to write songs; catching a yoga class.

Unfortunately, Greg's downtime inevitably conflicts with the Sunday morning "call to worship." As a result, the end of the week finds both of us gripped by guilt. I dread another Sunday where I sit through a worship service that fails to represent the sacredness of the day for me. Greg faces two choices: first, joining me, inevitably enjoying the service as tepidly as I do, and swallowing his frustration at never having time to relax; second, not joining me, sharing morning elevator rides with clean-shaven seminarian spouses heading to church with their partners, and fighting the guilt of not supporting his spouse—all the while worrying whether others see that his spiritual life appears out of synch with mine.

The constant need to visit new churches, then, is balanced against nourishing my marriage. Nathan, Brad, and Mauricio choose their field placements before I do. Their choices reflect who they are and, in some cases, what they feel about their calling. Nathan has a difficult time deciding. The rector at a midsized active parish on the Upper East Side wants him to be the youth program director. But Nathan really likes the new priest at a small church that in the past two decades has shrunk from one of Manhattan's thriving congregations to a church with fewer than sixty members. Ultimately, only Nathan can construe his choice so that the smaller, more struggling congregation is the place where he finds "the most learning opportunity." Few people I know would choose to embrace this "learning opportunity" and feel they were making no sacrifice.

Brad wants to find a congregation that "actually does something." He is tired of churches that debate whether a raffle or a bake sale should launch the stewardship drive or what nonalcoholic beverage to serve at the Shrove Tuesday pancake supper. He signs up for Holy Apostles, the church across the street in Chelsea with New York's largest soup kitchen, serving over a thousand meals a day, five days a week.

Mauricio isn't looking for an experience, he just wants a job. He is not rounding out his résumé or seeking personal growth. He has an education to pay for and phone calls home to Costa Rica to finance. As a Spanish-speaker and the only ordained person in our class, Mauricio does not take long to land a curacy at a parish in Jackson Heights, Queens. Soon he is preaching, offering pastoral guidance, and starting programs. When it looks as if one church will be unable to pay his salary, he wastes no time transferring to another. Mauricio spends little time agonizing about finding the perfect place.

For me, the reality of the resurrection seems to grow more distant with each 11 A.M. service. I agree with Mary, who, after a lifeless Easter Vigil service at The Chapel of the Good Shepherd, phones her parish in Beverly Hills and announces to her rector that, despite the time difference, Jesus has still not risen in New York. Where is the Good News that one preacher I heard called "the kind of news that neighbors threw open their windows to shout at one another across the street"? Where is the joy in discovering that God has not died? That God is real, could touch you, knows your name? This was the news that breathless Mary Magdalene had run to tell the other disciples.

The message of resurrection had brought me to seminary—but now, in the Easter of my first year, it sounded remote. If, in a city with more Episcopal churches per capita than almost anywhere else in the country, I could find no place where this News rang true, what made me think I would hear the message anywhere?

A Call from the Desert

My preaching professor, Canon Susan Harriss, works at the Cathedral of St. John the Divine in Harlem. So, in addition to exercises in extemporaneous preaching and full-length sermons of our choice in the chapel, our whole class rides uptown to Amsterdam Avenue and 112th Street, just west of Morningside Park and a few blocks south of

Columbia University. From the cathedral pulpit, we will have an opportunity to say a word to each other and to a few wandering tourists.

Approached from the south, the Cathedral of St. John the Divine does not exude the external grandeur one might expect from the world's largest cathedral. (St. Peter's in Rome is bigger but technically is not a cathedral or "seat of the bishop.") St. John's looks shabby and slightly underdressed. The bald dome covering the crossing is exposed; both transepts—the lateral arms of a crucifix-shaped church—are missing. Both of the two front spires stand unfinished, and scaffolding covers the southwest tower—not because of construction, but because there's no money to take it down. The stone is the same soot-streaked gray of most buildings in the surrounding Harlem neighborhood. St. John's reminds me more of an old European church than of the well-polished exterior of Washington's National Cathedral—my only other American cathedral reference point.

The cathedral's axis runs east to west, and a tangle of trees and tall shrubbery in the garden below obstructs the view coming up Amsterdam Avenue. Pedestrians stumble upon this vast house of worship rather than being drawn to it as to a beacon.

Possibly because it is not well coiffed, there is something plainly genuine about St. John's. The grounds at the base of the cathedral encompass a few city blocks between Amsterdam Avenue, Morningside Drive, 110th and 114th Streets. They remind me of T. S. Eliot's unkempt flower garden in his poem *Burnt Norton*. Turning in from Amsterdam Avenue, I cross uneven sidewalks scattered with cherry blossom petals. On the right is Diocesan House, offices of the bishop of New York. On the left, surrounded by overgrown boxwood hedges, stretches a leaf-flecked lawn with a chunky stone cross sunk into the ground at the far end. Reaching that end of the lawn, I turn left uphill toward the side of the cathedral, in front of which sits the early nineteenth-century orphanage from which the land for the cathedral complex was bought originally; rising behind it is the massive side wall of the nave. On the day our preaching class visits, a peacock reposes between the classical columns of the old orphanage, his royal purple, green, and blue tail feathers draped delicately from the porch.

Standing on the walkway in front of the orphanage, I look to my right and see the Cathedral School and Biblical Garden, just off the back corner of the nave. To my left, shadowed by seventy-five-foot-high flying buttresses, the walkway continues along the length of the cathedral wall back toward Amsterdam Avenue. Beneath the buttresses an abandoned stone yard is scattered with incomplete friezes and haphazard piles of rough-hewn granite slabs. Are these stones still awaiting the master masons, or have they fallen off the cathedral? Either way, the earth is rapidly reclaiming them.

On my first visit, I did not know that much of the stone in the nave is schist blasted out of tunnels bored for the New York subway system. Nor was I aware that the cathedral's fireproof tiles are of the same variety that line Grand Central Station. Still, early on, it feels to me as if the cathedral has grown out of the ground, its roots firmly anchored in the dirt and bedrock of Manhattan Island. It is a living organism, vital in a way that no other house of worship in New York has appeared—its external signs of decay seem part of a living process that can include renewal.

The day of my preaching class visit, we tour the darkened interior to see modern religious art announcing that the Cathedral of St. John the Divine is no relic of the past. As we pass through the front doors, Canon Harriss explains that we are walking beneath a pantheon of Old Testament prophets carved by a team of sculptors that includes young people from the Harlem neighborhood trained by a nonprofit group,

Cathedral Stoneworks. She shows us a giant quartz crystal weighing more than a ton, placed there to celebrate the natural order, as well as a large, handmade medicine wheel and Keith Haring's valedictory piece before his death from AIDS—a bronze triptych of the Last Judgment. We can pay our respects at altars for victims of genocide, for those who died in the TWA Flight 800 disaster, or, most recently, for victims of hate crimes across the world. Art gives lively meaning to the cathedral's Gothic and Romanesque architecture.

There is a living spirit in the cathedral's service and educational programs, too. Going downstairs on any Sunday, Canon Harriss says, we will have to sidestep children's art projects in the Children's Abbey, modeled upon the Benedictine rule. We might meet a group of teenagers carrying knapsacks and sleeping bags after a night spent "locked into" the cathedral for the Nightwatch program. A long line of homeless men and women awaits breakfast at the cathedral's weekly soup kitchen. The old orphanage also houses Cathedral Community Cares, a drop-in center and outreach program for poor people. The new stone capital of Nelson Mandela glimpsed overhead offers further evidence that the gospel and the world as I know it seem to meet gracefully within the stone walls of St. John's.

We spend the afternoon in a small chapel just behind the altar, critiquing each other's sermons. Back in the main sanctuary, one by one we give three-minute readings from the imposing main pulpit. I climb the marble steps and hear my voice echo thunderously through the vaulting. The grandeur of the cathedral's pulpit demands profound words; speaking from it has the irresistible appeal of making it seem as though you are delivering a state of the union address—with the added attraction that one can discuss God there, rather than trade policy.

The cathedral is a vibrant place. I can imagine inviting out-of-town guests or non-church-going friends to come and visit. The cathedral is institutionally recognizable, yet distinctly countercultural in its commitment to the gospel. It is traditional without being out of touch with the world. It is what I hoped for in Christian ministry.

BEFORE the cathedral even offers me a place, I begin to doubt my fitness for the job. Misgivings begin when I realize only one other person from my class has expressed interest in working there. Perhaps I've overlooked a red flag. Maybe, as with my first experience of the liturgy, what is obvious to everyone else about the difference between evening prayer and evensong is a mystery to me. Perhaps Episcopal seminarians are not *supposed* to do fieldwork at cathedrals. Possibly this cathedral, a "House of Prayer for all people," is not Episcopal enough. Doubtless I missed some vital piece of church information.

I fail to trust the idea that the church, like the world, is a wide and diverse place and that God respects all sorts. The childhood story requirement in our preaching class reveals how many people in my class have grown up in close-knit, church-based communities. Others are the sons or daughters of priests or bishops. By contrast, my own stories of childhood formation include an earnest letter-writing campaign to the prime minister of Canada about harp seal hunting. Church-based activity was more the exception than the rule as I was growing up.

Considering the differences in our lives that put liberal urbanites like Mary and me in the minority, it should have been no surprise that different seminarians felt called to different parishes. At the time, though, my solitary preference for the cathedral seemed only to suggest my own shortcomings.

Eventually, as places begin to fill and other classmates choose their internships, one of my professors inquires if I would like a paid position as assistant to a rector at a midsized Manhattan church he knows. I could explore partnerships with community service groups, businesses, and other churches and synagogues, he says. This church has an extremely friendly congregation, a strong outreach program, and they need a seminarian. The job description seems to match some of my strengths, so I accept the placement. Whenever I mention my choice, it feels like describing someone else's future plans.

Under most circumstances, the Sunday installation ceremony the priest has planned for me would be a wonderful way to begin an internship. But I feel like a bride who is having second thoughts only days before her wedding. In the back of my mind the cathedral stands tall, with its flying buttresses and excellent Web site. Because it has housed anti-Vietnam protests and environmental compact-making with equal catholicity, St. John's reminds me of why I came to seminary. I'm watching it slide out of my hands for no other reason than that I lack the salt to respond when my name is called.

WHAT IF Mary Magdalene had demanded more evidence before following her calling? What if she had not responded to the sound of her name by immediately throwing herself at the feet of the risen Jesus? We take for granted her joyous response. She hears her name called by the Lord, who she thinks is dead, and without hesitation she rushes to embrace him. Mary's faith in herself was strong enough that she needed to hear her name only once. Once was enough for her to witness the gospel for the remainder of her life—and, by some scholars' accounts, to offer strength and leadership to the male disciples, including Peter. To take action, she required no further demonstration of proof than this direct experience of the resurrected God.

The Bible, however, is filled with examples of people who hear God call their names—granted, in more austere tones—but whose response is far from joyful or immediate. Moses protested in Exodus that he was not eloquent enough to lead his people out of Egypt. Upon hearing the Creator call their names, both Ezekiel and Jeremiah were reluctant to act. Jonah, when he did eventually respond to God's call, boarded a ship that sailed in the opposite direction from the place he was ordered to go. With the exception of early Calvinists, who thought a divine calling was in itself efficacious, most people believe that following a vocational call from God requires a voluntary response.

The same is true in secular vocations. I sometimes have difficulty remembering that people I know who appear to have successful careers in the arts, law, or journalism were not preordained to those positions. Each swam heavily upstream at times and took what felt like huge risks to follow their hearts—putting off law school to try making it as a jazz musician, or ignoring family pressure to enter banking in order to report freelance from overseas. These were biblical acts in part because they required faith and willing risk.

Luckily, most decisions in life do not emerge from callings. If I had to discern whether I am called to eat pasta rather than fish every night, my health would suffer. Labeling most choices—even ones as apparently pressing as a seminary course schedule—as parts of "a calling" overdetermines ordinary decisions. Such grandiosity is impractical and, worse, self-important. If I had to find a calling in order to preach on a certain text or to finish my Greek assignments, both my congregation and my Greek would languish.

Despite this qualification, I use the words "discernment" and "calling" here to describe the process of figuring out an internship because for a seminarian field placements demand a large number of waking hours each week for two years. The church, not the classroom, is where most of us will work after graduation. At the field placement parishes, therefore, the rubber meets the road—if with less impact than in our first jobs. Moreover, seminarians are a dime a dozen in many big New York Episcopal churches; they sit lower on the totem pole than curates, associate rectors, organists, directors of children's education, or anyone else on the payroll. In these congregations, we are no longer high-potential seminarians applauded by our home parishes but worker bees who must discover if we can deliver on our promise.

As THE day of my midtown installation approaches, it takes a powerful image to cure my paralysis.

Before coming to seminary, I had spent the summer in Los Angeles with Greg, who'd been working on a media consulting job in North Hollywood. In July, I had gone on a weekend retreat to a Benedictine monastery in the Mojave Desert. As part of the monks' hospitality ministry, the monastery, an oasis in an arid stretch of Joshua trees and dust, offered quiet weekends to anyone in need of respite. The monks had built a large pond and constructed twelve stations of the cross leading into the desert; they also sold crafts and ran a few small businesses on the side. I remember enjoying delicious meals with the other guests, attending a few services, and talking to the brother in charge, who was completing his doctorate in theology from Oxford.

One evening during my retreat, I walk into the desert hills above the monastery. Wanting to photograph Joshua trees against the evening sky, I mount the ridge behind the monastery. Several hundred yards along the crest, a huge stone arch is silhouetted against the sunset. Beneath the arch stand almost forty plain stone crosses. The words "brother" or "oblate" are carved into each one, marking the graves of monks from the community below.

I stare at the simple crosses. How strange that no giant mausoleum, no marble memorial or National Historic Preservation sign honors these men who chose lives of great self-sacrifice. This desert cemetery offers none of the recognition that I believe should come to anyone who dares to live bravely at odds with many values of mainstream society.

This is what it comes down to? Nothing but a few plain crosses?

It struck me at the time that the promise of the resurrection was not a well-attended, end-of-life press conference. These monks had not become modern desert fathers in the San Fernando Valley so that when they reached the end of their lives the world could applaud their sacrifice. Most of them probably had not taken vows of obedience, stability, and conversion of life for the approval such a step would attract. Their motivations lay elsewhere.

Many of the people buried under those crosses knew that the crucifixion and resurrection of Jesus Christ did not take place at the center of society two thousand years ago, either. Now, under the influence of centuries of Christian art, we imagine the whole world gathered at the foot of the cross. We see the entire Roman Empire torturing Christ and his mother, while hundreds of onlookers weep. From a theological perspective, angels and devils were, no doubt, fighting it out in the sky above him. But to the everyday eyes of people living in first-century Palestine, Golgotha lay on the outskirts of the city, a place more like a freeway exit than a town square. While the crucified Jesus recalled with agonized remorse his words about the coming kingdom, most passersby on the road below were probably rushing too hurriedly to buy Sabbath provisions before sunset to heed the cosmic struggle by the roadside. If the crucifixion happened today, bystanders would be fixing a flat or herding their kids into McDonald's.

The crosses on the desert hill had seemed preposterous because they witnessed that the people buried there shunned worldly accolades. The monks had conducted a living experiment in a community where it was not supposed to matter whether you had a Ph.D. in philosophy or a certificate in sales—where someone's educational background, the part of the country he grew up in, his IQ, skin color, or ability to carry on an interesting conversation about politics mattered, but were far from decisive in confirming human worth. What counted in the end, according to the monks, was your relationship with God and how you treated other human beings.

The monks buried under the crosses in the desert had gone where God led them. They had trusted their calling to the religious life as an invitation to the richest sort of human experience. As selfless as I thought anyone who was drawn to religious orders must be, some degree of self-love and confidence was clearly required—along with the gumption more often associated with explorers and entrepreneurs. These monks had followed a calling that resonated so deeply that others' opinions were of marginal importance. The headstones on the hillside asked no one's approval.

THIS IMAGE of desert crosses comes strongly to mind on the weekend of my installation at the midtown parish. I awake on that Sunday morning, flooded with the same peace and confidence I felt in the desert, yet uncertain what the day will hold. I dress, give Greg the church's address, and head for the subway.

About two-thirds of the way through the sermon, I decide against taking my vows. I can communicate this decision to the rector only during the few verses remaining in the offertory hymn. Uncertain if I might be struck by lightning—or what the repercussions will be if my Commission on Ministry finds out—I cautiously skirt the altar and whisper my change of heart to the rector, asking if we can skip the installation vows. He nods, and the service proceeds on course.

My timing is appalling and my mode of operation reprehensible. I spend most of the following fall drafting letters of apology. Bolting from a vow at the altar is not a responsible action by anyone's definition. It should not, as the professor who had recommended me for the job pointed out, become a habit. "One should be a bit careful about doing exactly as one feels at a given moment in front of the congregation," he explains, before describing a priest who, from the pulpit Sunday morning, told his wife he wanted to end their marriage.

My spiritual director is equally surprised, if somewhat more bemused. Brother Clark witnessed firsthand my agonizing during the previous few months. He suggested that I imagine myself as one of the disciples who, like everyone on earth, had to make choices large and small. When Peter and Andrew dropped their nets, they chose to follow a calling that would close some options and open others. Even Mary Magdalene, who responded instantly when she heard her name called by Christ at the empty tomb, had probably at one time considered the costs and benefits of discipleship. We, like the disciples, were free agents, responsible both for small decisions and for larger choices about our calling. According to Dostoevsky's Grand Inquisitor, "man has no more tormenting care than to find someone to whom he can hand over as quickly as possible that gift of freedom with which the miserable creature is born." We past and present disciples were called to be living proof that the Grand Inquisitor was wrong.

After the service I explain to the rector why I had asked to skip my installation. Then I call Canon Harriss at the cathedral and discover that St. John's still has a place available if I want it.

Vest for Success

My first-year field placement responsibilities at the cathedral include preaching occasionally at Sunday evening vespers and the 9:00 A.M. Sunday service, assisting each week with the Children's Abbey, and participating in the 11:00 A.M. main service as a chalice bearer and subdeacon. Although my original attraction to the cathedral was its great diversity of ministries and its self-chosen appellation as "A House of Prayer for all people," I plunge straight into the bread and butter of ordained ministry.

At the cathedral, I slowly come to understand that for an Episcopal priest, learning how to move around the altar and deliver a sermon is the equivalent of a lawyer learning how to write a brief or a painter learning how to stretch a canvas properly. I could not fail to master these aspects of the trade. For much of the year, liturgy in the Chapel of the Good Shepherd has felt like playing church. At the cathedral, the mechanics of priesthood suddenly begin to matter. In the space of a few weeks, I learn several valuable lessons essential to a clerical calling.

Bring your own alb.

Don't let your disdain for tacky clergy vestment catalogues or for classmates who spend hours at the R. J. Whipple display table deliberating over collar sizes and shirt colors blind you to the importance of appropriate, well-fitted attire. There is no need to be a clerical fashion maven, but, paradoxically, attention to attire can remove it as a distraction from worship. Liturgist Aiden Cavanaugh quotes a Zen Buddhist monk who says that the teacher (or the priest at the altar) should be "like a clear glass of water" through which light can be seen. By this standard, I'd call as much unnecessary attention to myself by neglecting my appearance as I would by overscrupulous attention to it.

This thought occurs to me at 10:40 A.M. on Easter Sunday while nervously preparing to serve as a chalice bearer at the cathedral. The sacristy, a room about the size of a large kitchen where clergy robe, is crowded with at least twenty-five people—ten deacons, four canons, five visiting clergy, seminarians, acolytes, the dean of the cathedral, and the bishop of New York. After the final head count, the canon in charge of worship points to a large diagram of the cathedral floor plan taped to a vestment cupboard. With military precision, the canon tells us where to pick up our chalices, which of eighteen communion stations we will work, and how to signal for refueling when consecrated wine runs low. Even the bishop, mentally preparing for his address to 4,000 people on the most important day of the Christian year, looks up from his corner to listen intently.

This does not seem the best moment to inquire if anyone has a size seven alb, so I open my advisor's closet, find a white robe, and slide it over my head. A fellow seminarian informs me that all the extra cinctures—the white knotted ropes that serve as belts—are in use. As we move out in double file to join the choir for the procession, I realize that during my first public appearance at the Cathedral of St. John the Divine, I will be fighting an alb many sizes too large.

The forty-person procession includes a verger, torchbearers, crucifers, choir members, chalice bearers, deacons, clergy, and the dean. We complete nearly a full circumambulation of the two-football-field-long building before halting at the great doors at the front of the cathedral, where the bishop joins us. As ten men in uniform gradually swing back the forty-foot bronze doors, long shafts of sunlight stream into the cathedral. The bishop stands in the giant doorway holding a gold crosier, his olive-shaped miter and long robes of gold and red a dramatic contrast to the gray of Amsterdam Avenue.

The symbolism of the scene might have overawed me—the age-old tension between the church and the world, the splendor of the church and its mission to serve the poor—if I had been worried less about whether my oversized alb would survive walking up three flights of stairs from the base of the crossing to the top of the high altar. (The high altar, my partner in line whispers, is where we sit.) My goal is to ascend the stairs without falling or appearing like a mincing medieval lady trying to keep her skirts free of mud.

Although I reach my seat at the high altar without mishap, my thoughts are not on the mystery of the resurrection and the joy of Easter, as I hoped. Watching the sea of worshippers stretching across the arched Gothic space of the nave, I am simultaneously moved and relieved to have no more steps to negotiate. Much of the bishop's Easter message is lost on me as I fret. How do I look? Who is watching? Can I avoid embarrassment? So much for the "clear glass of water."

Remember that the Eucharist is a mystery.

Do not worry if you don't fully understand the Eucharist. Do not despair if you are dry-eyed when the priest hands you the consecrated wafer and wine. Have no fear if you find your mind wandering during the words of consecration or if you secretly look forward to walking to the communion rail because it is an opportunity to stretch your legs. You won't always feel refreshed on returning to your pew from the sacrament. Don't fear getting it wrong. Don't worry about not getting it at all. The Eucharist is a mystery.

During Lent, I was troubled by the fact that the Eucharist did not always provide the immediate spiritual gratification that, as an aspiring priest, I hoped it would. A good sermon, by contrast, was like the interesting academic lectures I had heard growing up. It inspired, refreshed, stimulated ideas, and scattered specks of color over the weekdays ahead. The liturgy of the sacrament during this period became the test of endurance whereby I earned the right to enjoy the liturgy of the Word.

Sometimes I felt vaguely repulsed by the idea of being invited to eat the flesh and drink the blood of Jesus Christ. Of course, the fact that I noticed this disquieting element of the mass, which Ellen found deeply disturbing during her infrequent visits to Sunday services, meant that at least I was paying attention. More upsetting from a vocational point of view was my frequent disengagement from this portion of the service. I tried different techniques to remedy the situation.

Sometimes I visualized Christ in the upper room of a house in Jerusalem and the stunned reaction of his disciples when he first said, "Take, eat, this is my body which is given for you. Do this in remembrance of me" (Luke 22:19). If I could just imagine myself back into the historical moment of the first Eucharist, I would appreciate the ceremony more.

On other occasions, I recalled class work about the differences between the Anglican doctrine of the "real presence," the older Catholic idea of transubstantiation, and the broader Protestant view. Maybe a clearer understanding of the theology would make the Eucharist's transformative properties more immediately apparent.

Once in a while, I meditated on the physical journey of the wafer itself—how the chewy, Styrofoam-textured circlet grew pasty on my tongue and slid down my throat; how enzymes then attacked and broke it down from starch to sugar, which entered my bloodstream and eventually fed cells in my muscles, skin, or hair. One thing I could be sure of: that wafer would help fuel a forehand on the tennis court or promote a particularly explosive firing of synapses when debating Luther and German nationalism. Often this process seemed far more miraculous than anything that happened to the wafer when the priest held it high. But since I was training for the priesthood, not an advanced degree in human biology, I needed to address the mysteries of the altar as well as my digestive tract.

Once again, the cathedral—specifically, the Children's Abbey—taught me not so much to understand the mystery of the Eucharist as how to engage in it.

In addition to my liturgical duties, I serve as part-time assistant to Gina Bria Vescovi, a Roman Catholic cultural anthropologist, author, and mother of three who runs the cathedral's Sunday morning Children's Abbey. Based loosely on the rule of life in a Benedictine monastic community, the "abbey" itself is a wide hallway at the foot of a stone stairwell leading from the corner of the first floor down to the basement of the cathedral. Every Sunday morning at 10:15 a group of children signs in with huge felt-tip markers and gathers on the stone steps for a sung psalm and a story about a prophet's life. The combination of biblical storytelling, art projects, and child-led worship makes the abbey wildly different from any Sunday school I'd known.

Much of the program's magic emanates from Gina, whose warmth and radiance make her an abbess with attitude. I look forward to her appearances at the top of the abbey steps—a vision in dark velvet; piles of dark, wavy hair pinned loosely atop her head; shopping bags, picture books, pens, and pipe cleaners suspended from each arm; a child balanced on her hip; two more kids in tow.

The week before Easter at the Children's Abbey, we hold a rehearsal of first communion for Sue Ellen, Mary Ellen, Elizabeth, Tatsuo, Heidi, Peter, and Donald. Gina brings in extra candles, and one of the deacons loans us a special tray of sacred vessels from the sacristy upstairs, plus a roll of unconsecrated wafers. On a small wooden table, the children help set up an altar that looks as much as possible like the one upstairs. Gina asks me to explain the objects on the altar and the prayers before, during, and after the breaking of the bread.

I try to define for the children the sacrament I do not fully understand myself. I sail through an explanation of how the Eucharist is really a meal, based on the Passover service we celebrated the week before in honor of the Jewish holiday. The "corporal," I say, holding up the large square of linen that the priest places on the altar before beginning communion, is a kind of tablecloth. The slightly smaller "lavabo towel" that he or she uses to wipe hands after the acolytes wash them resembles a hand towel. The priest uses the smallest piece of linen, the "purificator," to wipe the lip of the chalice after each person drinks. These cloths are all napkins, in a way.

"Yes, but why are we *eating* in church?" one of the children asks.

Hesitantly, I begin to explain about anamnesis and how through a sacred meal the death, resurrection, and ascension of Jesus Christ become a present reality to Christians. When I notice how intently everyone is examining the wafers—poking and pawing at the silver paten—I look to Gina for help.

She swoops into the crowd of children, reaches into the dish to remove the large, round priest's host, and holds it high overhead. Everyone falls back from the altar.

"What am I doing?" Gina asks the crowd. "What is the priest doing when she holds up this wafer like this in the service?"

We wait with bated breath.

"Look at this thing!" Gina says, pointing to the wafer. "Look at how small and thin it is. How could God, who is everywhere all the time, all over the universe, possibly fit inside this little piece of food? I mean, really! How could this happen?"

We don't know. It seems like it might be a tight squeeze.

"So when the priest is standing up there behind the altar holding this little wafer above her head, what is she doing?" Gina continues, still holding the wafer aloft. "The priest is asking, '*Please,* God, will you get in here? Will you just come and get in here, please! We know you can do everything, God, so will you *please* just come here and be in this wafer now!'"

I had never thought of the words of *epeclesis,* the summoning of the Holy Spirit to make the gifts of bread and wine "to be for your people the Body and Blood of your Son," as a request. I wrote them off as magic words. Gina's explanation makes much more sense—a heartfelt plea for the presence of the God of supernovas, who, in the words of Job, "binds the chain of the Pleiades and looses the cords of Orion," to come and be there for us in a small thing that we can taste. Her words capture centuries of human desire for a God who can get under our skins. I understand that desire, which pulls me into the rest of the rite. Whether the consecrated bread is spiritual or real or really spiritual is beside the point. Something more compelling lies in this entreaty for God to join us in the bread.

The other abbey participants seem drawn in, too.

"Does that mean that when you eat the wafer, God is in your stomach?" Heidi asks.

"Exactly," replies Gina.

Being a chalice bearer on Sunday morning underscores what I learned at the abbey. The intimacy of the rite is more apparent from the other side of the communion rail. In my view, feeding another person is an in-the-family activity, so offering the cup to a group of strangers in a public place is a challenge. This view aside, in the task of helping people sip from the chalice, I discover that I have a lot to learn about the particularity of God.

During my first communion in this new capacity, I offer the cup with the words "the blood of Christ, the cup of salvation" to elderly people, children, teenagers; to African Americans, Hispanics, and whites; to the disabled, the well-dressed, and the shabby. Some want to hold the cup themselves, but others refuse to touch it. Some look happy as they approach the rail, others desperately sad. Some smile and look up; others sip and make a quick getaway.

My clearest memory is of three teenage girls who approach the rail in awkward self-consciousness. The first one takes the wafer, puts half in her mouth, and glances sidelong at her neighbor. Her shoulders begin to shake, and soon all three are giggling. I do not know for certain what they're laughing about, yet their response seems appropriate. The Eucharist itself rests on the mysterious, almost absurd notion that God can shrink into a piece of bread. Their laughter seems as genuine a response as any.

The Holy Spirit is an essential ingredient for a good sermon, but no substitute for time in the library.

Just because great preachers tell you that they owe their most memorable sermons to the Holy Spirit's inspiration does not mean that they failed to flip through the commentaries or agonize over their diction. Although a few great preachers may owe more to direct assistance from other-worldly powers than to heavy research and drafting, these paragons should NOT be imitated when a seminarian prepares for her first sermon.

Before going to seminary, I heard a lot of talk about the Holy Spirit's influence on preaching, particularly on strong preaching. When a congregation dissolves in tears or responds to a sermon with choruses of "A-*men*," when they're moved to take to the streets in protest of injustice or to turn their lives over to God, the Holy Spirit is given most of the credit. Little is said about the preacher's cleverly disguised exegesis, deftly woven into a gripping story; or about the number of drafts she has written, edited, or filed in the wastebasket; or about the years of practical experience she draws upon as she stands before large crowds like an improvisational actor, exercising her ability to think on her feet.

A week before finals, I gain a different perspective on sermon preparation and delivery. Having successfully completed one preaching course and garnered a handful of preaching experiences, I am overconfident of my ability to deliver under pressure. When a fellow seminarian asks me to substitute for him at the cathedral's Sunday vespers, I quickly agree, jotting down the sermon date to worry about after finishing term papers.

The next thing I know, it is 1:00 P.M. Sunday afternoon on the day of my vespers sermon. I sit in a coffee shop across the street from the cathedral staring at the screen of my laptop and scanning one of my least favorite Gospel passages from John:

> "Lord, we do not know where you are going. How can we know the way?" Jesus said to him, "I am the Way, the Truth, and the Life. No one comes to the Father, except through me."

I dislike the implications of this passage for the souls of non-Christians—those who have never heard the Gospel, are dedicated practitioners of another religious tradition, or simply good people who do not place their faith in Jesus Christ.

I have six hours to write and print out my sermon. I am familiar with this text. Part of the reason for my last-minute preparation is that

I plan to lift a large section of an old class presentation on the historical context of the fourth Gospel. Now, as I face a blank computer screen, conscious of the clock, cutting and pasting this ten-minute sermon becomes a daunting prospect.

I type the date and center the title—"Vespers Sermon"; nothing is worse than a blank screen. I can't launch immediately into my prewritten explanation of the early Johannine community and the Council of Jamnia; a grabbing opener needs to come first.

I begin to copy the text. The text is always a good place to start. And it will have to print in at least 18-point type, or I may not be able to read it in the dimly candlelit cathedral:

> **"Lord, we do not know where you are going. How can we know the way?" Jesus said to him, "I am the Way, the Truth, and the Life. No one comes to the Father, except through me."**

I order another cup of coffee. Snippets of sermon-writing tips flit through my mind. *Bring the congregation with you.... Don't preach at people in the pews; explore the text together.... Make sure the congregation wants to hear your exegesis before you offer it to them.*

I decide to start with a clear illustration of the problem in this passage. Taking the text's message to its logical conclusion can serve as the opener:

> **No one comes to the Father, except through me. No Jews, no Buddhist saints. No Gandhis, no Dalai Lamas, no people born before Christ, no people born in countries the gospel has not reached or in nations where it cannot be preached. None of our Muslim friends. No one who is not baptized in the name of the Father, the Son, and the Holy Spirit. No one who does not profess Christ as his or her personal savior.**

I play with sentence structure, debating whether to replace "Muslim" with "Jewish" and "friends" with "family." Or is that too personal? I wonder if the periods should become question marks and worry about an overly ironic tone. Then I admire the cadence of the paragraph, repeating it several times aloud, ignoring a nearby woman's peevish glances from behind her Sunday *Times.*

A glance at my watch jolts me unpleasantly back to the present. I dash off another paragraph about how difficult these words are for people trying to love their neighbors in a complex, democratic, religiously and ethnically plural society. Passages like this have been used to justify horrendous acts in our own century, such as "ethnic cleansing" and genocide. I finish the introduction by observing that the historical misuse of passages like this often makes them greater liabilities than assets for people of faith who wish to spread the gospel.

Now I need a transition to my presentation on the early Johannine community and the influence of the rabbinical Council of Jamnia at the end of the first century A.D.

So where do we begin in our understanding of these words?

Great. Here comes the segue I need:

The place I would like to start is back in Palestine in about 90 A.D., when scholars think the Gospel of John was actually written ...

With intense satisfaction, I open my computer file on the "Fourth Gospel Presentation," copy a large chunk, and paste several paragraphs into "Vespers Sermon." My original presentation described how the decision of a group of Jewish rabbis at the Council of Jamnia in 85 A.D.

would have forced the Johannine Christian community to choose between fidelity to the gospel and membership in the synagogue. The unique, uncompromising tone of the Gospel of John that this passage reflects, I argue, may have been a result of the Johannine Christians' isolation after being thrown out of the synagogue—an experience unknown to the earlier Christian communities of Mark, Luke, and Matthew. Amending and enlarging the font blessedly makes my sermon two pages longer.

All is well, except that I have only an hour to polish and print the sermon, do a run-through, and vest for the service. Although I usually do the trial run after finishing my conclusion, the press of time urges reading it over in the absence of a punch line. I read it to Greg over the phone.

He listens attentively, then chooses his words carefully, knowing his precarious position at such moments: "That's great. I like your opening. Your projection is excellent. It's certainly a difficult passage. I'm thinking, though, that there might be a little something missing."

"Missing?" I reply irritably. "Like what, besides a conclusion?" My annoyance is greater because Greg points out what I already know.

"Well," he begins cautiously, "the scripture passage is definitely challenging, and you've given a very interesting historical explanation for the origins of that challenge, but, I mean ... well, so what?"

"So *what?*"

"Yeah. So what? Why should these ideas matter to people in more than an abstract way? What's the take-away? What can they apply to their lives after they leave the service tonight?"

My heart sinks. Another refrain from my preaching instruction semester echoes. *Always know what you want the congregation to walk away with at the end of your sermon before you begin to write it. As a rule of thumb, write your conclusions first.*

Unfortunately, this good advice arrives too late. In twenty minutes I need to be in the cathedral putting on my robe. I sit down again, straining to express how the same estrangement that affected the Johannine Christians and later religious or ethnic minorities—an estrangement sometimes grounded in a grossly distorted interpretation of this very Gospel—might be present in society today. On the last page of the sermon draft, I write:

—Say something about social divisions and alienation in high schools and its relation to violence.

—Ignoring crazy people on subway = more violent crimes caused by alienated schizophrenic people?

—Isolation is bad because ...

—Conclusion

People believe that the most powerful sermons are the work of the Holy Spirit. Jesus even said that the disciples should not prepare in advance what they would say to the magistrates who tried them. Many anecdotes recount great preachers who rise to give prepared sermons but in the pulpit are suddenly moved to say something completely different. Well, I muse ruefully, here is my opportunity to depend heavily upon the Holy Spirit—a chance to see if, in the pulpit, the normal laws of good public speaking might be suspended for God's weighty Word. Although it's unlikely that a divine flash of insight will strike as I speak, still, the odds are slightly better than for delivering a stump speech. Anyway, there's no choice. I shut my laptop and race to the copy shop.

Processing into the vespers service, a solemn line of acolytes and choir members moves slowly through the darkened nave of the cathedral, bearing candles and chanting in Latin. The officiant always walks at the end of the line. At the foot of the great choir, where the service takes place, he or she peels off and takes a position among the stalls. The choir continues up the center aisle, forming two short lines facing each other a few yards below the steps to the high altar. The great arches flicker in the vespers candlelight during the moments of silence before the first prayers.

"O Gracious Light," I begin, wondering if the mike will pick up my thumping heartbeat, "pure brightness of the ever-living Father in heaven ... you are worthy at all times to be ... glorified through all the world." I try to steady my voice. Sitting as the choir begins to sing the psalm, I listen to the Gospel reading with the same sick apprehension that preceded my balance-beam routine at childhood gymnastics meets.

"Here ends the lesson," the verger says. My time has come. I walk slowly up to the lectern at the foot of the high altar, clutching my text. I adjust the mike and peer into the black cavern of the cathedral, which seems to stretch for miles into the distance.

"In the name of the Father, and of the Son, and of the Holy Spirit ... please be seated." There is a short rustle of coats and shifting bodies as the hundred or so vespers attendees in the stalls to my right and left sit down. All sense of engaging with the congregation quickly dissolves. I can barely see the people, let alone make eye contact. The only clear sensation is my own voice echoing over the public address system through the yawning darkness below. Having next to no idea of how this sermon will end, I grasp each word like a lifeline, slowly drawing it out. But with every page the rope is closer to running out. Within moments I will be dangling helpless over the abyss.

Near the end, I speak more and more slowly. On the final page, sweat beads my forehead and my throat goes dry. I will each phrase on the page about school violence to become a complete sentence. Eventually, after a few faltering attempts, I say "amen" and stop.

It is over. I walk down the center aisle staring at the flagstones, my face burning. How can I have let this happen? The whole congregation must be excruciatingly embarrassed. I feel rising shame to have dishonored this majestic setting and the subject matter with my shoddy preparation. Here is solid proof that I will not make it as a preacher. Busy reviewing other career options during what remains of the service, I start the wrong version of the Lord's Prayer and discover halfway through that I am reciting it alone. In the sacristy after the service, I say a quick prayer with the choir and dash from the room before anyone can console me.

In my rush to escape, I collide with a woman standing outside the door. Before I can apologize, she takes my arm. "Thank you so much for your words. That was a very powerful sermon." I stare at her blankly, wondering if she knows she's talking to the wrong person. I thank her and continue down the hall to the sanctuary, where Greg throws his arms around me and congratulates me on a great sermon. My confusion deepens when, after examining him closely, I see he is offering a genuine compliment, not merely being a supportive husband.

"But it completely floundered at the end," I protest, desperately wanting to be contradicted.

"Really?" Greg asks, smiling. "I thought that you were just extremely emotional about the topic and that you slowed down because you were so moved." Another stranger approaches to thank me for the sermon.

I left the cathedral that night with the conviction that there is no substitute for a thoroughly prepared sermon—but also with a sense that no matter how much I sweated beforehand, the ultimate effect of my preaching would be determined only by a higher authority. Although that night the Holy Spirit may not have inspired the preacher's words, it had sharpened the listeners' ears. Skeptics might argue that I should have been more grateful to the PA system, but I knew otherwise. Spirit and cogitation would both be essential ingredients when I tried to illuminate the Word of God—but probably never in predictable ways.

Pastors in the Public Square

I was elated to be working at the Cathedral of St. John the Divine. Besides being vocationally fulfilling, St. John's offered movingly simple Sunday evening vespers services that Greg and I enjoyed together. The cathedral also drew me in by its powerful presence in the public square; it was more engaged in the social, political, and cultural life of New York City than many other Episcopal houses of worship I knew.

As a child of the 1980s, not the '60s, I found somewhat novel the idea that faith-based liberal opinions had a place in debates about social policy, race relations, and economic questions. Growing up in Cambridge, I had not known that Walter Cronkite's decision to become an anchorman may have been shaped by his strong Christian commitment. Nor was I aware that Mr. Rogers of *Mr. Rogers' Neighborhood* was a Presbyterian minister. During high school in the '80s, although I worked locally for nuclear disarmament, I was ignorant of the leadership roles that Christian ministers and activists played in the movement. I didn't know that one of the experts on nuclear arms policy during the Reagan and Bush administrations, and a member of the Council on Foreign Relations, was a Catholic priest, Father Brian Hehir. Even in college, I was only vaguely aware of the pivotal role the church had played in ending communism in Eastern Europe and apartheid in South Africa.

Many of the people I read about who called themselves Christians were protesting abortion clinics, organizing against gay rights, or embezzling their followers' donations. Religious leaders were more likely to be interviewed for their opinions on the "scandal" of presidential infidelity than on what the dean of the cathedral once called the "outrage" of homelessness or the "obscenity" of poverty. Christian witness in America had seemed limited to questions of personal morality or the ethics of reproduction. Religious leaders with a visible impact on politics—the Moral Majority or the Christian Coalition—I associated with the extreme right of the Republican Party.

As I became more involved with the church, I came to believe that our Christian witness is most vigorous when we build up our communities and stand up for issues of social justice. So, when the cathedral and the Episcopal Church joined a diverse assortment of other New Yorkers to probe police brutality, this strong affirmation of the church's place in the public square was woven inseparably into my experience of Easter.

LIVING on the Lower West Side, my husband and I reaped the benefits of our mayor's anticrime efforts. Helped along by demographic change and a nationwide decrease in violent crime, these efforts were partly responsible for the lowest crime rate in decades. We walked our dogs late at night without fear and enjoyed the public spaces in lower Manhattan free from the anxiety long associated with life in New York City. In the spring of my second year at seminary, however, I became aware that the costs of our mayor's crime crackdown were very unevenly distributed among city residents.

During spring break 1999, I had lunch with a reporter friend who had recently interviewed a group of protesters at One Police Plaza. They were part of a demonstration against the tragic killing of Amadou Diallo, an unarmed West African man, by a group of police officers who had shot at him forty-one times outside his Bronx apartment.

The protesters, according to my friend, showed up every weekday at lunchtime, marching or participating in civil disobedience that blocked the doors of police headquarters until they were arrested for trespassing. Demonstrators included doctors, high school students, public school teachers, legal advocates, union leaders, and lawyers—a mix of races, economic backgrounds, and professions. One of the organizers had told my friend that protesters were calling for the indictment of the four police officers—who still had desk jobs—and the fulfillment of recommendations, including a one-year residency requirement for all officers in training.

A commission on police violence had been appointed the previous year, after the torture of a Haitian, Abner Louima, in a Brooklyn police station. The commission's recommendations were later ignored by the mayor, who had appointed the panel. This failure to act fulfilled the preconditions for civil disobedience that Martin Luther King outlined in his "Letter from Birmingham Jail"—that legal redress of an injustice must first be pursued without success.

Although I disagree with most of the organizers' politics on other matters, I am compelled by the clarity of their goals, their diversity of support, and the well-organized, imaginative nature of the protest itself. Shortly after my lunch conversation, a picture of police arresting the former mayor of New York appears on page one of the *Times.* Also arrested are the head of the NAACP, a few film stars, several members of Congress, and several city council members. The organizers plan to continue using themes such as "lawyers' day" or "trade union leaders' day" or "state legislators' day" in order to show widespread support and keep the pressure on. Supporters of all backgrounds are welcomed and encouraged to wear coat and tie and register their names ahead of time with the police.

"There was a time when I might have gotten involved in something like this," I think ruefully, anticipating my imminent return to classes, "but now I'm confined to the Ivory Steeple."

To my surprise, however, when classes resume the following Monday, there is much talk about the protest taking place at police headquarters. Over lunch, someone mentions that an "Episcopal Day" demonstration is planned for noon at the end of the week and that maybe a contingent of us should go down to One Police Plaza. A letter is circulating signed by the bishop of New York, with a supporting note from the dean, that encourages Episcopalian New Yorkers to take part in the "Episcopal Day" protest.

Soon we are sending advance delegations down to the square to find out if both in-state and out-of-state driver's licenses are acceptable for fast-track processing and what sort of bail we may need to post. To facilitate police processing, members of the administration whose usual job includes making sign-up sheets for volunteers to steam-iron hoods at graduation are making a list of community members who want to be arrested at One Police Plaza. Suddenly the question around the Close is not *if* you will attend the protest but whether you plan to be arrested.

"No way! Are you kidding? I have other things to do besides getting deported by the INS, thank you very much!" exclaims Mary, when I inquire what she will do. Her proudly held Canadian citizenship is a liability when it comes to committing acts of civil disobedience in the United States. Mauricio, too, regrets that U.S. immigration officials may not take kindly to his expression of conscience when he wants to renew his student visa from Costa Rica. Three people definitely want to get arrested, and a group of others plan to demonstrate but are disinclined to tangle with the law due to small children or out-of-state licenses. Brad's instructions over lunch to "*Go*, girl!" in whatever way I see fit typifies the support most of our community offers.

I am uncertain what to do.

Personal risks and benefits aside, the newspapers—and my own experiences as a chaplain at Bellevue Hospital—suggest strongly that the New York Police Department, particularly the Special Street Crimes Unit that was largely responsible for cutting crime in poorer neighborhoods, has consistently violated the civil rights of minority citizens. The reported number of African American and Hispanic young men who have been stopped and frisked for little or no cause has increased dramatically, along with the number of complaints filed after incidents of police abuse. The Brooklyn case is an extreme example, but less well publicized incidents such as the unprovoked harassment of a Hispanic assemblyman illustrate a trend. Laws favor the enforcers, like the unique forty-eight-hour rule that gives immunity from legal questioning to police officers for that amount of time.

Although most police officers are hardworking, dedicated people with an enormously difficult task, it does not seem fair that safe streets come only at the cost of ignoring the rights of poor and minority citizens. Just because I personally face no danger of being frisked or beaten does not mean I should fail to protest very strongly the police abuse of others in my city.

On the other hand, as my mother points out, where were all the demonstrators at One Police Plaza when children in poorer New York neighborhoods were dying in their schools because school violence ran rampant during the previous administration? Has anyone bothered to ask what parents and grandparents in the worst areas of New York think of the current mayor's tough-on-crime stance? Indeed, the day before the Episcopal Church's planned protest, I hear a Brooklyn woman call into a radio talk show to condemn the protest organizers as political opportunists who care nothing about day-to-day life in poor neighborhoods and only want to unseat the mayor. Who am I to say that occasional injustice at the hands of the police is not worth the good of less crime for poorer communities, if those very people believe it is?

Also, I have to consider the personal costs and benefits of taking part in the civil disobedience campaign, not just the demonstration. Although at the time I did not put them on paper, my list of the pros and cons of getting arrested on "Episcopal Day" ran like this:

PROS	CONS
Support Episcopal Church in standing up for a just life	Ruin life? (i.e. — have a police record)
Will have finished studying for church history midterm	Might be distracted during exam
Show leadership at seminary (get the Social Action Committee involved in something besides being the recycling police)	Further solidify reputation as knee-jerk, bleeding-heart liberal from Cambridge
Reinforce academic learning (i.e. — test NT prof.'s thesis on Gospel passages from Matthew about "turning the other cheek" and their connection to nonviolent resistance)	Lack of moderation
Jesus would have done it (application of the WWJD test)	Jesus also raised the dead
Spontaneous	Impulsive
Take a risk	Take a risk

Then there is the categorical imperative—the irksome principle that any action should be universalizable to include any person in any circumstance. If I were willing to break the law to express my conscience, would I be willing to extend the same prerogative to antiabortion protesters expressing *their* consciences by violating the buffer zone around clinics? In the Christian ethics course, Immanuel Kant, author of the categorical imperative, had been a minor player compared to Augustine or Plato, but he had figured prominently in my upbringing.

At some point, however, as more and more elaborate arguments weight both sides of my mental scales, I decide that the search for perfect knowledge is becoming an excuse for inaction. I throw in my lot with Cardinal John Henry Newman, foe of nineteenth-century Darwinian skeptics who sought to debunk religious faith on the grounds that it could not withstand scientific proof. Arguing that "Reason requires rigid proofs, Faith is satisfied with vague ... ones," Cardinal Newman thought that the salvation of one's soul is so important that it requires only the *slimmest* evidence to prompt action. The greater the gravity of the action, the smaller the amount of proof required to support it. As one of my professors said, this principle means that a niggling suspicion as you drive off for a three-week vacation that the iron in your kitchen is still plugged in can stimulate a U-turn—while the 100 percent certainty that the beds are unmade probably does not justify the same action.

After discussing the question with Greg, Brother Clark, and a number of others, I decide that the question of police brutality is more like the iron than the unmade bed. The standard of proof required to prove the unassailable correctness of joining an act of civil disobedience is lower than for other actions. I am arranging an experiment in truth that may do more good for me than for victims of police abuse, but probably it will do no harm to justice. Besides, one sure thing I'd gleaned from three semesters of Gospel exegesis and of close readings of Paul's

Epistles—Jesus Christ and his apostles stood squarely on the side of those who lacked power in the dominant social systems of their day.

Some people seemed critical of how smoothly the demonstrations were running—as if moral authority rested on spontaneity. The enterprise became suspect to some, because this organized civil disobedience even gave the police arrest sign-up sheets in advance.

For me, the public relations finesse of the demonstrations at One Police Plaza clinched my decision to participate. The awareness of our late-twentieth-century context was one of the things that made this protest sound like a biblical calling. The organizers' recommendation that everyone wishing to be arrested bring in-state driver's licenses to speed police processing reminded me of theologian Walter Wink's observation about Christ's keen political awareness.

For example, when Jesus told his followers to give up their undergarment (χιτών) and their outer garment (ιματιον) if they were sued, he must have known of the Jewish practice of giving the outer garment as a pledge in a court of law and of the problem of indebtedness among Galilean peasants. Jesus must have also recognized the taboo of nakedness in Judaism; if a defendant suddenly stripped naked in the middle of court proceedings, members of the Roman imperial court system would be shamed.

Similar political acumen appeared in the demonstration at One Police Plaza. The point was not to antagonize the police by unduly complicating their work but to keep public pressure and attention on an administration that had repeatedly ignored the concerns of minority leaders and citizens.

Demonstration day does not produce the intense drama of conflict with the powers that be that I expect. After finishing my church history exam, I ride the subway with Nathan and Mary to join others at One Police Plaza. I feel rather despondent on the ride, absorbing all the answers I've missed on the exam. I can't adequately answer Nathan's questions about why I want to be arrested. As we walk toward the plaza, I wonder if my engagement may have ballooned out of proportion. Only when we hear the chanting and begin to recognize a surprising number of people does my frame of mind improve.

The first hopeful thing is to watch the diocesan bishop of New York (who rarely appears at protests) link arms with three other bishops to lead a march of priests, deacons, seminarians, and lay people around the plaza to the cheers of hundreds. In the "get arrested" line, I discover a few more seminarians; Barbara Crafton, the priest I'd worked for at St. Clement's; and most of the cathedral clergy, including my mentor, Canon Susan Harriss. It is moving to see this great gathering of clerical collars—a concentration usually seen only around the altar at Easter or Christmas—in the grit of the public square.

The excitement persists for about fifteen minutes as several dozen of us join hands to walk slowly toward the police station past crowds of demonstrators, reporters, and photographers who stand behind barricades lining the plaza. People cheer. Flashbulbs pop. Television crews stick mikes under the noses of a few protesters. At the building, we divide into two lines, one for each door. Several officers instruct us to crowd against the doors and turn around. Over the din of the crowd, a police officer shouts through a bullhorn.

"You are now obstructing police property. Anyone who chooses to leave at this point will not be arrested."

No one moves.

"Would anyone like to leave?" the officer asks again.

No one stirs. The officer waits about ten seconds before continuing.

"You are now under arrest," he shouts. "Please proceed inside the building."

There is an unpleasant moment as we are ushered through the glass doors, divided by sex, and separated into groups of six. It is odd to hear myself referred to as a prisoner. Within a few minutes, however, Susan Harriss, another seminarian, and I are grouped with three others and reassured by a friendly looking officer.

"Hello, ladies," the red-headed young man says courteously. "My name is Officer Bedell. I'll be your officer for the day. Please proceed to the left for your handcuffs." We are escorted downstairs to wait in line for the police wagons that will take us to other precincts for processing. Clearly we will be treated to a first-class tour of police detention facilities—and we'll receive a level of service unknown to most customers of this establishment.

"Officer Bedell, party of six. This way please."

The male seminarians who are arrested report that not all the demonstrators were treated so civilly. Nonetheless, I find it difficult to justify the brief celebrity status we have been granted. A few fellow inmates doubt that near-concierge treatment would greet a "real" protest.

In the police wagon, along with Canon Harriss and the other members of the Bedell party, I meet another seminarian and an elderly white lady who lives on Park Avenue and wears an antimayor button. She has extras and passes her bag around the bus. We introduce ourselves while some people complain that the wagon has no seat belts.

After arriving at a precinct on Canal Street, our wagon load of twelve joins another fifteen women in a small cell about twenty-five feet square, where we remain for most of the afternoon. Our driver's licenses and identification cards are taken to check if we have outstanding warrants in other states. We settle in, say a quick prayer, and dig into our respective spots. Younger women stand or sit on the floor while older women occupy the bench against one wall. We take a group photo after our handcuffs are removed and pass a pad around to make a list of everybody's name and address—a networking opportunity not to be missed.

By midafternoon, defense attorneys from Legal Aid arrive as promised. Two Asian American lawyers assist us with our rights and help secure trips to the bathroom and access to the vending machines. They also make phone calls for us.

"Here, this is my husband's number," says an elderly African American parishioner from a Bronx church whose handbag contains an endless supply of chips and candies that we snack on all afternoon. She hands the lawyer a slip of paper; elbowing her friend with a grin, she says, "Tell him he'll have to make dinner for himself tonight!"

A younger woman from the same Bronx church gives instructions on how to contact her office. "Tell them I'm . . . well, you know . . . 'tied-up,'" she says, to snickering around the cell.

Canon Harriss has tickets to see a musical that evening with her husband and kids. She is betting on being let out in time to be late for dinner but not too late for the show. The lawyers get only an answering machine at her husband's work, so she decides to wait until she sees him in person to explain. Spending the afternoon in jail had not been on her to-do list.

The situation is a little different for me. I briefed Greg about the possibility of arrest. He knows exactly where I am when he receives the precinct's call. He has no qualms about spreading the news, promptly telling his secretary and most of his officemates that I'm in jail, but his return message is comforting.

After a few hours, in which I have time to discuss my field placement with Canon Harriss and catch up on St. Clement's, we are brought upstairs, handed our summons, and released with Officer Bedell's strict warning that if we are arrested again for the same offense, we can look forward to a nasty night in the Tombs with career criminals. Canon Harriss, the other seminarian, and I take the crowded rush hour subway to our various family dinners.

BACK AT the seminary, for every person who congratulates me on being arrested, there is at least one who thinks I've acted rashly and probably hurt the cause to boot. Moreover, the following week, an article about the shooting from the perspective of the officers involved describes how they broke down when they realized the victim was unarmed. I realize the hell these officers and their families have entered. However despicably they had acted and however unjust the system, the officers are entitled to a fair trial. After all the publicity and protest, I wonder if they'll get one. It has not been a demonstration for revenge, but, I realize after the fact, the goals of our protest can easily be interpreted as vengeance.

Despite residual doubts in the following weeks that make my afternoon in jail seem simple, my participation in this act of nonviolent protest has firm biblical grounding. Moreover, standing up for a victim of injustice is arguably a more authentic initiation rite into Christian ministry than anything that we do in chapel.

It is an Easter epiphany to realize that the cathedral and much of my church have solid foundations in the world. The vaulted ceilings and lovely hymns I enjoy in cathedral services become more inspiring when grounded in the city's ordinary life—a muddy, complicated life that nourishes the church's aesthetic, abstract blossoms. Like the Children's Abbey and other basement programs—the soup kitchen, the arts and crafts center, the Nightwatch program—this pastoral venture into the public square of One Police Plaza is another tendril probing deep into the Manhattan bedrock. This intricately woven root system below ground feeds the Cathedral of St. John the Divine and nourishes spiritual life in the worship space above.

Pentecost

The season of Pentecost covers nearly half the Christian year. The day of Pentecost, falling fifty days after Easter, was originally a Jewish celebration remembering the giving of the Law. In the Christian calendar, however, it commemorates the Holy Spirit's entrance into the hearts of a group of Jesus' followers gathered in a Jerusalem home. The beginning of the Book of Acts describes how the group began speaking in tongues, marking this moment as the birth of the church. The time between the feast of Pentecost in May and the beginning of the first week of Advent at the end of November is also called "ordinary time" in the church—not because the miraculous takes a break during the summer, but because we can know God both through great epiphanies *and* in the less dramatic but continuous divine presence in everyday life.

Ordinary time is more concerned with the daily living of Christian life and the role of the church in the world than with celebrating sacred history. Since the Counter Reformation introduced the four basic seasonal colors—red, white, green, and purple or blue—clergy have generally worn green vestments during Pentecost. Green symbolizes growth, but, as some liturgical theologians point out, it is also the default option when there's no compelling reason to wear another hue.

During my first year at seminary, Pentecost coincided with an eight-week program in Clinical Pastoral Education at Bellevue Hospital. My finals in Greek, church history, and Old and New Testament concluded at the end of May, but in case I thought that seminary was simply about mastering theology, General had arranged a summer's worth of practical education in pastoral care. Maybe I could put classroom knowledge to use.

Being an assistant chaplain in a teeming New York hospital for mental and physical illnesses was, to understate the point, the most emotionally challenging experience of my first year. God's justice never seemed more confusing nor the church more marginal than to an associate chaplain in a large public training hospital.

Described by one of my professors as a "kind of spiritual EMT," a chaplain works differently than a parish priest. Historically, chaplains are appointed by states or private bodies as religious functionaries working at secular institutions such as schools, prisons, hospitals, or in the military. Chaplains rarely develop the long-term relationships that connect a priest to her parishioners. They are more like an emergency room staff—ready to sew up spiritual wounds and pass the patient along to primary care providers. Clinical Pastoral Education for Episcopal seminarians resembled a medical internship. If we could cope with daily crises in hospitals, we might be able to handle the less frequent crises in a parish.

Clinical Pastoral Education, known as CPE, is open to anyone wishing to learn about spiritual care, and it's required for everyone entering the Episcopal priesthood. In 1925, the first CPE program enrolled four seminary students for summer study with the chaplain at Westboro State Hospital in Massachusetts. CPE was the inspiration of Anton Boisen, a minister who, five years earlier, had been hospitalized for "catatonic schizophrenia" at the same institution. After he recovered, Boisen—with the help of Boston physician Richard Cabot and others—founded CPE to teach clergy to care for the sick and dying through firsthand experience. Although the founders disagreed about whether mental disorders were spiritual or physical in origin, all believed that seminarians would benefit from daily work with psychiatric and medical patients.

Now, over seventy years later, Jewish, Christian, Islamic, and Buddhist students seeking ordination in their own traditions enroll in the program nationwide. My classmates and I will work in hospitals and hospices in the New York area, ranging from Christ Hospital in New Jersey, where Brad does thirty-two-hour shifts once every eight days and performs many sacramental functions, to Columbia Presbyterian, where Mauricio takes part in a very structured program with preaching opportunities and strictly delineated pastoral responsibilities. The rest of us scatter around the city—to Beth Israel, NYU Medical Center, and Calvary Hospice in the Bronx.

I want to do my CPE at Bellevue Hospital because, as Mary points out, to work in a large, ailing New York public hospital is guaranteed to be a "boot camp" experience. Also, our supervisor, the experienced Chaplain Ernst Joseph, has been running CPE for thirty-three years; this would be his last program cycle before retirement. Joseph chooses four of us from General, a Yale Divinity School student from the United Church of Christ, and a Benedictine monk who lives in Oregon.

Bellevue Hospital, located directly across town on First Avenue and Twenty-seventh Street, lies within easy biking distance. Founded to serve "lunatics and paupers" in 1736—forty years before the Declaration of Independence—Bellevue is the oldest public hospital in the country. The inspiration for films like *One Flew Over the Cuckoo's Nest* and *The Snake Pit,* Bellevue is the archetypal insane asylum. New Yorkers tell tales about great aunts and dipsomaniacal uncles carted off to Bellevue, and even the guides on Circle Line tour boats describe it as a mental institution, but Bellevue is a general hospital.

From the point of view of a seminarian stepping gingerly out of the Close, it's hard to imagine a building that contains much more of "the world outside." The locked psychiatric wards occupy only one small part of this 1,232-bed medical facility. In addition to the birthing center, medical and neurological ICUs, and dialysis clinic, Bellevue houses two libraries, a high-security prison, a fully accredited public school, a print shop, a Medicaid registration office, two chapels, a synagogue, and one of the city's best emergency rooms. The hospital also has a community board, a palliative care unit, and a world-renowned psychiatric program for survivors of torture and hostage taking. Alcoholics Anonymous and Narcotics Anonymous groups meet there, and relatives of schizophrenic and depressed patients also find support groups at Bellevue. Art therapy programs work with children and adults who suffer severe emotional disorders.

As a microcosm of New York, Bellevue contains the best and worst of life. It gives me a clear view of the city's underbelly. At Bellevue I learn things I could have lived a long life without knowing—and some days, I wished I had. Surreal bits of information come my way. Catholic chaplains are wary of giving out rosary beads because patients have used them to display provocative gang colors; Bibles are no longer distributed in the locked psychiatric wards, since patients sometimes use the pages as toilet paper.

My notions of right and wrong face challenges, too. Level one trauma centers like Bellevue depend on a steady stream of violent-crime victims to maintain the reputation of their ER residency programs. In psychological intake exams, many desperate people give answers that will guarantee admission because they'd rather spend an indefinite period on the psychiatric wards than on New York streets. I learn that prisoners sometimes commit crimes that will return them to jail because they cannot handle the uneasy burden of freedom.

During my Bellevue summer, I also see selfless professionalism. Here is a group of medical and social work professionals, often leaders in their fields, who had on occasion forgone more lucrative or prestigious places at well-endowed medical centers like Johns Hopkins to help care for the poorest people in our society.

Should the president of the United States ever need emergency medical assistance in New York, Bellevue is slated to provide it. The NY Police Department's officers and EMTs all ask to be brought to Bellevue if they're injured on the job. However, once a patient leaves the ER or an intensive care unit, the quality of care declines radically. Since the 1970s' massive cuts in city funding for Bellevue, New York's political climate has thrown its public hospitals into a struggle for survival. The rush to managed care hampers Bellevue's attempt to continue against all odds as a health care provider of last resort. The hospital might once have kept a homeless woman or foster child longer than necessary if she had nowhere else to go, but insurance companies now curtail hospital stays. Dedicated employees scavenge to meet their needs—on some floors, I saw conscientious nurses hoard clean towels and bed linens in private stashes for their patients.

At Bellevue, the *New York Times* metro section unfolds each morning. Traditionally, seven bells sound three times when there's a city disaster such as the bombing of the World Trade Center. While I was at Bellevue, my CPE group learned about the collapse of a residential building in Times Square when many victims among its elderly residents were brought in. Weeks before the district attorney launched an investigation, we knew about the appalling health care conditions on Riker's Island via prisoners who had been transferred from that jail to Bellevue. As I watched an EMT calm a Latino woman suffering a panic attack, I heard about a racket run by Chinese families in nail and hair salons where undocumented immigrant workers were let go simply because they weren't Chinese.

City politics shape life at Bellevue. When the mayor announced his decision to fight methadone clinics, Bellevue doctors and substance abuse specialists vocally opposed his stand. More than once, I spent my lunch hour with unionized workers demonstrating for better severance packages. Sixty percent of Bellevue patients were in danger of losing their benefits when Medicaid became privatized, and people without HMOs faced being assigned to medical facilities by zip code. At the same time, the staff was terrified to criticize the city government, fearing that protest might jeopardize their jobs.

Stepping out of our office after the daily morning debriefing, the other seminarians and I walk past rows of people waiting to register for Medicaid. Going into a patient's room later, we are as likely to be asked for spare change as for a prayer. Sure, it would be great to speak with a chaplain, a patient says. But first, would I mind calling his daughter to come over from Brooklyn? And could I pay the $20 fee to turn on his TV or, better yet, call the public notary from Medical Records so he could send a letter to his bank and bail his son out of jail? I would turn away, guessing that our heart-to-heart on spiritual matters might have to wait. "By the way," the patient adds, as I try for a discreet exit, "could you get one of the nurses to pick up my bedpan? It's been sitting here since breakfast."

Bellevue has a passing resemblance to the Tower of Babel. Over the intercom, I hear requests for interpreters of Spanish, French, Filipino, and Cantonese. In addition to the African American homeless woman who just learned she is HIV positive, I might encounter a highly paid model recovering from a heroin overdose or a Wall Street lawyer hit by a bicycle courier. People from every class, race, ethnicity, and nationality pass through Bellevue's halls. Upward and downward mobility, not to mention immobility, are all on display.

After receiving medical clearance and a brief orientation, our CPE group gathers with our supervisor in a small, sparsely furnished room on the ground floor next to the social work department. Having to choose between the air conditioner and being able to hear each other, we opt for a stuffy but silent room. We try to ignore the broken answering machine that jangles at odd intervals during our meeting, and we stop for a few minutes while two janitors assess the damage from a gaping leak in the ceiling.

Our instructor tells us a little about himself. Having grown up in a strict Mennonite family, Chaplain Joseph went through an extended period of religious doubt and struggle as a young man. At college, he studied history and theology and after graduation spent several years teaching in the Middle East. Upon his return home, he began working with the mentally ill. In the early 1960s, Chaplain Joseph came to Bellevue as a CPE supervisor, liking it so much that he decided to stay. Sensing he was "slowing down a bit," he planned to retire soon. His last day, he decided, would be on the last day of the twentieth century.

In a hospital where it's impossible to be shocked by anyone's appearance, Chaplain Joseph is an unassuming, quiet figure. He seems on good terms with much of the permanent staff—particularly the social work department. At the same time, he's a little removed from the hospital mainstream. One psychiatric resident describes him as "that very nice-looking elderly gentleman." Chaplain Joseph's affable air and the way he walks—one hand tucked in the pocket of his short lab coat, name tag slightly askew—reminds me of the gardener in the Peter Sellers film *Being There*.

Chaplain Joseph appears unassuming, but we discover over the summer that very little slips by him. During our hour-and-a-half morning debriefings, we each recount our interactions with patients in reports called "verbatims." Chaplain Joseph's way of intensive listening, eyes closed, is sage-like.

He usually waits for the rest of the group to respond, then offers a few acute observations about our motives or behaviors that we would never have admitted to ourselves. As Mary reflected wonderingly about our curious CPE instructor from Staten Island, "Who knew? I mean, who really *knew?*" this Chaplain Joseph. Mary said he reminded her of the father in the prodigal son story. Like the parable figure who welcomes his long-lost, delinquent youngest son with a banquet, our chaplain has a magnanimity that extends undeserved forgiveness.

CPE is a group process, so other summer assistants are critical to the experience. Besides Mary and me from General there are Naomi, a member of the class ahead of me, and Bob, the only Native American in my class of eighteen people.

In his late thirties, Bob is a tall man with a ponytail of long dark hair; he moves slowly, reads voraciously, and speaks laconically. His father was an Episcopal pastor on the Pine Ridge Reservation in South Dakota, where Bob hopes to return with his wife and two small children. Our resident expert on the productivity of silence, he says little. But when he does speak, everyone listens. I'd been rather intimidated by Bob during the school year, but I appreciate his wry sense of humor and look forward to getting to know him.

The other two non-General members of the CPE group are Thomas, a divinity school student at Yale, and John, a Benedictine monk from an abbey in Oregon.

Thomas, who is about my age, graduated from Amherst College and was a paralegal for several years before following a call to ministry. He grew up in Concord, New Hampshire, where his father was a physician. Very bright, earnest—and from the most scrupulously traditional Protestant background of anyone in the program—Thomas often single-handedly defends his ministry at CPE by reference to the Bible. For all of General's liturgical fundamentalism, few of us begin sentences with, "The Bible says..." It is eye-opening to watch Thomas unapologetically defend his pastoral decisions on scriptural grounds, while the rest of us trip over each other to see situations in murkier shades of gray.

John, the fortyish Benedictine monk from Oregon, plans to be ordained a priest. In addition to his monastic responsibilities, John has traveled around the world recruiting for the abbey's Catholic seminary. Before joining the monastery, he studied music in Germany and released a CD of a choral ensemble he had composed based on the Passion. Possibly because of his age, experience, and decision to wear a collar, John assumes a unique air of authority in the hospital and among our group. He soon becomes the confidant of several policemen at Bellevue and is called into rooms and sought out for advice. John's congenial, slightly reserved manner makes him more enigmatic than others in the group. Impressed by his religious vocation and captivating life story, I strive to put my best self forward whenever we talk.

Following brief introductions, Chaplain Joseph gives us our schedule. Many classmates at other hospitals spent days in role-play and other exercises before plunging into the working life of a large medical institution. This is not so with Chaplain Joseph. We must show up for a group conference at ten each morning and attend a few didactics each afternoon, but beyond that we are free to explore the hospital. I receive a white jacket with a name tag bearing the title "Associate Chaplain." As the summer weeks pass, Joseph assures us, we'll have plenty of time to discuss the chaplain's role and responsibilities; now, he wants us assigned to units and on our way.

Asked to choose among the dialysis clinic, a locked psychiatric ward, the delivery room, and a neurology intensive care unit, I decide to make the ICU my first port of call. Feeling official in my lab coat and badge, I board a staff elevator for the seventh floor. Down the hall I glimpse an orange door with a sign reading "Visitors allowed for ten minutes."

Thomas and Naomi wave good-bye and depart for the other side of the seventh floor. Hesitantly, I push through the swinging doors to my unit and stop the first nurse I see. "Excuse me, do you know if there are any patients here who would like to speak with a chaplain?" The nurse pauses half a second, then points toward a bed in one corner. "Try bed number four," she says hurriedly and continues changing sheets.

I walk over as confidently as I can, consciously choosing not to look at the medical chart clipped to the board at the nurses' station. The elderly woman is on a respirator, her face pale yellow, both eyelids swollen and bruised bluish green. Her chest rises and falls in an exaggerated way as the life-support machine pumps air into her lungs. Tubes trail everywhere. I don't know who she is, what has happened to her, not even whether she has a family.

I panic. How can I "minister" to a woman in a coma? I could ask her how she's doing and assume that she can hear me, as some pastoral counseling journals suggest. I could read a Bible passage—an act that seems uncomfortable and strange in this overwhelmingly secular setting—and hope no doctors overhear. I could leave and admit that although a person near brain death may be just as much a beloved of God as anyone else, I have no earthly idea how to give her pastoral care. Instead, I sit down in the bedside chair, shut my eyes, and pray for the woman's recovery.

Luckily, her husband did not return during the few minutes I sat awkwardly by his wife's bedside. Later, I learned that a bike messenger had struck her as she stepped from a car on her way to work at a well-known acting school where, for thirty years, she instructed performers, including Robert Redford and Dustin Hoffman. She and her husband had no religious affiliation and hadn't requested a chaplain. When it's decided the next day to remove her from life support, I wonder if praying for someone who did not believe in God had been presumptuous or disrespectful—a question that wouldn't have crossed my mind if I'd been working in a church, not a hospital. Much of my discomfort was connected with social class, I concluded. Only a few days into CPE, I noticed how much more I respected the privacy of patients I perceived as upper class or educated.

After a brief, awkward prayer by the woman's bedside, I summon the courage to move on through the neurological ICU. Walking down the row of seven beds, I silently rehearse an introductory line: "Hi. I'm from the chaplain's office. Is there anything I can do for you?" The next two conscious patients I approach appear receptive: they smile and nod; one makes the sign of the cross with his unbandaged hand. I soon discover that neither one speaks English.

My final stab at ministry that first morning was talking with a sixty-five-year-old Russian émigré from the Ukraine. An engineer in youth, he had come to the United States to live with his mother. We talk a little about his life as a Jew in Russia after the revolution, but he spends more time complaining about the staff, who are trying to persuade him to go into a nursing home. When I suggest that he ask about home care, a social worker appears from behind the bed curtain, assures me that she has things under control, and says flatly that I need not interfere with patient care.

Dispirited, I return to the chaplain's office on the ground floor. Far from taking the hospital by storm, I've finished my first visit completely bewildered. Whom should I approach, and how? When should I talk? When should I listen? In a hospital where so many people perform concrete tasks with tangible measures of success, what is my role, with only a mandate to "address spiritual issues"? Our group wrestles with this question all summer.

THOSE FIRST few weeks at Bellevue might have been less painful if I'd understood the highly political environment of a public hospital and where chaplains fit in this intricate hierarchy. According to the official brochure from the Interfaith Chaplaincy Department, chaplains "help to provide spiritual support to patients, their families and significant others as well as staff during times of illness." Full-time chaplains are considered "part of the health care team"; they can "reduce loneliness ... help facilitate communication between patients and staff ... be available to parents and families ... and offer sacraments, prayer etc." Pastoral counseling by a certified chaplain is supposedly available to patients of "any religious faith," and Catholic chaplains are on call around the clock.

The booklet is accurate to a point. But the *unofficial* view of chaplains in the eyes of other hospital employees is something else. I quickly encounter diverse reactions from staff in the lunchroom, elevators, and on the units. More than once I stumble across invisible lines of authority. Whether I announce myself at a nurses' station before entering a patient's room, or ask the nurses and social workers about a patient afterward, I learn something about the patient—and get a loud, clear message about how different staff members regard the chaplain.

The doctor. In the rare event that a doctor fully registers the existence of a CPE student, she or he understands that you're a student vaguely wanting to be helpful, so you might be assigned a useful task such as feeding a patient or fetching a glass of water. Bellevue's physicians—mostly compassionate, hard-charging professionals who support the hospital's teaching function—are one of its great strengths; at Bellevue, doctors rather than insurance company executives or hospital administrators remain the forces to be reckoned with. In matters of patient care, doctors sit at the top of the pyramid. Doctors are also difficult to approach, owing to the speed at which they circulate. When they aren't examining medical charts, questioning nurses, consulting with each other, or tending patients, they'll be answering questions from a gaggle of medical students trailing in their wake. Unless physicians find a gravely injured Christian Scientist or Jehovah's Witness in the emergency room, religious questions don't seem to cross their screens.

The psychiatrist. On the whole, psychiatrists are more harried and less friendly to CPE students than other doctors. Unlike at some hospitals, which forbid chaplains to enter psychiatric units, at Bellevue our Bible study groups and visits are tolerated, if not warmly welcomed. With the exception of the Bellevue Program for the Survivors of Torture, where individuals from several disciplines participate in meetings, most of the psychiatrists view CPE students warily. It's not so much that psychiatry is an enemy of religion as it is that chaplains become another marginal variable in the psychiatric staff's struggle to bring order to their ward and into their patients' chaotic lives. We are one more factor complicating their task. For my part, I feel ambivalent about throwing another unknown ingredient into the volatile compound that is a psych ward, especially because many schizophrenic patients express the so-called "positive" forms of their illness (hallucinations, voices, etc.) in religious language. Based on their clipped and frosty responses, I learn to ask few questions of the psychiatrists.

The resident. Residents may not be the most outwardly hostile group in the hospital toward student chaplains, but they seem the most confused by us. A chaplain is enigmatic—she, too, wears a white jacket, but has a suspiciously large amount of time on her hands and a fuzzy mandate in relation to the patient (dealing with "spiritual issues"). Except for a fellow alumna whom I knew from my college women's rugby team, most residents I meet hesitate to count chaplains as members of the health care team, no matter what the hospital brochure says. Almost my first staff interaction was a minor standoff with a young resident. I was angry that he wouldn't divulge the diagnosis of a patient whom I'd sat with for an hour in the waiting room and needed to write up for a verbatim. I, too, am a paying, certification-seeking graduate student who has come to Bellevue to develop skills I need for my vocation, but he dismissed me out of hand.

The social worker. The associates in Bellevue's extensive social work program are a hard-boiled, dedicated lot with forceful personalities and no qualms about confronting a chaplain who treads on their turf. The social workers are also the hospital staffers who best understand who we are and why we are there. Besides the patients, social workers are the Bellevue people whom we work with most.

The nurse. Like social workers, nurses clearly understand what full-time chaplains and we students are up to. We also offer a welcome pair of extra hands capable of adjusting beds, fetching water, or calling the TV repair guy. And we can occupy needy or lonely patients with conversation—time they might otherwise spend buzzing nurses for attention. Some Bellevue nurses are very attentive to their patients, giving care as if they were family members; others treat their patients roughly or neglect them altogether. Every nurse I met that summer, good or poor, was overworked and lacked necessary supplies and support.

The full-time chaplain. From my brief observation of Bellevue's vocational hierarchy, full-time chaplains fall somewhere between nutritionists and X-ray technicians. Among them, the three Catholic chaplains covered the largest number of patients; they were on call around the clock, and they were expected to respond to Code Red announcements over the PA system. The young Pentecostal chaplain attended ethics meetings with doctors and hospital staff and conducted Bible studies popular among some staff members. However, an Israeli family I befriended waited two weeks before the hospital rabbi showed up. In addition, although I was told that a part-time imam was available to Islamic patients, like other elusive characters at Bellevue, I never actually saw him.

Cleaning staff and cafeteria workers. Whether I am chief of neurological surgery or a high school volunteer seems to make no difference as long as I don't dawdle over making my choice between fried fish or fried veal for an entree. The women behind the cafeteria counters are not to be crossed. Besides a few people I met at one lunchtime union demonstration and the Vietnamese janitor who spoke little English and regularly interrupted our morning discussions to empty the trash in the CPE room, I had little interaction with the cleaning staff.

Over the summer, we chaplains-in-training form relationships with staff members, and suspicions break down. Some of the most difficult people, like the social worker on my first visit, become close allies. By the end of the summer, most members of my group have recounted the memorable moment when a doctor first stopped to talk with them. I felt I'd made strides when, during my last week at Bellevue, I walked through the emergency room and the head of the program summoned me—"Chaplain!"—waving in the direction of a distraught young woman bank teller who'd just been held up at gunpoint. After almost two months of feeling like a wallflower in the ER, I prized this summons almost as much as the woman's smiling thanks.

As CPE students at Bellevue, we could count our conversations with the doctors on the fingers of one hand, a fact that bespeaks the low status of associate chaplains at this public hospital. I envy Brad and other classmates from General. At Christ Hospital—the Episcopal hospital in New Jersey where Brad worked—switchboard operators track down CPE students if they fail to respond right away to Code Reds on their beepers. I listen with disbelief as he reports that chaplains are expected to participate in the weekly grand rounds on every unit. "I gave up trying to stop the staff from calling me 'Father Brad'—you're a CPE student and everyone just assumes you're a priest," he tells me.

Unlike Brad, whose position as a representative of the church automatically entitles him to responsibilities like counseling the families of the dying or helping make decisions about patient care, at Bellevue I feel privileged to be asked to serve a patient her dinner.

Beyond the diversity of its patients and its intimate connection with the squalor of city life, what made Bellevue so much the "world outside" was how little time it had for us students of the church. Since this world appeared to have a low regard for my role—my search for signs of external validation were fruitless—I had to learn to rely on myself to find the value in being a person of God working in a secular place. I had to discover this work and assign it worth, myself. This was my struggle in ordinary time at Pentecost.

God Talk in the Lockdown

To discover why a chaplain might differ from a social worker, teacher, or hospital volunteer, I turn first to theological instruction. After a year at seminary, I should at least be able to conduct an interesting Bible study in my assigned units.

It quickly becomes clear, however, that the only places in the hospital where patients have time or inclination to discuss theological questions are the locked psychiatric wards and prison units. I try running weekly study groups in both places, but on the psychiatric floors I can discuss my patients' prophetic apocalyptic visions for only a short time before wondering if I, too, should be committed. Patients tell me that God's voice, sounding "like running water," speaks to them; some tearfully implore Jesus to deliver them from captivity. Up on 18W, the border between schizophrenic disorder and religious experience becomes so unnervingly blurry that my discussions trouble me far more than they help the patients. Our CPE group's morning discussion about the close links between schizophrenic disorders and the behavioral characteristics of mediums and holy people in tribal societies doesn't help much.

Luckily or not, the inmate patients on 19S thus become the primary recipients of my theological instruction.

My early impression was that prisoners at Bellevue were of two sorts. Some I could identify by the shackles that attached them to their beds and the guard who sat outside their door. These people, scattered throughout the hospital, had been hurt before or during an arrest and were awaiting arraignment, the formal presentation of charges. They lay in a murky no-man's-land between two major bureaucracies—the New York public health system and the state Department of Corrections. In this ambiguous realm of both law and medicine, where neither authority is ultimately accountable, speedy arraignment becomes a privilege rather than a right. Basic amenities that other patients get for a fee, like phones or TV, are left arbitrarily to the discretion of the corrections officer in charge. Prisoners in this category had concerns like those of the young man I spoke to who claimed a police officer shot him in the leg after he'd been going for help during a holdup of his boss's Brooklyn construction company. He wanted to find out what he'd been charged with, get in touch with his family, and make sure a competent defense lawyer showed up when the judge arrived at the hospital. A Bible study on the possible natural causes for the parting of the Red Sea was not a high priority for this prisoner.

Another group of prisoners at Bellevue, however, had idle time on their hands. Residents of 19S, a small prison facility on the nineteenth floor, were almost all transfers from other hospitals or from Riker's Island, New York City's 16,000-person correction facility in the middle of the East River near La Guardia Airport. (On a New York subway system map, Riker's is located northeast of Manhattan, just under the subway color key.) These prisoners were almost all partway through their sentences or awaiting trial—for some, this ordeal could last many months. These inmate patients whose health problems had brought them "off island" had all the time in the world. Compared to Riker's, Bellevue is a resort spa.

The idea for a Bible study based on Bill Moyers's six-part PBS series on the Book of Genesis came during a meeting on prisoner's concerns in my second week at the hospital. The meeting included members of the hospital's auxiliary board, the Department of Corrections activities director, about eight patients, and the doctor in charge of the forensic unit—a classic Bellevue character who preached strict vegetarianism, led Bellevue's running team, and made deadpan jokes about his ex-wife in the elevators. (Needless to say, this department head was popular with his inmate patients.)

Toward the end of our hour together, during which we had discussed the patients' rights and privileges, I notice a weekly schedule pinned to a white board. Slotted into the video section is the program "Genesis: Part I." I'd missed the series on public television; a Bible study group based on it could be exciting. When I mention the idea to the activities officer, he's delighted to put a new program on the schedule, even for a few weeks. A weekly Bible class might get patients out of their rooms and allow them a bit of intellectual activity. From my vantage point, of course, I will enjoy a literally captive audience.

GETTING INTO the recreation room on 19W is always more interesting than entering units on other floors. Instead of the regular units' blue or red swinging doors and white signs, I face a walk-through metal detector, several officers, and two sets of electrically powered steel gates. As an associate chaplain, I may enter only with a staff member from the ward. After passing through the initial security, I wait at another set of bars for an inside officer with a large key ring to let me onto the prison ward. Walking down the hall, I peer gingerly into the glass-walled prison cells and call out "Bible study!" to anyone who looks awake. Typically, by the time Jeff, the activities director, and I have set up the VCR, four or five pajama-clad individuals shuffle or wheel themselves into the room, half of them dragging IVs. For the first few times, I bring notes from Professor Corney's Old Testament class and photocopies of whatever biblical passage corresponds with that week's episode. We usually spend far more time discussing the patients' reactions to the program.

Mary joins me for the first video to help keep the session focused.

As we watch, I sense the men's attention drifting. When some patients begin to lose interest and start chatting, I fear losing my audience completely and debate whether to switch off the television. But Mary might be sitting in her own living room. Her main concern is not to miss any of the program, so she doesn't hesitate to ask the prisoners to lower their voices. Hers is a very particular philosophy of Bible study. Mary doesn't conduct sessions to secure mass conversions. Instead, the fewer uninterested patients in the room, the better—biblical education, for Mary, is about quality, not quantity.

In the first video, a group of Christian and Jewish religious scholars sits in a circle discussing the stories of the Fall and the exile from Eden. What do they convey about God's character? One woman scholar observes that the story suggests that creation was perhaps more "trial and error" on God's part than we like to think. The Fall of Adam and Eve and the story of the flood, she muses, show that God had created a very unfinished piece of work. As to the Fall of Adam and Eve, another scholar describes God as a "nervous creator" who, like an anxious parent, is unsure how much freedom to give his child. A third commentator, gesturing with his eyeglasses, poses the much-debated view that the use of the first person plural in "Let us create man in our own image" (Genesis 1:26) might refer to human beings as cocreators with God. The scholars agree on one thing: the Book of Genesis—and possibly the whole Bible—is more concerned with framing life's great questions than with answering them.

This conclusion dismays the few dedicated patients who have stuck it out for the full hour. Sensing they have comments, I switch off the TV and peer expectantly at the remainder of our inmate audience, slouched on red and green plastic chairs around the dingy rec room.

"I mean, these people are *paid* to talk about this stuff, right?" begins Tyrone, a young, light-skinned African American with thick glasses who sat quite close to the TV set. Scoffs and disgusted looks registered his annoyance throughout the program.

"They're supposed to be experts, right?" he continues. "I mean, they've spent their whole lives studying this stuff, which is why they're on TV and we're not. Right?" Tyrone's logic is irrefutable. "So then why are they giving us all this stuff about not having any answers? I mean, it doesn't take a Ph.D. *not* to have answers! And if *they* don't have any answers, then who does?"

The other patients murmur agreement. A few people shift, and heavy plastic chair legs scrape across the linoleum. Tyrone had hit on a question that I realize could plague the rest of my ministry. How can anyone claim to be an "expert" in religion, when "expert" to most people bespeaks knowledge, replete with empirical facts? Ph.D.s in biochemistry don't get Nobel Prizes just for posing interesting *questions.* I ask if anyone else has comments before we start.

"Yeah, I have something to say," pipes up a man in a wheelchair from the corner. Robert is a soft-spoken, clearly intelligent older man with glasses, a peppery beard, and a soft smile. Apparently, he arrived from Riker's Island over a month ago, incapacitated by a severe stroke. Robert becomes a regular attendee of our Genesis Bible study.

"I think it was a very interesting program. Thank you. I also think that those commentators were a little naive."

"Naive?" Mary asks, interested. "Naive about what?"

"Well, they keep saying about how God lets himself get in a relationship with frail human beings, but what do they mean when they say 'frail'? Are they talking about people who overeat or cheat on their taxes, or are they saying that God's in a relationship with all those serial killers and people who beat their wives every day? There is a difference."

An older patient sitting to my left who's been surveying the group with distaste jumps in with an opinion that's clearly been bothering him.

"These people can say whatever they like. That's fine. But I don't buy all that stuff about God being nervous. I don't worship a nervous God. That's ridiculous!" He stands up and leaves the room.

This may be a good moment to move on, so I begin handing out copies of Genesis 2 and 3 and start my own brief interpretation of the Fall (rehearsed with Mary). I'm on my feet for about one second before a tall, lanky man sitting on the edge of his chair begins his own exegesis.

"See, this is what I'm telling you, man," he says, half to Tyrone and half to anyone else who is listening. "The Koran is the place to go for answers!" Not wanting to discriminate against other religious views, I don't interrupt. Particularly since Tyrone, who has begun to drift a little, looks interested.

"I'm telling you, I read the Bible one time, and it's fine, but it doesn't tell you what to do. I became a Muslim because the Koran has the most truth in it. You don't argue about what it means. You read it, and you know what to do. The prophet got the word *directly* from God."

"Is that right?" asks Tyrone. "Is that how it is? The Koran has more answers than the Bible?"

Taking my cue from Mary to keep going, I continue to hand out copies. Since time is short, I ask Tyrone to please read the second chapter of Genesis aloud. He does, and the passage becomes a launching pad into other historical understandings of the Fall and how they have changed over time. We discuss the view that the Fall was simply Adam and Eve's journey to adulthood, a kind of inevitable "adolescent rebellion" for the human race. Or does the Fall demonstrate a fundamental, evil flaw in the makeup of men and women? Early Christian theologians like St. Augustine and St. Iranaeus disagreed about this—sort of like the commentators on the Genesis program, I venture.

My purpose is to show the group that each word of the Bible need not be taken literally and that areas of gray are plentiful in biblical interpretation. This discussion is meant to be empowering—if the great saints of Christian history and today's academic experts differ about the meaning of scripture, then Tyrone, Robert, and everyone else can formulate their own opinions, too. That is part of the mystery and attractiveness of scripture, in my opinion. It's inspiring that a book replete with the marks of human limitation in both its creation and interpretation is also a vehicle of divine truth.

Most of the patients in 19S, however, don't share my fondness for ambiguity, least of all in the Bible. They want answers, not questions. I pique some interest in another prisoner study group by pointing out that not all biblical heroes were perfect—look at King David's adulterous affair with Bathsheba, Jacob's trickery, and Noah's drunkenness. Tyrone is amazed at this discovery and keeps repeating throughout the hour that he didn't know the Bible had *that* kind of stuff in it. Still, except for a few such astounding revelations, the more contradictions I point out in the Bible, the more the inmates decide there is no point in wasting their time with a religion that lacks answers.

At the end of our Genesis study, Robert sums up more politely than the others the probable impact of my eager theological instruction: "Questions, questions, questions. So many *questions*!" he mutters, smiling and shaking his head. "Very interesting—all those questions."

CHRISTIAN fatalism offers another theological dilemma pervasive in 19S and elsewhere in the hospital, which I feel it's my duty to combat. If someone's child is struck by a car, or he's injured on the job, that is God's will. God is the giant puppeteer in the sky; our fate depends purely on the Creator's whim. It would be pointless to make any effort to reduce the risk of violent injury in your own life or your family's by changing your lifestyle—kicking a drug habit or avoiding weapons and gangs—since everything that happens is God's will. If you believe the only thing that determines whether you survive a gang fight is whether it's your "time to go," why quit the gang? I was not the only person in my CPE group to hear a patient prove his tight relationship with God by pointing out that he'd just survived his fourth shoot-out with the police.

Sometime in midsummer, Rashid, a new prison patient, turns up for the Genesis hour. He's another alert young man from Riker's who has a medical condition that requires daily medication. After watching the episode on Cain and Abel, Rashid deplores God's preference for Abel's gift instead of Cain's. Why did the Lord lack so much tact in expressing his preference? The newcomer announces that God willed that Abel's gift was more pleasing, so Cain had the cards stacked against him from the start.

After our meeting ends, I talk with Rashid at length. He is a serious Christian, he assures me, who has read the Bible several times and prays regularly. He has no patience with people who don't respond to the Word of God. Why is he at Bellevue? Rashid stopped taking his pills each day and then got sick. He knows that he will "go when it's my time to go, and not before," so it doesn't matter whether or not he takes his medication.

"You don't think God would want you to take your medication?" I ask, horrified, finding it very difficult to take the nonjudgmental tone Chaplain Joseph recommends. The young man reflects, then shrugs. "Yeah, maybe. I don't know." Rashid begins watching the TV over my shoulder, heedless of my stern attempt to show on biblical grounds that God is no Big Brother in the sky.

I was not alone in feeling obliged to try and puncture the God-as-puppeteer belief among Bellevue patients. John, too, felt frustrated when patients ascribed their suffering—or recovery—purely to the will of God. In our morning meeting, John reported a conversation with an ex-prisoner he had come to know well. The man had found a construction job within a few days of coming out on work release and had begun turning around his life. After only two weeks, John's friend had cut off three fingers in an accident at work. Just as he had begun to change his ways, the patient lamented, just as he had begun working hard, gone off drugs, and shunned his bad old friends, "God made this happen."

Reading this story from his typed "verbatim" in the CPE room, John tells us how he jumped in to try and correct the poor man's mistaken notion about God "doing things to him." John explained to the patient that God does not directly cause or inflict evil upon us, but rather, life presents challenges that God grants strength to overcome. He tried to persuade the patient that he should not wish unrealistically for the immediate removal of his suffering; rather, he should pray for the ability to overcome pain and be transformed by it. John told the man not to worry so much about why this had happened to him but instead to think about how he might use his circumstances to make himself stronger and closer to God.

While John reads his verbatim aloud, I make many check marks in the margins of my copy. John articulates a view of God's work in the world that I have been trying to put into words for my inmate patients in 19S. I am about to ask him how and why he developed this theology of suffering when, uncharacteristically, Chaplain Joseph cuts in.

"What made you so quick to correct his views?" Chaplain Joseph asks.

John hesitates, surprised at the question. "I was afraid he'd start to blame God for what happened to him. It's too easy to blame God instead of accepting the situation and moving on."

"That may be true," agrees Joseph. "But tell us about the response of the patient."

John pauses again, then continues reading. The patient clung firmly to his view that God had ordained the accident in order to test him. John's advice almost led to a bitter argument. The end of the report covers John's doubts about how he handled the question of suffering. Had he been too complacent?

Each morning, Chaplain Joseph urges us to examine the degree to which our actions toward patients are motivated by our needs, not theirs. Now Joseph gives the impression that John could have argued for three years about the theology of suffering. This argument, however, would only have raised the patient's blood pressure and entrenched his views more deeply. John might feel better after their discussion, but does the patient feel better? In a Sunday morning parish Bible study, John's words would have been perfectly appropriate. It's difficult, however, to have abstract discussions about God with people whose limbs are missing. Joseph muses that "sometimes, even if their theology is faulty, it may be better than no theology at all."

I return to 19S with these words in mind. My attempts to correct the inmates' literalism and fatalism during our Genesis discussions have shed more heat than light. It is not lost on me that the apostles' healing ministries tended to have greater transformative power than their preaching—and my rhetorical skills are no match for St. Paul's. Our Bible study is stimulating, all right, but a prison ward is probably not the best place to convey a life-changing theological insight.

MY FINAL week in the program, I discover a deeper sort of connection beneath the lively debate of our Genesis group. With Robert, I forge a link not through theological instruction alone, but in my capacity as chaplain. It became a success in ordinary time—an insight not exactly scriptural, but nonetheless pastoral.

After our weekly discussion, I linger in the rec room and hear Robert, in an uncharacteristically disagreeable mood, complain to one of the nurses. She had reprimanded him for missing his physical therapy session that morning, and he retorts that no one showed up to take him to PT; besides, one of the volunteers didn't help him to the shower that morning.

"Sounds to me," she says, "that you're blaming other people for your own lack of initiative in getting down to physical therapy today."

Robert protests.

"I know you're upset about going back to Riker's in a few days, but a lot of your getting so much better here has to do with your good attitude. If you lose that and start blaming everyone for your own problems, you can't get your life back on track."

Other patients start nodding, and Robert stops arguing.

The day before he leaves to return to Riker's Island I come to say good-bye. We talk for the first time about his life before the hospital and his fears about returning to jail. Although I never knew exactly what Robert was charged with, he had been on Riker's for almost ten months without trial, and he explains that the case against him is unfair. All he wants is to get out of jail, find a job, and pick up his life where he left off. What can he do? How could I help him? How is he going to survive?

There was a time when I would have told him quite truthfully that I know a lot of people in the law and that I would try to use my connections to make sure he got a good defense lawyer to move his case. I would have called it outrageous that he was sitting helpless on Riker's, and I wouldn't just sit by. I really would have meant this, too. I'd have made phone calls and sent e-mails to friends who had public interest law jobs. These friends might have given me the names of their mentors—an influential defense lawyer or even a trial-law professor at a top law school, and these people might even respond. I would be helping to right the world's wrongs.

But something would usually happen to change the picture. In this case, perhaps this was Robert's fourth arrest, not his first, or perhaps he wasn't awaiting trial but had already been convicted and was awaiting sentencing. Gradually, the e-mails would dwindle; I would make a few embarrassed apologies to friends who had extended themselves on my behalf; and Robert would still be sitting in jail with still more dashed expectations and yet another reason for placing responsibility for his life on others.

Now, however, sitting by Robert's wheelchair on a red plastic chair in the recreation room of 19S, I suppress the urge to promise deliverance and try to ignore the internal critic who berates my apathy in the face of such *obvious* injustice. I also fight the impulse to lecture Robert—to tell him that God will save him or that justice will be done. These are all theological concepts that I want desperately to be true. Instead, I recall the nurse's words to him a few minutes ago and draw a lesson from the text of Robert's own life in order to help him.

"Robert," I begin, "it seems like your health has made amazing progress since you arrived at Bellevue several weeks ago." Many people have told me his rapid recovery after a crippling stroke is due largely to his own willpower. Couldn't he hold on to this experience in his mind when he returns to Riker's, using the improvement he made in his health as an analogy for what he could do with his spirits? Robert's chances of making it again, of getting his life together in the way that so many people talked about and found so difficult to do, would depend largely on his faith in himself. He would not have the power to determine what kind of charges he might face, but he did have the ability to determine how he would live out his options every day. Would he awake blaming the world and hating himself for his condition, or would he find something to learn from over the course of sixteen waking hours? Perhaps if he could just hold on to his time at Bellevue and remember how he had fought hard and admirably to improve his health —and succeeded—Robert could begin to believe that he had power over other parts of his life. God would be with him in his beginning-to-believe. I do not say all this, but it is my prayer for him.

Robert thanks me. He nods and thanks me again. He thinks a little, nods once more, and smiles. I give him a book of psalms I found in a back closet of the Catholic chaplains' rooms and get up to leave. Robert is smiling when I leave, much as he had smiled during our early arguments about the Bible and the experts with too many questions. Trying not to romanticize, I take from his smile and my response that we have made a deeper connection.

Later that summer I visited Riker's Island with a group of forensic psychiatrists. As we walked the halls, a guard yelled at the prisoners as if we were invisible. We saw one of the prison's suicide prevention strategies—forty-seven people under mental observation lodged in a single room. The Riker's psychiatric staff talked of male and female "populations," their "feeding times," and the retributions they received for "acting out," "malingering," or exhibiting "antisocial behavior." Walking through the jail's gray and green halls, I had few feelings, except a heavy exhaustion that settled in after an hour of passing checkpoints, metal detectors, and clanging iron gates. At the end of the day, our group, fatigue evident on every face, was getting into vans to drive back to Bellevue. Three Canada geese walked across the road in front of us. Their free presence struck me as a poignant reproach—to me, to the institution, and to the whole sorry human condition.

Now that I'd seen the grimy reality of Riker's Island, my hopefulness about Robert's chances of returning to a normal life after incarceration dissolved. How could I trust that my fleeting impressions of his smiles, expressions of gratitude, and our passing experiences of "connection" could help him in the face of the hard statistics about recidivism? Nonetheless, human connection was what I had to hold on to as a chaplain. And it would sometimes give me the same life-sustaining hope that I prayed would be granted to Robert.

Prayers and Psychoses

The Interfaith Chaplaincy's official brochure stated that chaplains could offer "sacraments, prayer, worship services, biblical readings, etc." Sacraments and worship services were really the domain of the full-time chaplains who conducted services in the two chapels on the second floor of the old Bellevue building. As a CPE student, my opportunity to offer the sacraments was minimal, but I could pray with people and read the Bible.

Initially, I disliked praying with patients. Before beginning work at Bellevue, Ellen and I had talked over lunch. How did she feel about the hospital chaplains she'd met during recovery from a serious operation during high school? Ellen laughed. The chaplain had been annoying—constantly asking if she wanted to pray or take communion, when the only thing she wanted was to be left alone to read. The only people she cared to see were her family or the doctor. This offhand observation confirmed my suspicions that chaplains could easily get in the way.

When I start going bedside to bedside in the neurology ICU and other medical floors at Bellevue, I often feel I impose on people's privacy. Why not just introduce myself, state my role, hand out my phone number, and keep moving? I gather from other CPE students that they, too, began with variations of my diffident routine. Several chaplains-in-training also ask if the patient would like to be prayed for. This seems the most forced question I could ask someone I've just met—a sick person whose religious views are unknown to me, apart from the most basic denominational categories that appear on the medical chart. I try asking, anyhow—mostly out of a sense of obligation.

The first few times I ask if a patient or the family would like to say a prayer, I realize that their positive responses spring from mere politeness. The prayer might happen because we both feel dutiful. Except for a blessing I gave at the birth of a child (which I had four hours of labor to rehearse), public prayers are not easy. It is distracting to pray publicly when nurses are checking someone's heart-rate monitor only a few feet away and attendings are conferring with residents behind the plastic curtain.

What worked best were the prayers that came unsolicited—at the patient's request—though these prayers, too, could disconcert.

I meet Isaiah the first time I visit 18E, the homeless adult psychiatric unit. 18E is not locked down like 19S—there are no automatic iron gates and no metal detectors, but the sense of confinement is almost more powerful. Locked double doors lead to the wards. Residents and nurses have their own keys, but I must knock on the thick glass square (a feature of every door on the ward) to get the attendant's attention. The nurse's station beyond these doors resembles an air traffic control tower—desk staff work behind glass panels overlooking the hallway. Patients have to tap on the glass to be noticed.

When I go onto the ward after a nurse's invitation to look around, patients who are not wandering aimlessly or arguing with the nurses are dozing or watching TV. I pass a thin black woman with a red kerchief on her head, hollow eyes, and puffy lips, who gestures frantically at no one in particular. A friendly looking Middle Eastern man with a childish, adoring smile is followed by a heavyset, graying man wearing an old pair of Topsiders who wants to know why I'm not his doctor. At the end of the hallway, I notice a dark, somewhat sinister-looking figure sitting against the wall. I must pass him to get to the final rooms, so I devise a brusque smile while preparing an introduction. Slowly his dark face comes to life. "Chaplain? You're a chaplain? Can you help me with my prayers?"

When he stands, I see that Isaiah is a tall, disheveled African American with unsettling light-blue eyes and a large gap between his two front teeth. He looks in his mid-forties, but it is hard to be sure. Eyelids drooping (the sedative effect of his medication, I learn), he speaks in sentences that trail off into incoherent mumble. Isaiah has no fingers on one hand and only three on the other; his hands were frostbitten during a harsh winter on the New York streets.

Nervously, I wait for Isaiah to retrieve his prayers from his room. As we walk together back down the hallway, he asks if I can get some green plants for his room. I'd ask if plants were allowed, thinking that probably I will forget. In the common room used for doctor-patient consultations, Isaiah produces his prayers for my inspection. Clasped between his palms are about twenty small squares of scrap paper with pencil-written prayers in large, childish handwriting. A few bring me up short:

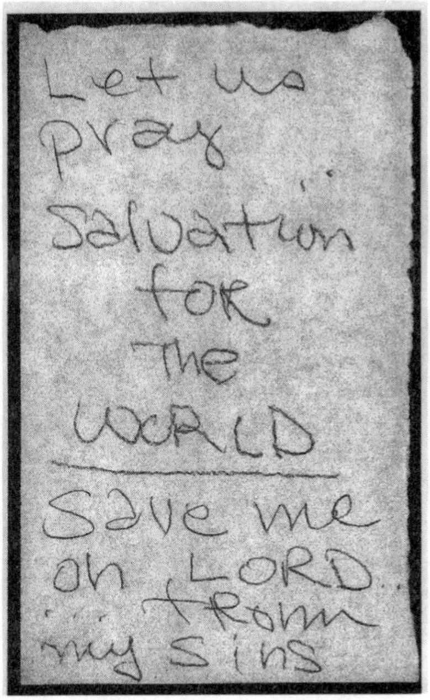
Let us
pray
Salvation
for
The
WORLD

Save me
oh LORD..
from
my sins

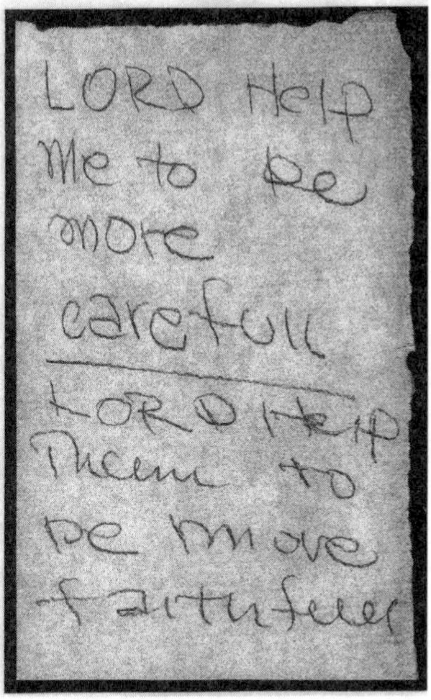
LORD Help
me to be
more
carefull

LORD Help
Them to
be more
faithfull

Other prayers are scrawled on other pieces of paper, and there are several scraps with the letter "P" written in neat lines. Among a group of nonsensical writings I see:

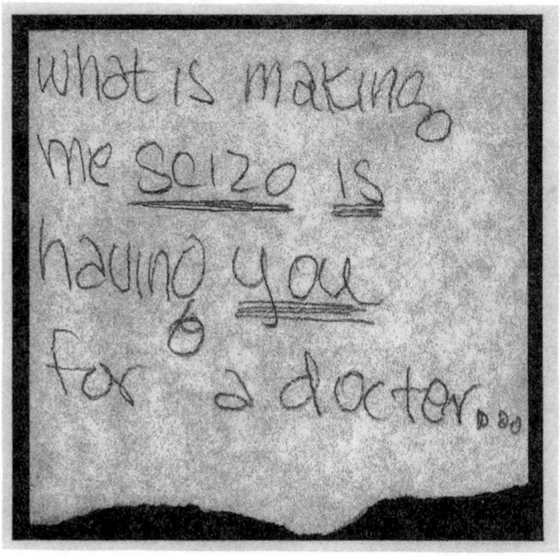

I gather from Isaiah and a conversation with one of the nurses that he grew up somewhere in the Midwest. He'd been an artist and may even have taught art. He mentions a couple named Steve and Melinda whom he claims to have lived with for awhile. From his medical chart, I see that Isaiah spent almost a decade in a New Jersey hospital during the 1980s. After his release, he must have lived for several years on the streets of New York. The chart explains that Isaiah was picked up at the end of May at Grand Central Station for "bizarre behavior." At Bellevue, he'd been judged a danger to himself or others and is being treated with antipsychotic drugs. Comments by the nurses on his chart call him "highly disorganized" and "delusional." Isaiah is far from a model patient. Like most patients on 18E, he suffers from a schizophrenic disorder.

After Isaiah shares his prayers with me, we develop a routine. Every other day, when I make rounds in 18E, Isaiah and I go over his prayers. Together, we might say one or two as we sit facing each other across the common room table. I am always slightly on guard in that area of the hospital and never lose the wariness aroused by my first glimpse of Isaiah. He is the one who moves our relationship forward—generally saying something surprising or interesting as we talk.

On my second or third visit to 18E, I find Isaiah extremely anxious, pacing up and down by the window of his room. I tell him to get his prayers and we'll go to the common room, where I ask him what's wrong.

"Prayer doesn't work for me anymore," Isaiah announces bleakly. "I prayed to make this itching go away, and it didn't go away."

I knew that the itching was probably a side effect of the drugs he took, but, as a chaplain, I am not supposed to give medical advice or offer explanations.

"Have you asked the doctor about it?" I ask.

"No. God didn't answer my prayers. I'm on God's hit list," Isaiah replies glumly.

I reflect that if I were locked up in a psych ward, getting large doses of medication with uncomfortable side effects, I, too, might feel well up on God's hit list. I do not contradict him. This is too interesting.

"But Isaiah," I continue, "why would God ever put you on a hit list? What kind of God would put anyone on his hit list?"

"Oh, God's just like anyone else," Isaiah answers impatiently. "You can't get mad at God or he will get offended and then he'll curse you. God used to answer my prayers, but now he doesn't anymore."

I try to tell Isaiah about all the people in the Bible who didn't get their prayers answered in the way they wanted. There is Job, and Jonah, and Christ himself when he prayed to have the cup pass from him in the garden of Gesthemane. That didn't mean they were on God's hit list, though.

Isaiah was having none of this. When would he get out of this hospital? He is sick of being inside and hates the way he is treated. He wants to get out as soon as he can, and he wants me to help.

Rather than answer, I begin asking what he liked so much about being outside. Why would he want to be on the street? Wasn't it a difficult way to live?

"Oh no," Isaiah answers. "I like being free to go anywhere I want. I like sitting in Grand Central watching people and bumming cigarettes."

"Why do you like people-watching?" I ask.

Isaiah peers narrowly at me, concerned that I am slow catching on. "People are interesting to watch, that's why." He sighs and thinks for a moment before adding, "Also, I like feeling the sun on me."

We sit together in silence for a while, before Isaiah asks to say a prayer together. Isaiah presses his palms together, and we pray that God may be with Isaiah wherever he is, whether he is inside or outside, in nature or in a building. Silently, I resolve to learn more about why Isaiah is being kept at Bellevue.

After our prayer, Isaiah's voice sounds thankful. "No one here understands me like you do. Everyone else here thinks I'm a joke." I am about to assure him that he is no joke, and everyone knows that, when he interrupts to ask if I know that President Clinton was born in New Jersey.

THE FOLLOWING week, I screw up my courage and approach the head physician on Isaiah's ward, who works closely with him. The Wednesday morning staff meeting I sit in on occasionally shows me that the doctor in charge of the ward is a severe-looking woman who, like so many professionals at Bellevue, probably has a kind heart but disguises it well. With short dark hair, glasses, and pointed features,

Dr. Threadgill is all business. She speaks quickly in those meetings and isn't afraid to cut people off in midsentence. With some trepidation, today I'll ask her about Isaiah.

After a week of leaving messages and arriving at Dr. Threadgill's office on 18E minutes after she departs, I stand outside her office rehearsing my inquiry. She quickly answers my tentative knock and brings me into her office, where another doctor sits.

"Oh!" I start, "I'm sorry to disturb you. I wonder if you have time at some point to answer a question I have about Isaiah?"

"I have some time right now," Dr. Threadgill answers, in a way that suggests she doesn't. "What is your question?"

I blank and look nervously at the other doctor. I had not expected to be put on the spot. Both doctors wait for me to speak.

"Ah, I was wondering ... I know Isaiah's case is coming up for review, um, I was just curious about the factors that go into the decision of whether or not certain patients are a danger to themselves or others. I just want to learn more about how that sort of decision is determined—particularly in Isaiah's case. From some of the conversations I've had with him, he seems to think that he is ready to leave ..."

Dr. Threadgill interrupts.

"Have you looked at Isaiah's hands lately?" she asks curtly, in a way that is not really a question.

Hands? What would Isaiah's hands have to do with anything? Somehow, although I clasped his palms only a few days ago, I've forgotten that Isaiah lost his fingers to frostbite. Over the course of our conversations and prayers, I stopped noticing his handicap.

"Oh, yes, you mean the frostbite?" I say, mortified.

"Yes, the frostbite," she replies, dismissing me with a slight nod.

I feel very foolish. Chaplain Joseph has stressed that pastoral care means having one foot in the murky waters of your patient's world and the other foot solidly planted on firm ground. We can't reach a suffering person if both feet are on dry land, but, equally, we can't help by losing our own groundedness.

After the doctor's sharp reminder, I feel that I've swan-dived into the deep end in my dealings with Isaiah. How could I have lost my sense of objectivity so quickly? A chronically ill homeless man asks me to pray with him, describing his obsessional disorder and hallucinations in religious language, and suddenly I'm certain he's misunderstood by the medical professionals who are responsible for him. I am angry at myself and transfer that feeling to Isaiah.

I will not visit him individually so often—clearly, I can't handle someone so manipulative. As if he divined my conversation with his doctor, the next time I see Isaiah he is sitting alone in the common room, his prayers fanned out on the table before him. When I walk over to invite him to join the group that will soon convene in the room, he silently picks one of his old prayers from his pocket, carefully tears out the word "surprise," stuffs it into his mouth, chews, and swallows.

That was it. Ignoring Isaiah's complaints that I didn't visit him anymore, I steer clear of 18E. I make sure my occasional visits occur only in the context of some group activity. I know that Isaiah has caused problems for some nurses, and his medication must have been increased, because when he does attend my meetings he falls asleep in his chair.

The lesson is, be wary of praying with the mentally unstable. Prayer in this instance is too radically equalizing. It is too effective a reminder that God's love is like the sun and rain that shines and pours on good and evil alike—a concept that makes sense, but plays havoc with our need for order in the here and now. The prayer and conversation Isaiah and I shared made me feel the common bond of humanity between us —but what about our differences? One early Christian writer describes prayer as arrows shot at God, but most people are aware that prayer breaks down barriers between people, too. That summer at Bellevue, it might have been better if a few more barriers between me and my 18E patients had stayed intact. After Isaiah, I grew reluctant to pray in other parts of the hospital without knowing an individual's context.

I spent several weeks avoiding Isaiah, hoping that at least I might be able to chalk up our explorations in prayer to pastoral experience. I knew that he was due to be transferred to Rockland State Hospital, and I would be glad to see him go. Seeing him reminded me of my own gullibility and lapses of judgment.

SOMETIME toward the end of that summer, Greg and I rented the film *One Flew Over the Cuckoo's Nest.* I had never seen it, and everyone in my CPE group said it was a good way of gaining perspective on our work at Bellevue. Another perspective on Bellevue was probably the last thing I needed, but, nonetheless, I watched it.

The film affected me deeply. Jack Nicholson was, in many ways, a model chaplain. He relished life, expected a lot of his fellow inmates, and was determined to teach them pride and self-respect, whether through basketball or sailing. Nicholson's character saw the potential in his fellow patients through these activities in the same way I'd glimpsed Isaiah's humanity in our prayers together. After turning off the VCR, I knew that my discovery of dignity in mentally ill people did not entail a responsibility to break open the hospital's doors. I could empathize with a neighbor without ignoring his psychological limitation.

That evening, I remember that the first time we met, Isaiah had expressed a wish for a plant. I buy a small one with thick leaves that needs only a little water; it's rooted in a basket with a large handle that will fit over his wrist. I telephone the chaplain at Rockland Hospital to make sure they won't take the plant away from him when he arrives. Saying good-bye, Isaiah gives me the rest of his prayers, which he has arranged in a small book-like packet.

The last time I saw him, Isaiah was walking away through the heavy swinging doors of Ward 18E, escorted by a policeman and a nurse, the new plant basket dangling from his wrist.

Adam's Rib

I learned early that as chaplains-in-training we were not supposed to be instructors of morality—allies in moral struggles or facilitators of conscience, perhaps, but definitely not directors, or even teachers.

This lesson became clear as I listened to the verbatims of my group. Some accounts were more pastoral than others. For example, Bob's story about his relationship with a homeless alcoholic in recovery, an expert panhandler who divulged to Bob all the tricks of his trade, sounded more "ministerial" to me than Thomas's instructions to a man in similar circumstances. Thomas told this addicted individual, who turned himself into detox at Bellevue every few weeks when he needed a temporary drying out, that "God loved him and would expect more of him." Though Thomas had doubtless spoken the truth, his verbatim created an uproar in the CPE room. It left me feeling terribly sorry for the poor man whose low self-esteem could not have been boosted by a young chaplain implying that God, too, was disgusted by his behavior. Chaplain Joseph commended Thomas for being "real" with his patient but also stressed the difficulty of preaching morality from above—a practice that might work from the pulpit but was less effective on a ward. In contrast, the admirable trust Bob had generated with his patient was clear from the man's free telling of detailed life stories.

My own experience told me that trying to play the guardian angel who dispels a patient's demons was not a productive use of a chaplain's energy. I was very proud of my progress with Colin, a Rastafarian from Brooklyn who wound up in the neurology ICU after being mugged. Colin had solicited my help in his struggle between his religious principles, which required peace and forgiveness, and his instinct for revenge. I'd thrown myself into the part he cast for me—supplying him with the stories of several biblical figures who were rewarded for prevailing over temptation. All went well until one afternoon. We were role-playing how Colin might react if someone called him with a tip on his mugger's identity. The phone rang. "Where the *hell* is my money? I told you that's MY money! Where the hell is it?" Colin yelled into the receiver without stopping for breath. Later he explained he was talking to his baby's mother, as if that justified the outburst. Colin said he was relieved, too. He didn't have to worry anymore about violating his nonviolent principles because his brother had taken it upon himself to beat up the people whom he suspected of mugging Colin. Still, he hoped that I would return soon and read to him more about King David.

Despite such evidence that placing myself in the position of a finger-wagging instiller of high principles didn't work, it seemed impossibly hard to avoid. I fell into this trap more than once, though it was painfully clear that imposing my own ideas of morally admirable behavior on a patient was fruitless unless the patient was searching for guidance.

Take Adam, a patient I met in the neurology ICU. The harder I tried not to impress upon him my own values, the more transparent my earnestness became.

When I first meet Adam, he is not a pretty sight. His medical chart notes that Adam has "jumped/been pushed?" from the window of a large Manhattan apartment during a party. A livid surgical scar bisects his shaved head; one eye is swollen shut, and a yellow-green rainbow of bruises arches across his face, one arm, and side. Adam, who is being fed through a stomach tube, can barely speak because of the tracheal tube in his neck. He breathes laboriously and flails around so much that he must be forcibly restrained. Seeing Adam as a deranged patient who'll be sent up to 18E when his physical ailments heal, I approach gingerly and take his wild gesticulations and raspy calls for water as hallucinations.

I realize there may be more to Adam only when I arrive at his bedside one day and find an elderly gentleman, Adam's uncle, leaning over the bed. He calls gently, "Adam, Adam, it's me. Your aunt and I have sorted out your apartment; we've turned off the gas and will come by to check your mail. Everything is taken care of, so don't you worry. It's all going to be fine." I am shocked at how my perceptions change with this new framing. To see someone who knows Adam speak to him about homely matters, as though he could grasp the conversation, brings me up short. After that, I sit longer, deciphering his scrawled notes about being afraid and wanting to see his uncle or wondering where he is. A conscious, rational person lies behind Adam's appearance and wildness. Usually, I carry on a short, one-sided conversation about how everything was going to be OK. Please, Adam, try to relax and don't try to get out of the bed; I can't give you water right now because of your tracheal tube, but the nurse can definitely bring some relief.

The real miracle comes when Adam is transferred to rehabilitation. It has taken a few days to find him, and a weekend has elapsed between visits. When I enter his room, Adam is sitting in a wheelchair by the sink, swabbing his face with wet paper towels. The swelling has abated, and his bruises are fading. He looks up inquiringly.

"Hello," I say, "I'm an associate chaplain here. I've been visiting you upstairs. You look much, much better!"

"Ah yes," replies Adam in a slightly nasal voice, "my uncle told me about you. I understand you've been quite a faithful visitor," he continues, smiling wryly. "Thank you very much."

Adam is a financial analyst who lives on his own in Manhattan. He grew up in a large Roman Catholic family in small-town Louisiana and attended Princeton. He thought about being a doctor but decided on business school. Adam is well read, well traveled, and enjoys what he calls the good things of life—music, literature, food, drink, and the company of good friends. The Roman Catholic faith of his childhood disappeared during his first year of college, when he began to "understand the world as it really is." Now, Adam volunteers, the only time he believes in God is when he listens to Mozart. He respects people who are religious, but, honestly, the whole thing doesn't much interest him. Adam and I enjoy chatting. No doubt, our shared middle-classness makes it fun to socialize with him. I describe my interest in entrepreneurial public service programs, and we compare undergraduate experiences. I ask his preferred authors, and he tells me about his favorite New York restaurants and the great meals he's enjoyed in London and Moscow. Although Adam could be both arrogant and condescending, his dry wit made for entertaining talk. He hadn't, for example, been able to make the Bellevue psychiatrists understand that he didn't want "happy pills—just a small leg of lamb, *puh-lease.*"

Adam's continually irreverent, occasionally condescending ribbing about religion touches a sensitive spot in me, though. Added to queries from others in my CPE group, my reaction makes me wonder if socializing with Adam is inappropriate. I am supposed to be his chaplain, not his dinner guest. Shouldn't I try to probe deeper matters, even if they are harder to discuss?

After all, despite Adam's degrees and accomplishments, he is at Bellevue recovering from what I assume (with no proof) has been a suicide attempt. At the very least, Adam behaved in a reckless fashion that, I believed, pointed to serious emotional problems. Although he has told me and everyone else in the hospital that he won't discuss what happened the night he fell, it seems my duty to make sure that he acknowledges that something is missing from his life. I feel responsible for moving Adam to attend to his psychic wounds as well as the physical injury.

This will be my agenda with Adam. I resolve to disguise it well, as I know the dangers of imposing one's views on patients. But there has to be something to show for our relationship. I could consider myself successful at chaplaincy if I succeeded in having Adam admit his confusion.

One afternoon, Adam is explaining how amusing he finds the young residents who try to locate his pulse without success. "They couldn't find anything because they held both fingers on my plastic wristband," he chortles. Adam deplores how seriously the psychiatrists underestimate his knowledge of their field and satirizes the transparency of their questions.

"When you have had the background and education that you and I have had, Chloe," Adam confides, "you know a lot about how these things work."

I smile and stay quiet, trying to turn our conversation to the issues on my agenda.

Adam continues talking, almost in a reverie, about his recommendations for improving Bellevue—some basic things are needed, like less noise and more courtesy. He understands that a public hospital probably couldn't offer the amenities of a well-endowed private one. "But I'm really not used to this sort of atmosphere," he explains, adding that when he has to stay home with a cold, an army of retainers is mobilized.

"Usually, I have everything, meals and all, delivered in. My assistant makes sure I have the work I need. This is really a new experience. My friends are amused."

I spy an opportunity to investigate. "So who are these 'friends' you keep talking about? Are they close friends?"

Adam catches me looking down my nose and replies vaguely that they are people who understand him—some from Princeton he's kept up with over the years, more recent acquaintances from around the city.

Suddenly he is defensive. "If I really wanted to leave here, you know, I could. I would just call up all my friends, and they would come and get me right away. I know how to get things done. If I really wanted to get out of here, I could fly right out that window."

I nod, and we sit in silence. Much later that afternoon the significance of his threat strikes home, and I am seriously alarmed.

"I've learned," says Adam then, switching subjects, "that I'm being prayed for from all over the map. People in all fifty states are praying for me, according to my aunt. I found out that a group of forty women I don't even know is praying for me. It's very sweet, I think, don't you? En*dear*ing."

I remember how worried his aunt was when she and her husband visited Adam in the ICU. She had asked me to anoint him with holy water, even though I wasn't Roman Catholic. Adam's condescension angers me.

"Why are you glad they're praying for you if you don't even believe in God?"

"Oh, I think it's great that some people believe in religion," Adam says airily. "I respect it very much. It's just that I don't think God exists for me. I don't know very much about it. If push came to shove I think there's about a fifty-fifty chance that God exists—so probably I do believe. But, I've told you already, religion doesn't interest me that much. I enjoy talking about other things."

I deliberately ignore the hint and keep probing. "So you don't care if I pray for you or not?"

Slightly exasperated, Adam says, "You should pray for people without money, without any kind of education. Pray for those who get trampled by the world and don't know to push back. They need your prayers. Me, I know how to push back a little bit. I know how to get things done. I've learned how to say 'no' or 'not right now,' or 'no thank you very much,' or just 'NO.' It works."

I back off. Has Adam imagined the first thing he'll do when he leaves the hospital?

"I'm going to have a huge party and invite all my friends and everyone who helped me to recover," Adam replies dryly, looking past me out the window.

On the way to the elevator, I feel ambivalent. It did not occur to me that Adam was egging me on. I could not let his last comment go by. Just as the elevator door opens, I resolve to confront Adam right away. I turn back and knock on his door.

"Adam, I just thought I should let you know that I've thought about what you said about throwing a party, and it upsets me a little bit. I mean, isn't that how you ended up coming here?"

The minute the words come out, I want to swallow them whole.

His back to me, Adam bursts out angrily, "I told you in the most diplomatic way I could that I did *not* want to talk about the accident. I don't know what happened to me that night, and I'm not going to discuss it till I get better physically and am at home and will seek expert advice. I can take care of myself, thank you very much, and, technically, this is none of your business. You are out of your league. Good-bye."

IT TURNED out that I had not destroyed the fragile trust remaining between Adam and me. I summoned the courage to return and found his manner almost the same. He accepted my apology, and our usual conversation began. He complained that the nurses were unsympathetic when he insisted that visiting family was more important than "spending another half hour jumping around on a pogo stick in rehab." I manage a smile when he jokes about his "infamous welcome-home party" and invites me to attend with an oxygen mask and a stretcher, since I worry so much about his health. Adam and I remain on good terms until I leave Bellevue.

Still, I was disappointed and alarmed that I did not resist the impulse to preach at him. By the time I brought it up with my CPE group, I anticipated Chaplain Joseph's suggestion to hesitate before "rushing in where angels fear to tread." Too well I knew the answer to his question about whether my wish to hear Adam confess dark doubts had more to do with Adam's needs, or mine. But how could I—so proud of my open-mindedness and ability to embrace diversity—be perceived as "pushing the religion stuff a little too strongly," as Adam scoffed. I had indeed "rushed in" to the life of someone who was perhaps spiritually wounded, but also perhaps mentally ill beyond my powers to assist. I *thought* I understood the concept of pastoral engagement in moral questions, but clearly not well enough to put it into effect.

Pastoral engagement stayed mysterious. How I could get involved with a patient's moral dilemma without, on one hand, agreeing with everything he said, or, on the other, without imposing my own views? The choice still seemed to me to lie between relativism and close-minded dogmatism. Although I never worked out a satisfactory answer to this puzzle in my own pastoral work, one of Mary's experiences let me glimpse a solution.

MARY HAD taken time off from the neonatal ward to visit the obstetrics ward. A nurse on the ward pointed out a young woman who had just had an abortion; her mother sat beside the bed. Mary went over to introduce herself and began talking with the patient, an African American in her early twenties.

Tashi wondered if she would be "forgiven" for what she'd done. Noticing the "confession" and "forgiveness," language, Mary inquired further.

The young woman and her mother had arrived at Bellevue a few days before, seeking an abortion for Tashi after the baby's father disappeared. She and her mother feared that Tashi wouldn't be able to bring up her child alone. The mother was adamant on this point. At Bellevue, all had gone according to plan, until they discovered after the operation that Tashi had been carrying twins.

"I don't know," Tashi told Mary tearfully, "somehow when I heard it was twins it seemed like this was a gift. Something really special."

Mary caught the inconsistency. Twins would have been twice the work and demanded twice the resources of a single baby—all the more reason for their choice, if Tashi and her mother really meant what they said about being too poor to raise a child. Now Tashi cried that had she known she was carrying twins she might have kept them.

Then Mary did something pastoral. She pursued her curiosity and asked the young woman if she could elaborate on her feelings.

Again, Tashi said it was because twins felt like a gift, a special thing.

Mary suspected there was more to the story. From the overbearing quality of the mother, she gathered there was heavy maternal pressure on Tashi to keep up appearances even within their own family, most of whom had no idea what had taken place. This pressure must have weighed heavily in the hasty decision to seek an abortion—and getting rid of the child was the tragic means of saving face and avoiding shame.

Not once, however, did the church's or Mary's personal position on the morality of abortion enter their conversation. "Right" or "wrong" was never mentioned. By inquiring with sensitivity, compassion, and natural curiosity into Tashi's situation, Mary engaged the young woman and her mother in an honest conversation about the abortion—a conversation they probably would not have dreamed of having with someone in the church. Mary heard Tashi express her sorrow in the language of Christian faith, and she opened the way for the young woman to continue talking with a priest or pastor who might help her to move beyond regret. Listening to Mary, I thought that the tragedy was not so much the abortion itself as it was the fact that such a large decision had been made so hastily and with no outside guidance. The church was the last place Tashi and her mother felt they could turn.

Mary's story recalled the last time I had thought deeply about the morality of abortion, at a pro-choice march in Washington, D.C. Now the difference between a pastoral approach and other approaches to moral issues grew clearer. Mary had not been discussing an important "issue" in the abstract, she'd had a poignant conversation with Tashi. In a pastoral setting, Mary's own views or the church's views on the morality of abortion in principle were far less important for the young woman's life than uncovering Tashi's own feelings of remorse. Tashi was the one who would ultimately have to be reconciled to herself in order to move ahead. She alone would know how God's forgiveness would allow her to embrace her own life again. And Mary, the good chaplain, had shown Tashi that reconciliation was worth pursuing.

Ordinary Time

In the Gospel story of Mary and Martha, Jesus is welcomed into the home of two sisters. While Martha hastily prepares dinner for the honored guest, her sister Mary sits at Jesus' feet and listens to his teachings. Martha, irritated by her sister's unhelpfulness, demands assistance in the kitchen. Jesus reprimands her, saying, "Martha, Martha, you are worried and distracted by many things; there is need of only one thing. Mary has chosen the better part."

No matter how often I hear preachers say that everyone possesses both Mary- and Martha-like characteristics, I still hear Jesus esteeming contemplation more than action—in CPE terms, he commends the "be-er" not the "do-er." As a Martha myself, and one for whom advocacy comes naturally, this passage is a blow. Like other Marthas, I'm quick to pick up the phone or write a protest letter. I assume that the world's problems—from environmental degradation to domestic violence and political oppression—can be solved if we awaken enough consciences, tap the right pro bono lawyers, fire off enough well-timed press releases.

Although Jesus doesn't say so explicitly, I believe Martha's natural tendencies are more helpful in some contexts than in others. For example, my own lifelong Pavlovian reaction to others' distress was unconstructive when set down in a big, busy public hospital. My advocacy impulse was triggered by every passing wheelchair but lacked any backup nonprofit organization or public-interest lawyer to support it. I began to feel frenzied—like a computer receiving an e-mail virus that multiplies exponentially throughout its system.

My activist gene made the social work function of chaplaincy rather easy for me. If a meeting needed to involve physicians, social workers, family, and friends in a medical decision, I'd organize it. If a patient in the hospital's lockup worried about losing her lease, I'd call the landlord. If a dying patient wanted a phone call from her son in jail, it was an exciting challenge to arrange that call. Few requests were too trivial to champion. Even menial errands like paying the TV rental man could feel more productive to me than sitting in uncomfortable silence by someone's bedside.

Possibly detecting a frenetic quality in some of my activities, Chaplain Joseph and the rest of the group react tepidly to my reports of how busy I am. Although I expect a cold shoulder from the social workers who resent encroachments on their territory, my own group's lack of enthusiasm surprises me. Why do these people rarely think that mobilizing resources or calling in experts is the right way to relieve suffering? What kind of internship is this, where my resourceful attempts to contact public defenders are called defense mechanisms or avoidance techniques?

Invariably, my reports of social work touch off another debate about whether chaplains should always "do" things for our patients—or was it better to "be with" them in their pain or fear? It's not my activity alone that generates this recurrent debate. If Thomas calls a nurse at a patient's request he might be accused of "doing" something for the patient, rather than "being there" for him. If Mary spends half the day on the phone tracking down a public notary, she might be avoiding the far more difficult task of simply "being with" the patient who asks this favor.

Defending himself during our morning discussion, Thomas exclaims, "It seems a little indulgent that while everyone else in this hospital has a lot of tasks to accomplish, our job is simply to be present to our patients." I agree. Coming from a world that judges people largely by their productivity, it's difficult to spend months in a place where there is so much suffering and injustice present, yet where I am asked mostly to "be."

One reason for my skepticism is that the call to "be" becomes a convenient alibi for not doing anything in a place where it is difficult to get anything done. When John, for example, reports comforting an elderly Latino woman who claims that the resident who operated on her hip made a mistake and refused to admit it, my warning bells go off. John's analysis almost exclusively records his "being" with the patient—how he recovered his presence of mind after an early faux pas and prayed harmoniously with the woman for strength and guidance before he left. Although she told John that she had a second opinion and that she was not being treated well, he made no move to follow up—to call patient advocacy, a translator, or the resident who performed her surgery. How well they had gotten along during his twenty-minute visit seems to matter more. To me, John's "being" with the woman as a calming presence was no substitute for taking action to make sure she was treated properly.

My own energy-intensive attempts at righting wrongs at Bellevue, though, often produce little more than dashed expectations. The time I spend getting transferred from department to department, or sitting on hold with the hospital switchboard, might have been better spent drying tears. When Chaplain Joseph said that ultimately "God is love," I took him to mean that our responsibility as chaplains was to create acts of kindness, not struggles for justice.

Simply "being" felt a bit forced, but if I practiced hard enough I might learn to excel at it. Part of the problem was that even when I was trying my best just to be, I was still always doing—speaking to a patient, thinking of something to say, wishing that I hadn't said what I did say. I worried about listening closely enough, worried about listening too closely, worried about being overheard, and worried that the conversation would fly from my mind the moment it was assigned as a write-up. All this "doing" took most of the few minutes of a short talk. Perhaps "being" simply meant speaking more slowly or trying to relax when no one can find the right thing to say.

Of course, recalling the Tibetan Buddhist monks I had taught English to in South Asia, I knew that "being" wasn't about doing nothing. "Being" did not dictate that we ignore social problems or give a spiritual stamp of approval to the hospital authorities. When Chaplain Joseph talked about "being," I think he meant overcoming a fear of silence, becoming mindful, learning to listen, and—when taking action—not letting one's own desires to act supplant a patient's need for comfort. This was no passive way of being.

ACTING IN light of the patient's sense of purpose rather than your own embodied the most authentic social-work function of a chaplain. For me, it was most severely tested by someone I met early that summer and continued to agonize over until my last day at Bellevue.

Antony K. was one of the neediest, most irritating patients I met. I first came into contact with him while visiting one of his many roommates, a sixty-five-year-old Russian Jewish emigrant who had taught engineering in the Ukraine and was recovering from a stroke. Antony's pleading gaze and incessant requests to get him a nurse or a glass of water became more and more difficult to avoid as I went in and out of the room. At one point he asked me, "Sometime can you come and visit me, too?"

A stout man in his late fifties, with graying hair and a flaccid, pudgy face, Antony grew up in Brooklyn. He attended City University, joined the navy, started a graphic design business, and married young. At some point during his late thirties or early forties, however, he became manic-depressive. His marriage ended; he lost his job; and he lived on the streets for a couple of years. With the help of Jewish social service organizations and a dedicated social worker, Antony had gotten medication and moved into his own apartment near Times Square. For the last couple of years, he had lived with his girlfriend. He attended meetings of his psychosocial club for formerly homeless people and lived on benefits he received for his depressive illness and from the military.

Antony's life was still in semishambles when he was admitted to Bellevue for treatment of blurred vision and headaches. His girlfriend claimed he'd abused her, taking the opportunity of his departure to move out herself. Still, his life was more stable than it had been on the streets.

There was a cloying quality in Antony's manner that fit a large toddler better than a middle-aged man. Whether he was sitting upright in bed or lying down with the back ratcheted up, his eyes were almost always trained on the door, mutely appealing for something from someone. His bed needs adjusting; his food is cold; or he's asked a nurse three times for his medication, and she still has not returned. Whatever I've been discussing with Antony leaves his mind the moment I make a move to leave. A kind of clawing panic sets in. Suddenly, Antony needs me to do three vital things—two of which involve phone calls. I can't leave without telling him the day and time I'll return.

ANTONY is in Bellevue because he has a large brain tumor. On four separate occasions, having given his permission for a biopsy, he has revoked it moments before entering the operating room. His social worker is at her wit's end; the nurses are completely fed up. Antony's friends from the psycho-social club seem at a loss to know how to help —particularly since Antony indiscriminately asks everyone who enters his room for advice about the test. The whole cast of characters around this patient—myself included—feels addled by him. Unattractive qualities and all, Antony is very difficult to ignore.

When I ask about the biopsy, Antony claims he received incomplete information from his neurologist, so he refused the operation. He wants his old social worker, the doctors, his friends, and me to all sit down with him to help him decide. He will probably get no new information, but—like everyone else—I feel Antony should act, so I agree to organize this huge meeting.

About a week later, with a friend, his old social worker, and two doctors finally assembled around his bed, we all get a clear view of the enemy. The doctor puts on the light box the X rays of Antony's head in cross section, showing a tumor filling nearly a quarter of his brain. The doctor recommends an immediate biopsy to determine the type of tumor, but even the most medically illiterate among us realize that Antony has only a short time to live. I am not in Antony's good graces that day and am not allowed to stay in the room for the ensuing discussion of his future.

Later I ask what he thought when he saw the X ray.

"Well I know I wasn't born with it," Antony says, beginning to weep. This is one of only a few moments of genuine empathy with Antony. A small sliver of neighborliness appears between us as we share our fear of death. I will try to comfort this dying man, no matter how objectionable he is.

Although most of my resolution dissolves the next time Antony orders me off to find a nurse, I manage to keep one aspect intact. Greg and I are still house-training our two small puppies. Antony spoke fondly of a dog he once owned; between errands, I had related the diabolical antics of my two shih tzu puppies. He seemed to enjoy tales of the latest rug destruction and the pair of slippers gnawed to a wet pulp. Reflecting on Antony's X rays, I decide to smuggle one of my puppies into the hospital one evening to surprise him.

I spend a hair-raising evening packing the less frisky puppy into a knapsack, riding crosstown, and walking as nonchalantly as I can past hospital security—praying desperately that the dog won't begin barking in the elevator. Seeing my white jacket, the unit's desk nurse waves me on. Antony is awake and gazing at the door. Luckily, his roommate is asleep. When the puppy tumbles out of my knapsack, Antony is delighted, petting the dog while it licks his hands. They commune for about a minute and a half before I'm scared that a nurse will arrive.

The puppy is zipped back in my pack and I'm heading out the door when Anthony shouts, "Didn't you say there were *two* dogs?"

Further evidence of the potential treacherousness of doing something for patients that reflects merely one's own notions of what is good for them came just a few weeks later. Thomas, who had been on call over the weekend and visited Antony, told me that the patient had asked to be brought communion—an important thing to do, at last.

I looked forward to the first opportunity to give communion in a hospital. Maybe the sacraments would help Antony end his denial of death. With my supervisor's approval, I take the elements to his room —juice and wafers consecrated by the Catholic chaplains.

Antony is lying in his bed, as usual, facing the door. His eyes are half shut, and he seems groggier today. Receiving more pain medication as the tumor grows, he tends to drift in and out of sleep during conversations. I touch his arm to make sure he's awake and show him the communion wafers.

Opening his eyes wider, Antony nods slowly. He seems incapable of sitting up, so I adjust the bed and help him turn onto his back so that he can recline slightly upright. "Do you want to take communion?" I ask again, and he nods slightly, so I know he hears me. I open the communion set, say a blessing, make the sign of the cross over the bread, and offer it to Antony.

The juice goes down smoothly as he lifts his head and swallows. The communion wafer, however, becomes a problem.

I can't remember if I placed the wafer on his tongue, or if he put it in his mouth himself. I do recall that the wafer stayed there a very long time. At first, when I see Antony's mouth half open, the wafer resting delicately on his partially protruding tongue, I think he may be contemplating the solemn moment, and I take the opportunity to pray myself. When I look up again a few minutes later and see that motionless wafer, panic rises.

This is a chaplain's worst nightmare. What if Antony has gone into a coma? Was this like his biopsy—Antony thinking he wants communion, then changing his mind? What if he's dead? None of these possible explanations is appealing—and, regardless, we are still celebrating a supposedly sacred moment. What shall I do?

I stare at the wafer, wondering how long before it dissolves on its own. Centuries pass. Finally, after six or seven motionless minutes, I lean forward to shake one chubby arm: "Antony, are you all right?"

Sluggishly, the patient opens one eye. Without changing expression or position, he gradually closes his mouth.

During our debriefing the next morning, I remain deeply unsettled by the communion incident. Something was wrong, I report to the group. Whether he'd fallen asleep or not, Antony seems deeply ambivalent about the Eucharist.

Silence in the room. From the corner, Mary says tentatively, "Um, didn't you say a few weeks ago that Antony was Jewish?"

Everyone looks at me. This can't be true, I think.

But Mary's words ring a faint bell. When I first met Antony, he said his family had been Jewish but he and his girl liked going to Christian churches because of Jesus. I didn't check his chart, but now I remember his social worker mentioning a rabbi. Oh no, I decide, *this* is definitely a chaplain's worst nightmare.

After we break from our meeting, I race back to the seventh floor and rush into Antony's room.

"Antony!" I practically shout. "Why didn't you *tell* me you were Jewish before I gave you communion? Why would you want communion if you're Jewish?" I envision explaining to Antony's rabbi and friends that my last pastoral act has been to give him the Host.

Taken aback, Antony replies: "I like all religions."

"What do you mean, you like all religions?" I stammer.

Antony looks down at his lunch tray for a few moments. "It's sort of like a good meal. You don't just want to eat one thing all the time, you want to taste a little of everything. You know, like a big buffet. That's how I like religion."

I am speechless. I try to argue that even at a buffet you eventually have to choose the dish you like best, but I know my analogy doesn't work for Antony. It doesn't even fit buffet behavior. Of course you couldn't treat religion like a buffet. That is heresy. Isn't it?

EVEN IN the final days of my CPE course, my well-intended actions toward Antony were thwarted. He continued to do things that didn't fit my idea of how life should work.

A week or so before the summer's end, early one morning, I run into his social worker in the elevator. Antony is dying, and I'd better hurry if I want to say good-bye. I rush to the seventh floor, arriving in his room to find a resident and two nurses performing emergency resuscitation. Antony appears to be slipping into a coma. Some toxin has been found in his blood, and they're not sure he'll survive. If Antony doesn't revive, the doctors have decided to give a Do Not Resuscitate order.

I arrive at our ten o'clock group meeting flustered and out of breath. I tell the group Antony's news and wonder what to do.

"What about baptizing him?" suggests Thomas. "He told me he was thinking about getting baptized."

"Perhaps you could just sit with him for a little while and read him a prayer," says Chaplain Joseph. "He might find that calming if he can hear you."

Other people have ideas, but I'm too distracted to listen closely. Thomas and I leave the meeting early and go directly to Antony's room. Asleep, he is lying peacefully on his back. I read the Beatitudes, remembering how much he liked them. In these circumstances, it doesn't occur to me that reading the Gospel might be similar to giving communion. Thomas, too, says a prayer aloud before leaving the room. I stay for a time that afternoon, going over everything Antony has told me about his life, holding what seemed his happiest moments in my mind. I contact his friends and the ex-social worker; they should come right away and bring the rabbi. It seems wrong that someone, however motley, with Antony's history—someone who has steered navy vessels, planned business ventures, earned a higher degree, and tried to share his life with people—should die all alone.

I can't help wondering, though, if my presence by his bedside in the last hours of his life makes any difference. How much had he taken in over the past few weeks? Did Antony remember the shih tzu puppy? Could he hear the Beatitudes, and if so, did the words have any meaning beyond their sound? With Antony in a coma, all these were unanswerable questions, or so I thought.

As it turned out, the next day Antony surprised us by reviving—not recovering, of course, but coming back just enough to continue as he'd been.

ON MY LAST DAY at Bellevue, I spent the morning saying good-bye to all the patients with whom I still had contact. I gave a picture of my dogs to Antony, who had been moved to another floor after his remarkable recovery from blood poisoning. He wondered, as I waved good-bye, could I contact a nurse about the alarm clock he left behind? I brought an almond croissant to Adam, who was now eating solid food and had become a model patient. I paid a quick visit to 19S and 18E to take my leave of the Bible study groups. Since Isaiah's and Robert's departures, I had not spent much time in either place.

Little had changed at Bellevue since my first day. Still an institution of intense human drama, the hospital operated by its own sense of time, its own set of universal laws. I left with a fund of stories from a cross section of human beings who would otherwise have remained statistics, not people, to me. My chaplaincy had not reformed the hospital. Though I hated to admit it, I wouldn't be missed. The church—in this world, at least—was not the forerunner of social justice and institutional transformation I had hoped for. Instead, its work had been a barely audible, nearly invisible knitting of relationships that, at best, gave a glimpse of meaning to people in bewildering situations. It had been a reminder that God, too, does commonplace work in ordinary time.

THE STRUGGLES of ordinary time at Bellevue were the struggles of my whole year.

I had arrived in Chelsea Square twelve months earlier, expecting to be utterly changed. The formation process, I imagined, would purify me of the unclean elements of my previous life. Holiness was about spotlessness, and seminary would be the place where those old blemish-making habits and experiences of an earlier existence would be smelted away in the refiner's fire. I would step from my former world into this new kingdom—a purer, holier, more beautiful person. In this place, angels would sing and the streets would be paved with gold. All this, priestly formation would disclose.

I would be swept off my feet in the same way that Esther had been by the royal summons of King Ahasuerus, who wanted her as his queen. Taken from humble origins and dressed in royal robes, Esther is suddenly surrounded by beautiful things and lovely people, given maidservants and anything she wants. Esther's former life becomes only a shadow prefiguring the glory of her bright new world.

I, too, imagined a new world opening in the first year of my preparation for ordained ministry. The church was to be a glorious new kingdom—free, as I myself would be, from the imperfections that mar secular vocations. All the ragged edges and confusing gray situations of my family life, high school experience, college years, and early adulthood would pass like cloud shadows, now that I had found the place where real life truly began.

Like Esther, however, I soon discovered that entering the kingdom does not shut out the past. As her uncle tells her, Esther's special privileges in the king's household will not protect her from the fate of her people. She cannot remain in isolation, leave behind or forget the place she came from. Esther's true entrance into the kingdom comes only when she wagers her life and position of dignity in order to serve outsiders, the people of no importance. The kingdom, she realizes, is not the palace, its jeweled hallways, or the esteemed status she occupies. Her kingdom, to be complete, must embrace the lives and well-being of those who live outside its golden gates.

My first year at seminary offered no escape from the ambiguous situations and difficult decisions that preoccupied me in the secular world. Family dinners did not suddenly become simple. My insecurities about falling behind in the race to get ahead, which had been the hallmark of my university years, did not suddenly disappear. Doubts of my future and the correctness of the choices I'd made stayed by me. They were as omnipresent in my first year at seminary as at any other time in my life. Haunting me, too, were a continuing passion for social justice and a sheer avidity for learning.

No wings had sprouted to carry me soaring above my circumstances. My life was the same life it had been before entering seminary; my personality had not changed, either.

I did eventually give up trying to transform seminary into heaven, however. I got tired of being disappointed each time I leapt off a pew bench in ecstatic contemplation—only to land on the Pine-Sol and wax-smelling chapel floor. The seminary's streets weren't paved with gold, as the dog days of Lent had shown. My entrance into ordinary time during Pentecost at Bellevue helped this realization along. As in Esther's real kingdom, nothing in human experience was missing in ordinary time. If God's grace could be present in a place where the church was as marginal as it had been at Bellevue, then the unchurched parts of my life were also embraced by God's "ordinary"—the jurisdiction of the divine, as the church defines this word.

I had spent many summer weeks trying to show other people that their struggles were sacred—all of them were sanctified, whether they were inner battles about abortion, biopsies, or unanswered prayers, whether they were expressed in tongues that were Episcopal, Jewish, psychotic, or Cantonese. In my own life, I gradually stopped segregating the acts and moments that are sacred from those that are profane. I gave up deciding what parts of me—past, present, and future—were of God and what parts didn't qualify.

Only after my first full year at General Theological Seminary on the ordination track for priesthood in the Protestant Episcopal Church of the United States did I fully realize the deep truth that *any* vocation, pursued with grace, can become a path toward God. Two years before, I had glibly assured my Commission on Ministry that I believed this truth, but in fact I had little idea what I was saying.

The full force of my vocation struck me only as I began my second year on the Close. All the petition drives, magazine ventures, and unfinished projects of my life before seminary—which I had sloughed off dismissively a year ago as the ill-fitting carapace of a directionless, secular life—were as precious to God as anything I did under the roof of the place we call "God's house."

My blessing from God—bestowed upon me through my spiritual director; family; mentors; Mary, Nathan, Brad, Mauricio, and other friends—was the strength to accept the past. For a change, my whole life returned with me to seminary when the second year began in Advent 1998.

Ministry came easier when I stopped trying so hard to be a priest. Knowing there is nothing extraordinary about preparing for priesthood—no magic elixir to imbibe, no special vestment to squeeze into—I could begin studying for ministry in earnest. No interest is too obscure, no experience too secular, for God to use to advance the work of justice and reconciliation. My job is to uphold my past experiences and present interests for the uses they might have, instead of trying to hide or bury them. The church, like the world, will be wide enough for me.

The real kingdom Esther found after she offered up her place in the palace and carried her past through the gates into the city was one that looked worth serving, I thought. This kingdom will be realized only when people in the institutions of power—churches, corporate empires, government offices, or royal courts—serve others and outsiders, not only themselves. If I, like Esther, had come into the kingdom "for such a time as this," then it would be because I, too, was able to risk the safety of my place at the high table in order to include those without a seat.

Acknowledgments

This book would not have arrived on the shelves without the dedicated hard work and intermittent hand-holding of my agent, Loretta Barrett. I am deeply grateful for her faith in the manuscript throughout all its various incarnations and particularly during the times when I myself had doubts. Further, the insightful comments and support of my editor, Jo Ann Miller, and others, including John Donatich, Donya Levine, and Jessica Callaway, made Basic Books a great place to complete my first book.

In addition, I am thankful for the early professional assistance of Henning Gutmann, my first editor, and Liz Maguire. I am grateful to Ed Cohen for planting the seed for this project after I left *Who Cares* and for all the encouragement along the way. Among my friends outside the Close who offered helpful comments and suggestions for the manuscript, I am particularly indebted to Hillary Lifton and Amy Waldman. I continue to benefit from the example of the Reverend Barbara Crafton, whose book *The Sewing Room* and work at St. Clement's shows the world that writing and ministry can be compatible vocations.

Acknowledgments

For sheer endurance, I would like to thank my advisor, friend, and inside-the-Close editor, church history professor Robert Bruce Mullin. Dr. Mullin's exhaustive knowledge of Anglican history and tradition, pastoral insights, tact, humor, and patience with rough-draft errors that might have upset a more squeamish scholar gave me fortitude to complete the first lap.

The Close bears the imprint of Judy Dollenmayer's editorial expertise from beginning to end. Because she edited my original proposal and then helped me hammer out the final round of drafts over five years later, Judy is truly the alpha and omega of this book. Judy's delight in the English language and ruthless intolerance of "issues," adverbs, and lists of three has imbued me with respect for well-crafted sentences and with great admiration for her own generous spirit.

I am indebted to my spiritual director, Brother Clark Berge, S.S.F., for his sympathetic presence and inspiring words. Our conversations and the retreats at Little Portion Friary have been helpful indeed. My bishops, the Right Reverend Ronald Haines and Jane Holmes Dixon, have also been a great support to me. They and their staff have been generous with their time and patience for this project—receiving faxes and e-mails of drafts at times when there may have been a few other things to do at Episcopal Church House in Washington, D.C.

I am grateful also to Dzogchen Ponlop Rinpoche and his family, who sat patiently through many hours of interviews in the middle of a Washington summer when this book was in a previous incarnation. I am thankful for Buster Yellow Kidney and his wife, Liz, who did the same on the Blackfeet Reservation in Montana. I treasure the memory of Bransford Eubank, who died at the age of one hundred before this book was finished, and am grateful to him and his wife, Eloise, who opened their home on the ranch and adopted me as a kind of grandchild of the spirit.

My final thanks go to my family. My husband, parents, brother, and sister never flagged in their support for this project or failed to offer good-humored perspective as it gradually transformed from "the book proposal" to "the book project" and, finally, to "the book" without qualifiers. Also I am grateful to Jack and Judy Scholl, Elsie Lewis, and Eleanor Scholl for welcoming me and my portable office into their home and for tolerating my regular disappearances between meals over the course of several holidays.

A Note on the Type

The text of this book has been composed in a digital version of Perpetua, a typeface designed by English stone-cutter and sculptor Eric Gill (1882–1947). A student of calligrapher Edward Johnston, Gill spent his early career as a tradesman, inscribing tombstones, head-pieces and initial letters for fine presses throughout England and the Continent. In 1925, Stanley Morrison, then typographical advisor to the Monotype Corporation, commissioned Gill to design a new serif type based on the chiseled quality of his stone-cutting. After several years of revisions and trial cuttings, the type was readied for commercial use. In 1928 Gill's typeface was used for the first time in a private printing of *The Passion of Perpetua and Felicity*, one of the earliest accounts of Christian martyrdom.

Book design and composition by Mark McGarry,
Texas Type & Book Works, Dallas, Texas